MARKETING IN THE 21ST CENTURY

Marketing in the 21st Century

Interactive and Multi-Channel Marketing
Volume 2

William J. Hauser and
Dale M. Lewison
Volume Editors

Bruce D. Keillor, General Editor

Praeger Perspectives

Westport, Connecticut
London

Library of Congress Cataloging-in-Publication Data

Marketing in the 21st century / Bruce D. Keillor, general editor.
   p. cm.
  Includes bibliographical references and index.
  ISBN-13: 978–0–275–99275–0 (set : alk. paper)
  ISBN-13: 978–0–275–99276–7 (vol 1 : alk. paper)
  ISBN-13: 978–0–275–99277–4 (vol 2 : alk. paper)
  ISBN-13: 978–0–275–99278–1 (vol 3 : alk. paper)
  ISBN-13: 978–0–275–99279–8 (vol 4 : alk. paper)

  1. Marketing. I. Keillor, Bruce David.
  HF5415.M2194 2007
  658.8—dc22   2007016533

British Library Cataloguing in Publication Data is available.

Library of Congress Catalog Card Number: 2007016533
ISBN-13: 978–0–275–99275–0 (set)
ISBN-13: 978–0–275–99276–7 (vol. 1)
ISBN-13: 978–0–275–99277–4 (vol. 2)
ISBN-13: 978–0–275–99278–1 (vol. 3)
ISBN-13: 978–0–275–99279–8 (vol. 4)

First published in 2007

Praeger Publishers, 88 Post Road West, Westport, CT 06881
An imprint of Greenwood Publishing Group, Inc.
www.praeger.com

Printed in the United States of America

The paper used in this book complies with the
Permanent Paper Standard issued by the National
Information Standards Organization (Z39.48–1984).

10 9 8 7 6 5 4 3 2 1

Contents

SET INTRODUCTION

It is my privilege to introduce this four-volume set, *Marketing in the 21st Century.* Given the myriad changes that have taken place in the area of marketing over the past several years, and the increasingly dynamic nature of marketing as a business discipline, the publication of these volumes is particularly relevant and timely. Each volume deals with an aspect of marketing that is both a fundamental component of marketing in this new century as well as one that requires new perspectives as the marketplace continues to evolve.

The set addresses four of the most compelling areas of marketing, each of which is changing the foundation of how academics and businesspeople approach the marketing tasks necessary for understanding and succeeding in the changing business environment. These areas are global marketing, direct marketing, firm-customer interactions, and marketing communications. By using recognized experts as authors—both academic and business practitioners—the volumes have been specifically compiled to include not just basic academic research, but to speak to business people in terms of how they can translate the information contained in each chapter into long-term success for their firm or organization.

Volume 1, *New World Marketing,* edited by Timothy J. Wilkinson and Andrew R. Thomas, deals with the salient aspects of the global marketplace. More specifically, it focuses on the realities of the 21st-century global market and then moves into how to identify emerging markets of opportunity, operate in these markets successfully from the perspective of the customer, and develop global strategies that are grounded in the concept of constant improvement through the use of value-added strategies. Authors of numerous books and articles related to international marketing, with extensive experience in executive education in international/global marketing, the editors are uniquely qualified to create a cutting-edge volume in their area of expertise.

In Volume 2, *Interactive and Multi-Channel Marketing,* edited by William J. Hauser and Dale M. Lewison, the focus shifts toward the various mechanisms through which firms and organizations can establish a means for direct interaction with their customers, whether individual consumers or other businesses. Using a two-step approach, Volume 2 discusses in great depth issues related to understanding the various direct-marketing options and then moves on to the application of these options to maximize results. As Director and Associate Director, respectively, of the Taylor Institute for Direct Marketing at The University of Akron, the leading institute worldwide for direct marketing, the editors have the ability to draw on the knowledge of the "best and brightest" in this rapidly emerging and influential area of marketing.

Volume 3, *Company and Customer Relations,* edited by Linda M. Orr and Jon M. Hawes, tackles the challenges of not only establishing and maintaining a functioning relationship between company and customer, but also how to sell successfully in the 21st century. Along the way, they deal with thorny issues such as when to disengage customers and where technology fits into what are, typically, personal interactions. Dr. Hawes is a well-recognized expert in building and maintaining customer trust, while Dr. Orr has a wide range of business and academic experience in organizational learning. This combination of perspectives has resulted in a volume that deals head-on with issues of immediate concern for any business organization.

Finally, Volume 4, *Integrated Marketing Communication,* edited by Deborah L. Owens and Douglas R. Hausknecht, addresses the various means of creating a basis for communication between company and customer that goes well beyond the traditional approaches of advertising, public relations, and sales promotion. The volume begins by considering how the new age customer "thinks" in the context of consumer behavior and then segues into methods to construct an interactive communication platform. Both editors are widely recognized in business and academic circles as experts in the field of marketing communication. They are also known for their ability to view traditional marketing communication tools "outside of the box." The result is a volume that puts a truly fresh perspective on communicating with customers.

Each of the volumes in the set presents the most advanced thinking in their respective areas. Collectively, the set is the definitive collection of the necessary new paradigms for marketing success in the 21st century. It has been my pleasure to work with the volume editors, as well as with many of the chapter authors, in bringing this collection to you. I am convinced that, regardless of your area of interest in the field of marketing, you will find *Marketing in the 21st Century* an invaluable and timeless resource.

Bruce D. Keillor, General Editor

Part I

THE MANY FACES OF INTERACTIVE MARKETING

CHAPTER 1

ANYWHERE, ANYTIME, ANYWAY: THE MULTI-CHANNEL MARKETING JUGGERNAUT

Dale M. Lewison

Future success in the highly competitive and diverse marketplace will require a carefully conceived process that is capable of formulating a unique business concept that is adept at gaining access to newly defined markets through uniquely designed pathways. In this first chapter we introduce our model of a multi-channel marketing process that will assist you in the conceptualization and implementation of a contemporary business model that is well suited to the multidimensional behavior of the 21st-century consumer.

In the new knowledge/experience/service economy of the 21st century, the most relevant unit of business competition is not your company or your product line; rather it is your concept of how to conduct business in a fashion that is uniquely advantageous to your firm and its stakeholders. Now and in the future, intangible assets (for example, consumer perceptions of your distinctive way of doing business) will be as or more important to your success than tangible assets. The plasticity of multi-channel direct marketing practices allows you to create a concept of business that can be dramatically differentiated from the ordinary and overused "go-to-market" strategies of the past. The destruction of the mass market and its reconstruction into market segments, niches, micro markets, and markets of an individual customer demands that future business models tell an interesting and compelling story of how your multi-channel networks are capable of delivering a more customized shopping experience that is best suited to the individual needs and preferences of your targeted consumer segments.

Music Television (MTV) is so much more than a music channel. Launched in 1981 as a music video channel, MTV Networks today has become a multi-channel marketer in the complicated entertainment industry by operating a slew of channels targeting markets from toddlers to boomers. Cable channels, Web sites, and wireless services create the core of this network of channels that reaches 440 million households in 169 countries. MTV's portfolio of channels includes the following channels and their target audiences:

Noggin: Preschoolers 2 to 5 years old,

Nickelodeon: Grade school kids 6 to 11 years old,

MTV: Teenagers and Young Adults 12 to 34 years old,

VH1: All ages 18 and up,

Spike TV: Guys 18 to 49 years old,

Comedy Central: Laugh junkies 18 to 49 years old,

Logo: Gays and lesbians 18 to 49 years old,

TV Land/Nick At Nite: The nostalgic 18 to 49 years old, and

CMT: Country fans 25 to 54 years old.

To continue to grow, MTV will have to continue to expand its channel portfolio into other contact venues.[1]

Our multi-channel marketing model is based on a five-phase marketing process that will guide you from unearthing potentially new and promising customer needs (analytical marketing), to mining and converting raw data into useful information (database marketing), to formulating new and successful ways of filling customer needs (strategic marketing), to building and operating a collection of pipelines capable of extracting sales (multi-channel marketing), and, finally, to managing and adapting the relationships required to directly serve chosen market prospects (relationship marketing). The model is shown in Figure 1.1. We begin where one should always begin, with an exploration of the marketplace and its happenings.

PHASE 1: ANALYTICAL MARKETING

The first phase of the multi-channel marketing process deals with gathering, analyzing, and interpreting the marketplace intelligence needed to make informed decisions concerning the internal and external aspects of your marketing effort. Successful marketing operations necessitate a complete understanding of the following:

1. Existing and potential customers,

2. External and internal environments, and

Figure 1.1
Multi-Channel Marketing Model

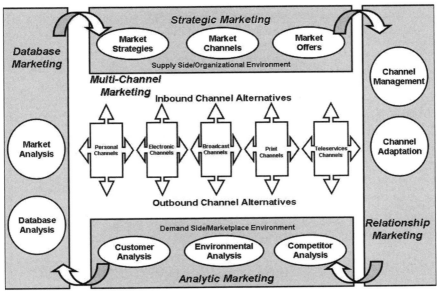

3. Levels, types, and degrees of competition.

We introduce these issues here and explore them in more depth in later chapters.

Customer Analysis

You need to know what customers think and how they act. Customer analysis is a hodgepodge of tools and techniques used in diagnosing past buying behavior and forecasting future buyer activities. Multi-channel marketers must continuously gather relevant information about what, where, when, why, and how customers buy and behave. You need to know how prospects and customers act and react to various situations involving the procurement of products and the adoption of ideas. The buying behavior of individual consumers and organizational buyers tend to be significantly different. How so? Let us find out.

Consumer Buyer Behavior

Consumers have become strategic shoppers with the knowledge and experience to go beyond simple searches for the cheapest or best-known products. Today, consumer buying activities have become multi-dimensional behaviors involving numerous marketing channels and a complex set of integrated and interacting forces. Consumer buying decisions, and the resulting patronage behavior, involve a problem-solving process in which consumers are swayed by a wide variety of internal and external influences. Figure 1.2 illustrates the relationships between the five stages of the buyer behavior process and the four categories of buyer influences.

The consumer buyer behavior process is a sequential series of actions that progresses from problem recognition, information consideration, alternative evaluation, response selection, to some form of a behavioral reaction and a purchase decision. This process is directed and influenced by a set of psychological, personal, social, and situational forces that have both a direct and an indirect impact on the buying behavior of consumer groups and individual buyers. The major categories of concern are listed in Figure 1.2.

Organizational Buying Behavior

Organizational buying behavior is the focus of business-to-business marketing. The types of products organizations buy and the methods used in procuring those

Figure 1.2
Customer Analysis

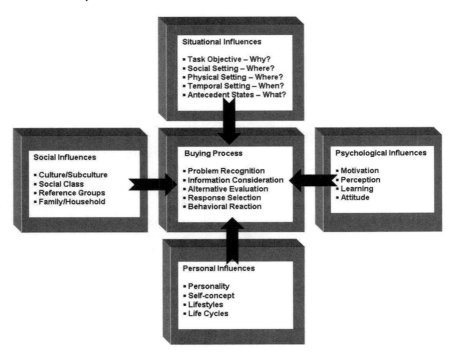

products are significantly different from the consumer buying process. The organizational market is composed of several different markets. For example, there are industrial markets (buyers who make purchases in order to produce other goods and services), reseller markets (retailers and wholesalers who secure products in order to resell them), government markets (local, state, and federal agencies that need products in order to provide those services they are mandated to perform), and institutional markets (public and private and profit and nonprofit entities that use goods and services to achieve their missions).

Organizational buying tends to be more rational, systematic, complex, professional, and direct. Organizations tend to use some form of multirole buying centers wherein need initiators, decision influencers, gatekeepers, decision makers, purchasing agents, and product users interact in a variety of ways to arrive at a purchase decision.

While the complexity of the organizational buying process is difficult to generalize, it tends to be a five-stage series of activities that is similar to the individual buyer buying process. The five steps of organizational buying typically consist of the following:

1. Need recognition and specification,
2. Vendor identification and consideration,
3. Proposal solicitation and evaluation,
4. Vender selection and order placement, and
5. Product inspection and performance evaluation.

Environmental Analysis

The second component of analytical marketing is assessing the external and internal environments that create the key possibilities of the competitive playing field and determining the core competencies of each market player. This analytic process is illustrated in Figure 1.3. External environment analytics requires a decision based on the opportunities and threats discovered in this assessment of the marketplace. In other words, what are the key possibilities or prospects offered by the market? The flip side of an external environmental analysis is an internal exploration of the firm's core competencies. What is the firm capable of doing? How do the firm's strengths and weaknesses impact its capabilities? Can the firm develop sustainable competitive advantages that will support the organization well into the future?

External Environmental Possibilities

Awareness, understanding, and appreciation of external marketplace environments are crucial steps in your successful detection of the key market possibilities facing your organization now and in the future. In this role, you become the eyes

Figure 1.3
Environmental Analysis

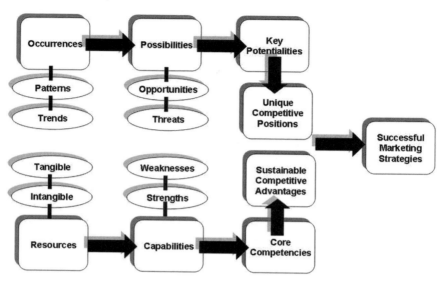

and ears of the organization's effort to monitor and interpret the patterns and trends that characterize the competitive external marketplace. Given the largely uncontrollable nature of this complex environment, you need to identify and react to these dynamics on a timely basis. As a marketer you have the best chance to detect pattern occurrences and emerging trends that define future market directions (possibilities) for a product or industry. Patterns and trends are systematic, repetitive, and detectable arrangements of marketplace phenomena that express a meaningful mosaic of occurrences that form consequential correlations, associations, or linkages between those occurrences and successful marketing outcomes.

The external marketplace environment encompasses all of the realities of the surroundings, conditions, circumstances, and forces that influence and modify the behavior of your organization. Typically, an external marketplace scan includes monitoring and assessing all relevant political and legal issues, social and cultural influences, technological and informational advances, economic and competitive forces, population and demographic trends, as well as, physical and geographical surroundings. Your analysis of the marketplace begins with the information gathering process we term "possibilities scan." Using the information from the scan, analysis should continue with the following:

1. The identification of the major influential forces that drive a particular pattern or trend,

2. The delineation of the opportunities and threats emerging out of an identified pattern, and

3. A discovery of the competitive advantages resulting from the opportunities and threats assessment.

Internal Environment Capabilities

Does your organization have what it takes to do what it wants to do, to go where it wants to go, and to be what it wants to be? You need to have a clear idea of you organization's potential—what it is and what it is not. In this internal analysis you need to understand your organization's capabilities in terms of its people, processes, systems, structure, and culture. "Know thyself" are the watchwords for conducting a scan of the multi-channel marketer's special abilities. The purpose of this inward-looking assessment is to gain an expansive view of the firm's core competencies and capacities for adapting to and taking advantage of selected key possibilities that make up the market.

What are your capabilities? A capability is any ability that you or your company possesses to perform a task or activity in an integrative fashion by deploying tangible and intangible resources in an efficient and effective fashion. In the knowledge/service/experience economy of today and tomorrow, intangible capital created by humans can often be the most important capabilities your firm possesses. In the economies of the future, your firms intellectual capital in terms of knowledge and know-how will create the core competencies needed to progress in the murky environs of tomorrow's marketplace. When conducting a capabilities scan, you need to identify and assess strengths and weaknesses of your organization that impact your firm's ability to survive and thrive in future markets. All organizations need the capability to resist negative forces in the environment and endure hardships. These embedded capabilities will allow you to overcome environmental threats and take advantage of environmental opportunities. Weaknesses prevent the firm from withstanding attack and reaping benefits of new marketplace opportunities.

How do you develop the core competencies package needed to deal with the uncertainties of the marketplace of the future? What can your firm do to establish recourse in responding to environmental situations? What courses of action will your firm have to rise to the occasion? The answers to these questions lie with the strategic value of the firm's resources to create capabilities, core competencies, and ultimately, the sustainable competitive advantages needed to outmaneuver marketplace rivals. In the misty realm of tangible and intangible assets, it may behoove you to understand and appreciate this "resource-based view" of business and marketing strategy. A full assessment of the wide spectrum of resources is beyond the scope of this chapter. In general, strategic assets include all potential sources of future economic benefit that have a capacity to contribute to a company's overall value. Assets have a distinct life cycle—a beginning and an end to economic value. Asset categories include physical assets (land, buildings, equipment, and inventory), financial assets (cash, receivables, debt, investments, and equity) customer assets (customers, marketing channels, and affiliates), stakeholder assets (employees, suppliers, and partners), and organizational assets (leadership, strategy, structure, culture, brands, knowledge, systems, and processes).

Competitor Analysis

The proceeding customer and environmental assessments can provide you with enough intelligence to determine the overall potential of a marketplace; however, it cannot provide you with one critical bit of information—what share of that total market you can reasonably expect to capture. Competitor analysis is concerned with profiling the competitive rivalry taking place in any market. Changing competitive actions and responses between rivals for a competitive market position is an everyday occurrence in the dynamic global marketplace. You will have to build and defend your competitive advantages and market positions on a continuous basis. What do you need to consider when conducting a competitor analysis? Competition can be characterized in terms of different levels, forms, and degrees. We examine these competitive nuances.

Level of Competition

One way to look at competition is to examine the directness and specificity of the competition you face. As Figure 1.4 portrays, competition can be head-to-head direct competition between two competitors for a specific product item. At the other end of the continuum, the competition is fairly general and indirect; nonetheless, it can be quite significant and disruptive. As seen in Figure 1.4, competition can fall along a continuum from item to category to substitute to generic competition. The narrowest perspective on competition is item competition—the rivalry among firms selling the equal or similar products to the same target market at comparable price points. Item competition is specific because it involves direct competition among product items in terms of brands, styles, sizes, models, and features. Category competition consists of rivalry among marketers of closely related lines of products with similar features. For example, toys, books, apparel, home electronics, office supplies, home and garden, and arts and crafts are all product categories where heated competition is common. The big-box category killers such as Best Buy, Barnes & Noble Booksellers, Dick's Sporting Goods, and Michaels, The Arts and Crafts Store are all engaging in this level of competition. Substitute competition is less specific and more general; where two different products (for example, a movie or a football game) try to satisfy the same basic need (entertainment). Finally, generic competition can best be described as the general competition that exists among marketers of different goods and services for the limited income and patronage of the consuming public. If the consumer

Figure 1.4
Continuum of Competition

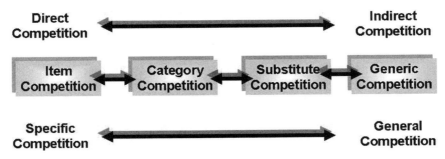

buys a new CD player, he or she may not have the money to go out to dinner and a movie.

Forms of Competition

The nature and structure of the relationship among various members of the marketing channel of distribution can greatly impact the form of competition that any particular firm might encounter. Within channel and between channel competition, as well as competition between two or more vertical marketing systems is common. Intratype competition is the rivalry between two marketers from different channels that occupy the same level with their respective channels of distribution. Wal-Mart and Kmart engage in intratype competition. When competing parties from different channels use unlike business formats to serve the same target markets with comparable product offerings, the competitive form is referred to as intertype competition. The competition between Sears, Roebuck and Company and Baby Gap in infant apparel lines illustrates this intertype rivalry. There are times when you will have to compete with a member of your own channel of distribution. Vertical competition is the rivalry among members of the same channel—an apparel retailer that stocks and sells Levi's jeans competes with factory outlet stores and direct marketing channels operated by Levi Strauss & Co. Systems competition is the rivalry among entire marketing channel systems; it is the competition that exists between two vertical marketing systems (an integrated production, wholesale, and retail operation). The Home Depot, Inc. and Lowe's are highly vertically integrated operations that compete as controlled and coordinated distribution and fulfillment systems.

Degrees of Competition

Competitive relationships range from hostile conflict to illegal collusion. The intensity of competition can be described along a continuum of competitor relations that reflect no competition to destructive competition. Figure 1.5 illustrates this continuum. Collusion is an illegal direct (person-to-person) or indirect (signaling) conspiracy to engage in cooperative behavior with the intent to injure a third party. Cooperation involves the consideration of a mutually beneficial relationship in which competing parties work together for a common goal. Indifference characterizes the coexistence strategy of competition—organizations seek to serve different core market niches and compete indirectly in peripheral market segments. By avoiding direct competition, coexisting competitors can pursue a live-and-let-live existence. Competition is an aggressive and confrontational degree of competition that will require that you meet or exceed customer expectations by developing a better marketing program that offers the customer greater value. The hottest degree of competition is conflict—a serious confrontation between competitors that leads to harsh reactions and retaliatory measures.

It should be your goal to develop a competitor audit using the above factors to understand the current actions of competitors and predict probable future actions. A successful competitor audit form is able to serve as a diagnostic tool in identifying the strengths and weaknesses of competitive enterprises.

Figure 1.5
Competitive Intensity

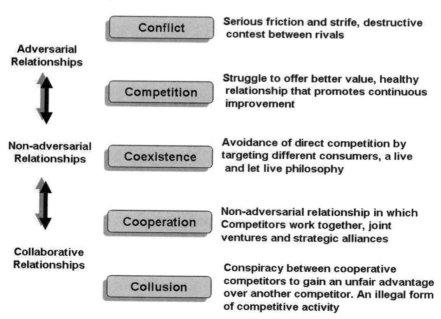

PHASE 2: DATABASE MARKETING

Database Analysis

Now that you have gathered and categorized information regarding your customers, competitors, and the environments and conditions under which you must operate, you need to change your static information into actionable intelligence. Extracting information from a database is more than just creating a new pile of facts and figures. Creating actionable intelligence requires that you first analyze and interpret the information, then use this new minted intelligence to develop the marketing strategies and craft the creative appeals needed to take advantages of those intelligence opportunities that have been identified in the analysis process. Database analysis is all about transforming data into useful intelligence that allows you to develop successful operational marketing programs.

A database is a compilation of data that you can access and organize using computers to make queries, sort data, and extract information through the identification of patterns and trends. Database marketing focuses on discovering relevant trends and patterns in customer and competitive behavior as well as identifying the opportunities and threats that are inherent in the marketplace environment. The most common forms of databases are those related to the following customer traits and activities:

1. Purchase history in terms of what, how, and when of the customer's buying behavior,
2. The type and level of response to previous offers,
3. Customer satisfaction levels with previous experiences,
4. Demographic characteristics,
5. Contact information, and
6. Psychographic (interests, lifestyles, and activities) profiles.

Database marketing is a highly regarded marketing tool that will allow you to closely monitor your customers and permit you to categorize them in terms of their lifetime value to your organization. It allows you to identify the most profitable customers as well as those who are not worth the expense and effort of retaining. Good database analysis is an essential tool to identifying market segments, selecting target markets, executing tailored marketing efforts, and developing cross-selling opportunities. Databases are very useful in providing a strong analytical foundation for your marketing plans and establishing the quantitative measures and successful implementation of those plans.

J.Jill, the Quincy, Massachusetts–based cataloger started its push in 1999 to become a multi-channel marketer by moving beyond its mail order roots, launching a Web site (www.jjill.com) and opening brick-and-mortar outlets. Over the years each channel developed its own database with little or no effort at integrating these sources of information. By keeping its information in separate silos, it was impossible to coordinate the marketing efforts of each channel. When J.Jill fully combined its databases in 2004, thereby going from a multiple-channel enterprise to a multi-channel network, the firm saw a substantial 20-percent increase in sales.[2]

Market Analysis

The important tasks of identifying and analyzing markets are essential prerequisites for developing a viable marketing program and a successful multi-channel approach to the marketplace. Poorly defined and profiled markets lead to poorly designed and executed marketing programs. Now we look at how we might define a market and effectively analyze it.

Defining Your Market

What is a market? We need to start with a common concept of what a market is. Our usage of the term "market" is very specific. As illustrated in Figure 1.6, a market has traditionally been a group of individuals or organizations (consumer population) who have needs and desires they want satisfied (consuming purpose) and who have willingness, ability, and authority to support a particular marketing effort by a given marketer. With advancing technologies and the availability of sophisticated direct marketing capabilities, markets no longer have to be plural; a market can now be an individual or an organization.

Analyzing Your Market

The goals of market analysis are rather simple—to simplify and organize the rather complex marketplace by first identifying individual consumers or clusters

Figure 1.6
Defining Your Market

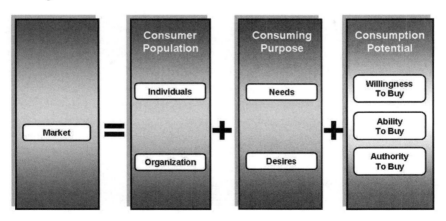

of customers who have similar needs and exhibit similar buying behavior patterns. By grouping customers into more meaningful submarkets, you can select and target those individual customers or groups of customers that best match your marketing programs and operating competencies. As we find out later in this chapter and in the book, having a greater understanding of the marketplace will allow you to gain a competitive advantage by uniquely differentiating and positioning your marketing effort with regard to the specific needs and desires of a more homogeneous market. The rationale behind this market delineation and assessment process is to assist you in focusing your efforts on some of the most promising target markets.

The essential steps in analyzing a market include market segmentation (dividing the heterogeneous mass market into more homogeneous submarkets), market targeting (selecting one or more market segments to be targeted and developed), and market positioning (creating in the minds of target buyers a distinctive position or image for your firm and its products and marketing programs). Market segmentation can be accomplished using one or more of the following approaches:

- Geographic segmentation—delineating and describing market segments in terms of their physical location and aerial expanse.
- Demographic segmentation—identifying and characterizing market segments based on the personal traits (for example, age, gender, race, education, income, and so forth) of the customers that make up the market.
- Geodemographic segmentation—linking demographic characteristics with geographic locations in an attempt to isolate more defined market segments.
- Psychographic segmentation—defining and profiling market segments using social class, lifestyle, and personality traits.
- Behavioral segmentation—outlining and describing market segments that reflect usage characteristics (user status, usage rate, usage occasion, and usage regularity).
- Benefit segmentation—identifying and profiling market segments on the basis of the primary benefit or benefits sought when buying and using a good or service.

Databases and modeling tools from such vendors as Acxiom Corporation, Claritas, and Equifax, Inc. have gone beyond providing basic geodemographic information for market identification and analysis. These sources and others offer detailed psychographic profiles that provide insight into what makes customer tick. Lillian Vernon, the Rye, New York–based cataloger of gifts, home goods, and children's products outsources the information gathering and assessment responsibility. It adds lifestyle, attitudinal, and behavioral information to its own customer transaction data from past and current customers to gain a sophisticated look at new and existing market opportunities. In the brave new world of multi-channel marketing, vendor programs such as MapInfo's *PSYTE U.S. Advantage* can identify customers and prospects who prefer buying online, ordering via phone, or shopping in a store. These tools and others are vital approaches not only in market segmentation and selection, but in developing contact strategy.[3]

Having gone to all of the work on collecting and analyzing market data and using it to discover and comprehend the mysteries of selected market segments, you now need to employ some guidelines that will assist you in selecting one or more segments that suit your particular situation. Consider these questions:

> How accessible is your chosen market segment? Is your market reachable using the firm's current communication and distribution channels. What marketing program changes will be required to access each consumer segment?

> Is your chosen market segment large enough to be profitable? What is the current and future sales potential? Are the financial rewards sufficient to warrant the development of a special marketing effort?

> How compatible are the needs and expectations of the chosen segments to your business mission and marketing objectives? Are the operational and marketing requirements for serving the selected market segments consistent with the resources and capabilities of your firm?

> Will the market segment respond favorably to your special offers that have been designed to meet their individual needs? Are you capable of developing a marketing program that is unique enough to capture the loyalty of these selected target customers?

> What relative advantages do you have in serving this market segment relative to the strengths of competitors? Do you have sufficient competencies to defend and grow your competitive position?

The final step in conducting a market analysis involves positioning all of your marketing efforts in the minds of your customers in a fashion that clearly distinguishes it from those of its competitors. Market positioning is one of the marketing strategies that we explore in the next section.

PHASE 3: STRATEGIC MARKETNG

Marketing Strategies

The purpose behind a well-conceived database marketing effort is its generation of intangible value that is created by being "in the know." An intangible asset (information) is a major source of wealth in the knowledge/experience/service economy of today. Marketing strategy is the force that drives this value-creation process. A well-articulated marketing strategy is a vital integrative tool for connecting the realities of the marketplace with the practicalities of a strong marketing effort. Good strategy can provide direction and focus to each marketing program, give meaning to the marketing effort by creating a unique identity, reduce ambiguity and inconsistency in decision making and action taking, align and integrate vertical and horizontal marketing operations, create value for all of the firm's stakeholders, and assist the firm in gaining a sustainable competitive advantage by finding the right strategic fit between the internal organizational capabilities of the firm and the marketplace possibilities of the external environment. There are several categories of marketing strategy; we discuss three of the more well-known categories—reference, growth, and market stage.

Reference Strategies

A reference strategy is one in which you make direct and indirect comparisons between your market offering and those of your competitors. Customers tend to think in relative terms when organizing their thoughts and assessing their choices. Consumers make assessments in terms of a good or service being better, faster, cheaper, or cooler than someone else's good or service. When developing a market offering for specific target markets, it is important not only to be different but also to establish a unique mind-set about the firm and its offerings. Differentiation is the marketing strategy of developing a set of unique and meaningful differences that will distinguish the firm's marketing programs from themselves and from the offering of competitors. You need to continuously ask yourself, What are my "points of difference" and are they important to my target consumer groups? The consumer buying process starts with buyer awareness and interests; having a differentiated offering is one of the best ways to build recognition and appreciation for it. Differentiation distinguishes your market offering from the sea of alternatives that make up the marketplace. Goods are differentiated by functional and aesthetic features and psychological benefits. Service differentiation is achieved by offering more service extras in a more consumer friendly manner (the way customers are treated, assisted, and served). Better value, greater convenience, and lower prices are three additional approaches used to create a difference.

Positioning carries the competitive referencing strategy to the next level. By employing the positioning marketing strategy you are attempting to establish a distinctive and consequential consumer mind-set with respect to your firm and its offering. While being different is important, positioning goes beyond this basic concept. Positioning is all about being more appropriate, more consistent, more personal, more relevant, and more desirable when compared to what has been tendered by competitors. Depending on the situation, positioning strategies can be either creative or adaptive. Creative positioning seeks to fashion a new and distinctive perception of the firm and its marketing programs in order to improve the likelihood that chosen market segments will judge the offering to be superior to competitive deals. Adaptive positioning focuses on altering how consumers think about the firm's current offerings. The goal of a repositioning strategy is to change consumer mind-sets in such a fashion that the firm's modified offering is viewed in a more favorable light than its past position and the new positions of its competitors.

Growth Strategies

Finding new and exploiting existing market opportunities is the core growth goal to be achieved through the implementation of market penetration, marketing development, and product development strategies. Long-term survival requires that you be able to redirect your efforts in response to environmental changes and to increase your organization's resources by identifying and pursuing profitable growth opportunities. Essentially, growth strategies address the question of "what should our business be?" Growth opportunities and the means available for harvesting new market prospects include intensive, integrated, and diversified marketing strategies.

Opportunities found within the organization's current portfolio of businesses are referred to as *intensive growth opportunities*—occasions when current products and current markets have the potential for generating incremental sales volumes. Your firm may be able to realize considerable growth potential by more aggressively marketing current products to existing markets (*market penetration*), by introducing current products to new markets (*market development*), and by developing new products for existing markets (*product development*).

Integrated growth opportunities are those that occur within the organization's current industry. Integration involves those occasions in which an organization establishes a strong position or a leadership role within a given industry by gaining greater control over its marketing channels of distribution or competitive business enterprises. By vertically integrating one or more levels of a distribution channel, marketers expect that resulting efficiencies will help them to increase sales revenues. A *vertically integrated marketing channel* is one in which a single channel member at one level controls and manages all or most of the functions performed by all channel members in all levels of the distribution system. Gaining control of competitors who operate at the same level (for example, the retail level) within the same channel is the marketing strategy known as *horizontal integration*.

If you elect to add attractive businesses whose business nature and format are dissimilar to current business concepts, you are pursuing diversified growth opportunities. *Diversified growth* is achieved by entering new markets with new products. The important question to answer in chasing this type of growth chance is "how new and different" should proposed products and markets be from our current business operations? You can elect to add new businesses and markets that are similar to and have numerous synergies with existing businesses and markets or you can venture into entirely new business concepts and hitherto unexplored markets. The further you get from your core businesses and markets, the more difficult it gets to develop the necessary expertise for successfully running the business.

Marketing Offers

To interact with consumers, there must be some bases for that interaction; that base is your market offer. As a mutli-channel marketer you must recognize that you cannot be all things to all customers. Successful marketing in the future will require a unique set of value propositions to a select group of customers. To implement an effective differentiating and positioning strategy, create a persuasive offer that speaks to the consumer's inner mind-set. Customers are more cynical, doubtful, and dubious about offers that do not grab them with something that they value; they want you to clearly communicate to them how the attributes and benefits of your offer represent a good "return on their investment" of time, money, and effort when buying, using, and/or possessing your product.

An *offer* is the total attributes and benefits package that you present to the customer as an exchange proposal. It is the deal, contract, arrangement, proposal, or proposition that you develop in hopes of soliciting a favorable response. In traditional marketing vernacular, it represents three of the four Ps of marketing; it is a unique combination of products, prices, and promotions. From the consumer's perspectives, the offer communicates what the customer gets and what he or she has to do in order to get it. A good offer provides the prospective customer with a good rationale for accepting it.

So, what constitutes a good offer? One that gets the right response. You can ensure a better offer response rate if you follow some simple guidelines. First, clearly articulate and communicate the importance of those attributes and benefits deemed essential by prospective buyers. Second, make sure that you have one or more points of difference that will attract attention and promote reaction. Third, your offer's affordability needs to match your customer segment's ability to buy. Fourth, be sure one or more of the attributes or benefits contained within the order is viewed as being superior to those offered by competitors. The fifth guideline suggests that you work hard to ensure that your offer is hard to duplicate—your offer should contain aspects that make it difficult for competitors to duplicate. Make your offer compelling is the sixth guideline to successful offers. Does your offer contain sufficient benefits and attributes to motivate the customer to respond now? If customers can see, feel, taste, hear, or smell an offer, they are better able to judge its merits. More tangible offers are usually more effective than offers based on fewer sensory cues. Finally, there is no purpose in creating an offer that will not generate a fair return on the effort. Profitability is the concluding guideline to more successful offers.

Marketing Channels

In recent years, as markets have fragmented and competition has intensified, the role of the marketing channel has become an increasingly important and vital element in the success of any marketing program. The concept of a marketing channel is thought of in broader terms today than in the past. The old view of marketing channels focuses on developing a physical distribution network that is capable of moving goods from producers to consumers in the most cost-efficient manner possible. Marketing channels were viewed as physical logistical challenges associated with moving products. As shown in Figure 1.1, the more current view of marketing channels is that they are a collection of inbound and outbound channel alternatives that serve as connecting pathways between supply side elements of the organization's operational environment and the demand side dynamics that characterize the marketplace environment. Designing the architectural structure of your marketing channel involves identifying and selecting your go-to-market strategies and tactics. Channels are the vehicles that promote two-way (outbound marketing and inbound response) exchanges between the marketer and selected consumer groups.

There is no doubt that marketers are doing the right thing in offering their customers more ways to buy their products and services. One estimate is that customers of multi-channel marketers spend considerably more (upward to 30 percent) than those who pursue a single-channel source approach. Proliferation of avenues for reaching and serving customers has created new and promising opportunities for market growth: the increased use of mobile phones, the growth of wireless networks, and 3G video calling all provide for new contact strategies. Imagine the impact on the personal financial services business if the customer could have a face-to-face conversation with the bond official using 3G video technologies. Some studies suggest that clients would be more inclined to engage in complicated transactions if they could use this form of personal channel.[4]

Marketing channels are viewed as operating systems because their architectural structures and designs satisfy system requirements of sequential linkages, nonrandom organizations, and goal orientation. Marketing channel links are comprised of a wide variety of participating partners organized to perform certain marketing, distributive, and operating functions at certain times and places. The marketing channel is typically viewed as two subsystems—the industrial (organizational) channel level and the consumer (final) channel. Industrial channels originate with the raw-resource producer, proceed through various jobbers, semiprocessors, and industrial distributors and terminate with the final manufacturer. Consumer channels are the communication and exchange pathways between the final manufacturer and the final consumer; wholesalers and retailers bridge the gap between consumer channel origins and destinations.

Successful go-to-market strategies of the future will require marketing channels designed as "borderless marketing systems" that incorporate the best collection of channel alternates that are capable of delivering a comprehensive marketing effort. The unbound nature of future channel structures is a logical outcome of the borderless consumer who uses different marketing channels to meet his or her needs at different stages of the buying process. A shopper may discover a new product by browsing through a magazine at Barnes & Noble, search for additional information about the product on the Internet, and place an order through an inbound teleservices channel. Being less mindful of channel boundaries, consumers are migrating from one channel to another in search of an acceptable combination that is best suited to their particular needs at any given point in time. Channel choices range from the traditional marketing channel designed as a single pathway between marketer and responder, to a multiple-channel structure where several channel alternatives are available as independent and separate avenues to the market, and finally to hybrid multi-channel marketing networks where an appropriate collection of channels is vertically and horizontally integrated to provide customers with their preferred choice of a channel alternative for supplying a particular task.

PHASE 4: MULTI-CHANNEL MARKETING

In traditional marketing channel architectures, channel members (jobbers, distributors, manufacturers, wholesalers, and retailers) operated in a self-serving fashion by jockeying for power and control of channel operations and market access. The limitation on vertical integration (between various levels of the channel) and the total absence of horizontal integration (between different types of channels) hindered most efforts at establishing a cooperative and coordinated channel effort. As suggested above, the dawn of a new era of multi-channel marketing will require most businesses to pursue a strategy in which they use several different channel alternatives that are both vertically and horizontality integrated. What are those channel alternatives? Your choices include personal, electronic, broadcast, print, and teleservices channels. We briefly examine each of these channel alternatives.

Do you prefer "face-to-face" communications and interactions? Personal channels feature one-on-one explanations and demonstrations of the attributes and benefits of an offer. Brick and mortar retailers and direct personal selling are the two most common forms of face-to-face personal channels. Electronic channels utilize the Internet for communicating and interacting globally. By using text, pictures, sound, and video, electronic channel marketers use the World Wide Web and e-mail to contact prospects and customers. Radio and television constitute the primary forms of broadcast channels. Because broadcast channels have traditionally been limited to outbound communication with little or no inbound interaction capabilities, they are poorly configured for direct customer response.

However, as part of a multi-channel strategy, broadcast channels play a vital role in a multidimensional marketing network. Print channels rely on words and visuals (pictures, tables, and graphics) to extend and accept offers. Direct mail packages, magazines, and newspapers are the principal print media for generating customer interest and response. The final channel alternative is teleservices channels. The telephone is a convenient and effective two-way communication tool; as such, you can use it to contact and interact with prospects and customers (outbound telemarketing) or have customers contact and interact with (inbound telemarketing) you. All of these channel alternatives will be explored in more depth later in the book.

PHASE 5: RELATIONSHIP MARKETING

What kind of relationship do you have with your channel stakeholders (customers, stockholders, employees, communities, business partners, competitors, and managers)? Relationship marketing is the channel philosophy that all channel activities be directed at establishing, nurturing, and building successful relationships with customers and additional stakeholders with a vested interest in the channel's success. While relationship marketing has historically been viewed as the partnership between the firm and its customers, multi-channel marketers must take a broader view, including the creation of win-win relational exchanges between the firm and all of its strategic partners (stakeholders). In this final phase of the multi-channel marketing process, we look at the issues inherent in managing channel operations and adapting those operations to new environmental conditions.

Channel Management

In the normal course of marketing channel operations, a large number of different types of interactions among different channel levels and between different channel types are necessary if the entire marketing effort is to be completed in an efficient and effective manner. Buying, selling, stocking, informing, financing, transporting, transferring, and promoting are the more common interactions that need to be managed.

A channel manager will be charged with the responsibility of managing the entire set of channel flows (activities and movements among channel members). Channel movements and activities are two-way (inbound and outbound) interactions. The more complex nature of multi-channel structures greatly complicates channel architecture. All channel partners with a multi-channel structure must deal with both inbound and outbound channel flows within and between channels. Communication flows must deal with both the inbound and outbound movement of information (informative facts and figures) and promotions (persuasive appeals and creatives) from one channel level to another within the same vertical marketing channel, as well as horizontally between various channel partners at different channel levels within different channel networks. The difficulties of managing all of these vertical and horizontal lines of communication are more than compensated for by the enhanced marketing capabilities and expanded market opportunities. Equally complex is the vertical and horizontal interaction flows of negotiations (offer propositions and responses), transactions (order placement and fulfillment), and relations (service features and actions).

Marketing channels can be characterized by a number of different structural designs. Channel structure describes the arrangement or positioning of channel partners within the marketing channel network. Channel structure is a function of channel length, width, direction, and multiplicity.

The length of the channel is the vertical dimension of its distribution network. Long channels are indirect structures that have several independent intermediaries (for example, wholesalers and retailers) between the channel origin (for example, the producer) and the destination (for example, the consumer). Short channels are direct pathways to the marketplace containing few if any middlemen. Shorter channels tend to be more vertically integrated than their longer counterparts. The operational efficiency and the marketing effectiveness of shorter channels offer competitive advantages that are superior to long, indirect structures.

Decisions regarding channel width are based on the intensity of market coverage the channel architect deems necessary to gain the needed exposure and degree of availability of your marketing program. Channel designers can plan market coverage densities that range from intensive distribution (readily available in as many outlets as possible), to selective distribution (available in a limited number of outlets), to a very restrictive and exclusive distributive network (one outlet per market area).

Channel multiplicity relates to the practice of developing several channel alternatives in an effort to reach the same or different market segments. As discussed earlier in the section on multi-channel marketing, delivering your marketing effort to diverse market segments will require hybrid channel networks made up of multiple channel alternatives that provide those functions best suited to their operating dynamics.

The multi-channel marketing network is an interactive system of participating members; as such, it is subject to the behavioral processes inherent in all social systems. Each channel partner's actions impact the whole system. The entire system benefits when individual actions are directed at cooperative and integrative behavior. Channel disruption and disharmony occur when individual behavior conflicts with the norms of the multi-channel network. Channels must be managed and controlled. We quickly review the types and causes of channel conflict, the means and methods of control, and the kinds of channel cooperation needed to build a highly integrated multi-channel marketing network.

Channel conflict occurs when a participating member of a multi-channel system believes that the actions of another channel member are interfering with the attainment of its goals (for example, reduction in cost of goods sold or better market exposure for new product introduction). A state of frustration and distrust on the part of one channel partner occurs when other participants restrict their role performance. Adversarial relationships occur as either vertical or horizontal confrontations. Vertical conflict occurs between channel members from different levels of the same channel, for example, a retailer who disagrees with the manufacturer over the amount of promotional support he can receive if the order size is increased. Serious disagreement between channel participants who occupy a certain level in one channel and channel members of a different multi-channel network at the same or different level describes horizontal conflict. An example would be a firm that uses both telemarketing to sell a product via a teleservices channel and direct mail catalog.

Why do channel partners disagree? The causes of channel conflict are many. Poor communications, different expectations, incompatible goals, limitations on resources, changing market conditions, cloudy delineation of reasonability, modification of channel structures and relationships, and lack of coordination of activities are a few of the more common causes of channel conflict. Channel conflict must be resolved and converted to channel cooperation. It may be your role to assume the position of channel captain by providing the leadership needed to build harmony and ensure collaboration.

How might you ensure cooperation between various components of your multi-channel network? Channel integration focuses on creating a unified marketing system under one leadership and one set of goals. The integration of the multi-channel marketing network can be accomplished through vertical integration [seeking control and coordination of intermediaries at different levels of the same channel), horizontal integration (managing channel operations of channel members who operate using different business formats (channel alternatives) at the same or different channel level]. The core purpose of this unifying process is to end the segregation of intermediary operations and their functional tasks.

Channel Adaptation

Your need to know where you have been in order to know where you need to go. Channel assessment involves the creation of a systematic approach to performance analysis and a better understanding of the contribution made by each component of a multi-channel network. Your systematic approach should include a sequence of activities from mining to organizing, analyzing, interpreting, and presenting information that reveals the trends and patterns that distinguish successful marketing efforts from those not achieving expectations.

Channel assessment leads to behavioral modification. You must understand and appreciate that adaptability and innovation are critical success factors for any multi-channel network architecture. Adapting to new and changing environmental dynamics can be accomplished through adaptive and generative innovation. The modification of existing channel structures and operations, in an effort to fine-tune channel network operations, defines the adaptive approach to behavioral modification among channel partners. Generative changes are modifications in channel structures and operations that represent new and unique approaches to multi-channel activities. It involves doing entirely new things in response to marketplace conditions.

Mobile marketing is a pending adaptation facing many new age marketers. Mobile phones are as common as credit cards, more so with the highly prized teen and young adult market. Mobile phone marketing allows the marketer to interact directly with the consumer and elicit an immediate response. The interactivity and ubiquitous access of this emerging channel invites serious attention. Because the mobile phone belongs only to one person, it is one of the most personal one-on-one marketing channels. It can effectively be used to support marketing programs delivered through other channels. Finally, one of mobile marketing's greatest assets is that the deliverability of the offer and the corresponding responses to the offer can be easily measured and quantified.[5]

PHASE OUT: SOME CONCLUSIONS

The preceding discussions have carefully articulated a process by which you can develop a successful approach to multi-channel marketing: from the systematic gathering of market intelligence (analytic marketing), to the processing of data into useful information (database marketing), to its utilization in developing effective marketing strategies and market offers (strategic marketing) that are delivered and responded to via several different marketing channels (multi-channel marketing) in order to build and nurture mutually beneficial relationships with your customers and channel stakeholders. Concluding the multi-channel marketing process is the need to adapt channel operations through continuous and dynamic improvement efforts.

NOTES

1. Tom Lowry, "Can MTV Stay Cool?" *BusinessWeek,* February 20, 2006, 51.
2. Ray Schultz, "Three's Company," *Direct* 16, no. 9 (July 1, 2004).
3. Ann Meyer, "Homing In," *Catalog Age* 21, no. 5 (May 1, 2004).
4. "Digital Demands Multimedia Tack," *Precision Marketing,* October 7, 2005, 12.
5. Robert Fuchs, "Mobile Marketing Has Its Advantages," *Marketing News,* October 1, 2006, 21.

CHAPTER 2

INTERNATIONAL MULTI-CHANNEL MARKETING RESEARCH

Ying Wang, William J. Hauser, and Timothy J. Wilkinson

With the advent of the World Wide Web and other seamless information and distribution technologies, more and more firms are entering foreign markets to search for growth opportunities. International marketing research plays a vital role in this process. In today's knowledge-driven business environment, management needs current and valid information in order to make strategic decisions in such essential areas as market entry, consumer understanding, product positioning, marketing mix, and competitive intelligence. The complexity of the international marketplace, cultural differences, and managers' lack of knowledge and experience in different global markets all make international marketing research more important than ever.[1]

Marketing research involves systematic collection, analysis, interpretation, and distribution of information related to marketing problems and opportunities. International marketing research has been defined as "research conducted to assist decision making in more than one country."[2] In foreign markets, the need for valid data and research is even greater than in the domestic markets as companies move away from their familiar knowledge base and venture into the unknown. International marketing research can provide key insights on how to achieve profitable growth by avoiding costly mistakes and enhancing product development in foreign markets.

CHALLENGES OF INTERNATIONAL MARKETING RESEARCH

At its core, the procedures and methods for conducting international marketing research are conceptually the same as for domestic research. For example, in both cases, it is important to clearly and precisely define the research problem. Also, appropriate sampling is essential to obtain valid results in either domestic or international research.[3] However, when undertaking market research across national/cultural boundaries, researchers and companies face some unique challenges.

First, the external environment plays a critical role in international marketing research. The complexity of the international environment makes international marketing research a challenging task. There are numerous social and political environmental considerations in the international marketplace including differences in culture, language, race, political system, societal structure, economy, market condition, religion, climate, and infrastructure. Among these, understanding cultural differences is of the utmost importance when trying to investigate similarities and differences across countries. Culture refers to all widely shared values, attitudes, and patterns of behavior within a large group of people. Culture is made up of both tangible (products and artifacts) and intangible (ideas, opinions, and beliefs) dimensions. Culture not only shapes consumer attitudes toward certain products and promotions, but also influences consumer behavior profoundly.[4] However, cultures are extremely complex and not only differ across countries, but also within a given country. Thus, while the researcher may think he or she has a good grasp of a given culture, he or she may quickly be confronted by the idiosyncrasies and nuances within that culture and the other cultures with which it interacts.

Many international marketing "blunders" have been attributed to lack of cultural understanding of foreign markets. For instance, a large U.S. soft drink company simply could not sell its products in Indonesia because many locals were not used to American-style beverages. They preferred a sweet coconut-based drink.[5] Levi Strauss & Co. jeans used its domestic "old West" appeal in its advertising campaign in Japan, which proved to be a poor decision because Japanese consumers did not share this heritage.

Market conditions are another important environmental factor to consider when conducting marketing research at the international level. For example, researchers may have to broaden their definition of competition to include not only the direct brand competition that is usually present in domestic markets, but also some unexpected indirect competitive pressures. For example, Chinese ice cream manufacturers may have to compete not only with other direct competitors, but also with vendors of traditional pastries and certain fruits that are extremely popular in that culture.

Another issue associated with international marketing research is the logistics needed to complete the research. Because of such factors as the need for exploratory research, as well as differences in research infrastructure and data collection techniques, the need for translation and long-distance travel, the availability and efficiency of research organizations, conducting international marketing research can be more labor intensive and sometimes costlier than domestic research.[6] In many developing countries, for example, telephone and personal computer ownership is low. Therefore, heavy reliance may need to be placed on personal interviewing. This requires the availability of trained interviewers fluent in local language(s). In addition, interviewers often must travel long distances to contact a representative sample of respondents.

The time and cost required to collect primary data may seem daunting for some firms and prevent them from undertaking international studies. This is especially the case for small and medium-sized companies in the initial stages of international market expansion. As a result, many firms expand globally with little marketing research, which in turn may lead to costly mistakes. In other cases, research is conducted too late, after mistakes have already been made, rather than prior to making a strategic or tactical decision.

Historically, the majority of international marketing research was conducted in North America or Western Europe where expected market size is large enough to justify the expense and where relationships exist with either local or international marketing research agencies. It has been only recently that systematic research has taken place in developing nations in certain parts of the world such as Central and South America, Africa, and the Middle East. Ironically, these are markets where companies have less knowledge and experience and are more likely to make mistakes.[7] Due to a lack of familiarity with foreign environments, international research should be viewed as an investment rather than as a current expense for a company. However, the payout period for international marketing research is usually longer than that of domestic research.[8]

Another challenge facing international market researchers is the complexity of research design, as well as the difficulties in establishing comparability and equivalence of data. First, in a multi-country research project, special attention is needed from the researcher to determine the appropriate unit of analysis. Countries are the most commonly used units due to the existence of national boundaries. However, in some studies, this may not be the most relevant unit of analysis.[9] For example, to answer a research question such as "what kind of advertising will attract teenagers who play video games across Europe?" the appropriate unit might be teenagers, a market segment with similar needs, interests, and behavior patterns throughout the continent. But even here, this market segment may also be affected by the attitudes and patterns of behavior in a given culture.

Second, achieving comparable results is one of the most important issues for multi-country research and one of the hardest to achieve. In order to answer questions such as "which country or countries have the most potential for the firm's products or services?" the researcher needs to be able to make valid comparisons between countries, which requires the comparability of the responses that are obtained with similar instruments. Jean-Claude Usunier and Julie A. Lee discuss various levels of equivalence in international research including conceptual equivalence, functional equivalence, translation equivalence, measure equivalence, sample equivalence, and data collection equivalence. To illustrate the importance of translation equivalence, the researchers used the following case. A European syrup maker hired a large international research firm to conduct a survey of the Swedish syrup market. Unfortunately, the word "syrup" was incorrectly translated to a Swedish term used for concentrated fruit juice, which is a local substitute for syrup but with much less sugar. Thus, the results of the survey were less than useful because the researchers did not investigate the product market of interest. Clearly an understanding of the culture and language were not in place prior to and during the research, and essential time was not taken to make sure that key variables were properly translated and back-translated.[10]

Third, another challenge centers on the lack of secondary data for many countries. Many times, data are not available even in the common areas of demographics, economics, and specific industries. In many cases, the data that are available are old and inaccurate. Also, there is no standardization on how the data are collected and no good understanding of the "politics" that went into the data collection. Fortunately, due to international policy and economic institutions, the data are becoming better, but are still subject to local problems in collection and interpretation.

Finally, one of the biggest challenges to international marketing research still exists at the researcher level. Personal bias about a culture and ethnocentrism directly affect how the researcher will develop and implement the entire research process. More importantly, personal bias has a strong possibility of tainting how the researcher analyzes and interprets the findings. While researchers are theoretically taught to exclude these biases from their research, in practice many find it extremely hard to do so.

THE PROCESS OF INTERNATIONAL MARKETING RESEARCH

Recognizing the paramount importance of marketing research information for the success of a firm's international business, as well as the challenges of generating this information in global markets, researchers need to set up systematic procedures to optimize validity, reliability, efficiency, and the economy of international research projects. In this section, we briefly discuss the essential steps of the international research process.

Step 1: Define the Research Problem

Defining the research problem or issue accurately is the most important step in a marketing research project. The more precise the objectives, the more likely the researcher will be able to get the necessary information while saving time and money. Thus, it is crucial that the firm discusses what the research effort is expected to accomplish.

International marketing research programs are often designed to identify potential foreign markets and suppliers, to learn about the business environment, to pinpoint problems, and to assess possibilities for profit. Specific *research* objectives and information needs vary from firm to firm due to factors such as the nature of the firm's international business, the nature of the product or service, the domestic marketing situation, and the company's financial status. For example, whereas identifying sources of needed supplies or materials is a frequent market research objective among firms engaged in importing activities, the research problem for exporting firms often involves identifying and assessing foreign market opportunity. That is, "What is the market potential in foreign markets for company products and services?"[11]

Let us assume a U.S. company is interested in marketing its instant coffee products outside the domestic market. The management might ask the following questions:

In terms of cultural, economic, political, and competitive environments, which countries or markets offer the most potential now and in the future for instant coffee products?

In terms of income level, education, cultural traditions, beverage-consuming habits, and lifestyle, which market segment of this country's consumers should be targeted for instant coffee products?

How would marketing mix (product, price, distribution, and promotion) have to be adapted to ensure a successful market entry?

These objectives are prioritized to generate data gathering in a cost-effective manner. This is where having secondary data on the country and a good basic understanding of its culture comes into play. If sufficient demand does not exist in the foreign market for instant coffee, there may be no need to carry out additional research or, if research is still appropriate, to change the methods and targeting of the research.[12]

Step 2: Develop a Research Plan

Once the key research questions and information requirements have been decided, the next step is to design a research plan. The research plan lays out specifications of the data to be collected, as well as the research techniques and instruments to be used, the sampling plan, and research administration procedures and analyses to be conducted.

On the basis of the information needed, researchers decide on the method of data collection. A cost-effective approach is to make maximum use of secondary research, especially during initial entry into international markets. In some cases, secondary data alone may be adequate to answer the research questions. In other cases, primary data collection is required in order to generate adequate information for management decision making.

For primary data collection, careful sample design is essential to ensure the desired degree of reliability. At this stage researchers select the sample source and number of desired respondents. It is sometimes difficult to obtain sampling lists in many countries because of the unavailability of basic information. Thus, using random sampling techniques may be difficult and nonrandom procedures are often preferable and more cost-efficient.[13]

A number of organizational and administrative issues should be resolved before carrying out the plan. Where primary research is conducted, an important consideration for management is whether to use outside sources or in-house staff. This decision is likely to depend on the size of the firm and its research staff, as well as its experience in international operations. Often companies handle the job in-house in order to save money. However, they may overestimate their in-house capabilities in experience and resources to conduct research in foreign markets. The reality is that many companies do not have specialized expertise in *international research, nor do they have a staff large and flexible enough to handle both domestic and international research.* Therefore, it may be wise to consider outsourcing the research project.[14]

Another important issue is how the global marketing research effort will be organized. Richard L. Sandhusen identifies three approaches: (1) a centralized approach, whereby company headquarters determines the research objectives and design and exerts control in local implementation; (2) a decentralized approach, whereby headquarters articulates broad research policies and guidelines and then delegates further design and implementation to local countries; and (3) a coordinated approach, whereby headquarters establishes overall research objectives, but local country managers provide input into these objectives, as well as the specifications of research design.

The centralized approach is appropriate when research is intended to influence company policy and strategy, and markets are similar. When markets differ from country to country, firms generally adopt a decentralized approach in order to be more flexible and to gain closer proximity to local markets. The coordinated approach represents the effort to organize marketing research functions in an integrative way to benefit from both central control and local input in global operations.[15]

Step 3: Collect Data

Next, the researcher should gather information according to the plan. Data may be collected through one or a number of secondary or primary research techniques. Whenever possible, a number of techniques should be used to provide in-depth information. This process is known as triangulation and provides the researcher with additional information and learning that may not be obtained by using only one technique or methodology.[16]

It is very important that the researcher understands which techniques will or will not work in a given environment. Techniques commonly used in the United States may neither be culturally acceptable nor feasible in a given country or culture. For example, telephone surveys and face-to-face interviews in a number of cultures would be considered an invasion of privacy. Likewise, focus groups may not work well in cultures where stating opinions in public is not considered a socially acceptable behavior. In some cases, nontraditional (by U.S. research standards) locations for the research may be needed to attract potential respondents. For example, during the mid-1990s a large American manufacturer of plastic housewares asked one of the authors to undertake comprehensive research in Western Europe to ascertain whether consumers would accept this company's products and which ones, in particular, would best fit their needs and living environments. In England, it was almost impossible to find a research facility in which traditional consumer "intercept" research could take place. With this in mind, the local research team recommended that a small community outside of London be selected as one of the research sites. On the day of the research, staffers went out into the town center and intercepted potential respondents. Those individuals interested in the research were then prescreened and sent to the great room of the local 800-year-old pub. The company's products, along with local competitive items, were then placed throughout the great room by categories. As the respondents entered the room they were met by interviewers who led them from area to area asking a small battery of questions about each group of items. At the end of the research "trail" the respondent was thanked and given a ten-pound sterling note (approximately U.S.$20). Not unexpectedly, many of the respondents went into the pub and used the incentive to buy lunch and, in some cases, a beverage or two.

Step 4: Analyze and Interpret Data

Once the data are collected, it is extremely important to analyze the data within the context of the environment in which it was gathered. Statistical techniques will help to define the data, but it is the interpretation of the findings that will make or break the research effort. First, the findings must be viewed through the eyes of the respondents. Trying to compare these consumer's needs, attitudes, and behaviors to American consumers may prove to be very misleading.

Second, and related to the first, specific cultural intangibles must be considered in the interpretation. For example, say you are researching the feasibility of selling designer women's jeans in Islamic countries. Your data suggests that the women who attended the research are very interested in the jeans. However, you also learn that these women may be a small group in a more progressive Islamic culture. At the same time, it may well be that while the women like the jeans, cultural and religious rules may prohibit them from ever wearing the jeans in public. So what seemed to be simple affirmation for the jeans by American research standards may be a series of complexities dictated by politics, culture, and, in this case, religion. Do you conclude that all women in Islamic countries will be prohibited from wearing the jeans and decide to forego the market, or do you dig deeper into the data to ascertain that in some moderate Islamic cultures women wearing jeans may be acceptable?

Third, the interpretation must now be linked with the strategic plans and goals of the company. The information gathered takes on a "nice to know but not worth the cost" status if it cannot be interpreted and integrated with the company's plans. This means that given all the cultural, economic, and political considerations, does it still make sense for the company to pursue this market? This is an extremely important role for international market researchers to play and one that makes them different than their domestic counterparts.

Step 5: Present the Findings

The final step of international marketing research is to communicate the *research* findings to management. The presentation may shape the perception of the entire *research*. Therefore, it is a crucial component in the *research* process. Following are some guidelines for making a successful presentation:

- Make the results clear to everyone.
- All interests should be represented since these presentations are often communicated to both headquarters and local managers.
- Be concise, avoiding lengthy analyses and demonstrations.
- Interpret the results at a number of different levels.
- Make sure presentations demonstrate how research results relate to original research objectives and are consistent with overall corporate strategy.
- Pinpoint particular problems or opportunities.
- Be accurate and avoid making extravagant claims.
- Put the statistics and technical information in an appendix.

Remember that after the initial presentation, follow-up meetings are often needed to clear up misunderstandings and answer additional questions. This is an extremely important part of the research process and another reason why a triangulated research approach is recommended. Usually follow-up questions ask for more detail or a more in-depth investigation of why a recommendation was made. By having a wealth of information that takes different "views" of the research problem you will be better able to provide the needed information for management decision making.

METHODS OF INTERNATIONAL MARKETING RESEARCH

Having discussed the research process, let us now look at some of the more commonly used methodologies and techniques.

Secondary Research

Secondary data consists of already existing information that has been collected by other researchers. It can be quickly accessed in order to provide background information about a country of interest, including macro environmental (that is, political, legal, demographic, and economic) and cultural information, as well as micro marketing data (that is, market size, distribution channels, competitors, and consumer information).[17]

Secondary data are a key source of information in international marketing research due to their ready availability, relatively low cost, and usefulness in providing background information relating to a specific country or industry. Secondary data can be collected quickly and are available either free or at low cost for researchers. Such data are especially valuable when research concerns countries where market potential is small and may not justify a full-scale primary study. Secondary data sources are also valuable in assessing opportunities in countries where management has little experience, and in product markets at an early stage of market development, such as emerging market countries. C. Samuel Craig and Susan P. Douglas pointed out that secondary data can be used to provide guideline in the following three key decision areas:[18]

- Selecting different markets to evaluate for initial entry,
- Estimating demand for a company's products or services in international markets, and
- Assessing market interconnectedness to guide resources deployment.

In addition, secondary data are essential where a multistage research approach is used. Secondary data can be used to further define the problem and identify areas that merit in-depth investigation. For example, secondary data might be used to identify which of a large number of countries in the world appear likely to offer the most potential for market entry or expansion. Secondary data can also warn the researcher that the project is not feasible or financially viable before more time and money are spent in primary data collection.

Secondary data, however, have some serious limitations including lack of availability, low accuracy and relevancy, and being outdated. In developed countries, various government and private sources collect an extensive array of secondary data on a regular basis. But, it is important to keep in mind that, for the most part, there is no standardized operating procedure for defining and collecting the data. Thus, factors may have the same name across countries, but the data for these factors may have different operational meanings or be collected differently. On the other hand, this may not be the case in many developing countries where even basic information like income and telephone numbers may not be available.

Even if secondary data are available, it may not have the level of accuracy that is needed for confident decision making. Some of the statistics may be too optimistic, reflecting national pride rather than practical reality. For example, Chinese businesses sometimes falsely report important figures like income and sales either to obtain government approval or to avoid taxation. Therefore, the validity of these data may be suspect.

In addition, secondary data may not meet the marketers' information needs because they were usually gathered for a different purpose than the one at hand. Secondary data are often outdated and may have been collected on an infrequent and unpredictable schedule. Hence, it is necessary for researchers to check the relevancy and timeliness of secondary data to ensure the effective use. When the benefits and usefulness of secondary data are exhausted, researchers must be prepared to explore the option of primary *research*.[19]

Primary Research

Primary data are information gathered for the first time to solve a particular research problem. They are usually more expensive and time-consuming to collect than secondary data. On the other hand, primary data have the advantage of being current and more relevant to the marketers' specific problem.

There are two main categories of primary research methods: qualitative techniques, such as observations, interviews, and focus groups; and quantitative methods including different types of surveys and experiments. Compared with quantitative research, qualitative techniques tend to be less structured, attempt to gather detailed in-depth information, and do not entail the imposition of the researcher's conceptualization on the respondent. Qualitative methods are useful in the international context and are particularly suited to research in emerging markets. Qualitative techniques can be used to probe the underlying motivations of attitudes and behaviors, provide understanding of contextual or situational factors, interpret observed differences, as well as predict future trends.[20]

There are a number of traditional qualitative research methodologies that can be used to research international markets. One of the most basic techniques is observation. This technique is extremely good for getting the lay of the land in a foreign market. Let us say you want to see how people shop for given products in the market you are investigating. Instead of an interview or survey, you may want to spend time unobtrusively just watching how people evaluate and select the products. Where appropriate, you may even want to play the role of being new to the area and politely ask the shopper why one product may be better than the other. It is important to keep in mind, however, that observation is not projectable to all shoppers in that country or even in that store. It is just a technique that helps the researcher gain a better understanding of how the culture works before designing and implementing more in-depth research.

A derivative of the observation technique has proved to be quite helpful in new international environments. This technique, commonly called "home visits," allows the researcher to visit a number of homes for a short structured period of time to see how products are used and stored in their natural environment. In order to do this, the researcher or local research firm must build enough trust with individuals willing to open their homes for a few hours to strangers. Once in a home, the researchers must be cognizant of customs and traditions and must not overstay their welcome. This technique served one of the authors well when studying the Japanese consumer market. A number of individuals agreed to let the researcher view the inside of their homes, especially their kitchens. Once in a home, the researcher was able to ask the homeowner questions about how she stored products and about her likes and/or dislikes in doing so. Not only did this provide useful discussion, she was able to actually demonstrate what she was talking about. In this case, it was easy to see that the American plastic food storage containers she had were way too large to fit into her cupboards. In many cases, the containers were too large to be placed upright and were stacked lying on their side. Besides having trouble removing the containers, the real problem was that many of the containers contained liquids and the seals leaked. But as with other forms of observation it is important to keep in mind that the findings here are anecdotal and cannot be projected to larger populations. They do, however, provide the researcher with a firsthand view of the culture that may never be obtained through more stringent research techniques.

Probably the most commonly used form of qualitative research is focus groups. Focus groups consist of 8–12 individuals coming together in one location for one to two hours in order to discuss their opinions in a group setting. Professional focus groups use a trained moderator who manages the conversation to make sure that the client's questions are answered and that all members of the group are participating in the discussion. Good moderators will go with the flow of the discussion, but maintain control and achieve the desired results. Focus groups are used primarily to generate ideas or to gather in-depth opinions in a group setting. Since focus groups cannot be construed to represent the overall population and the number of respondents is too small to be considered a random sample, they should never be used to predict behavior. Ideally, focus groups should be used in tandem with other quantitative measures.

On the international level focus groups can be challenging. First, many cultures have norms where it is not socially acceptable for individuals to openly state their opinions in front of other unknown individuals, especially if those individuals are perceived to be from another group, clan, or subculture. This could lead to personal embarrassment, conflict, and so forth. Second, even after they have been notified that the session is being taped, many individuals fear that their personal privacy will be affected. Third, in countries with heterogeneous populations and cultures, the relatively small number of groups normally completed and the small number of respondents in them may fail to speak for large segments of that country's population. Finally, the cost and logistics of doing focus groups can be prohibitive. Deciding where and how many groups are needed, who the respondents will be and how they are recruited, how much and what kind of incentive to give the respondents for participating, and finding the location(s) to hold the groups can be very time-consuming and costly. However, when all of these factors are handled properly and the findings of the groups are used to generate or enhance other research endeavors, focus groups can be a very valuable tool in the researcher's toolkit.

A final qualitative technique is one-on-one interviews. One-on-one interviewing provides the researcher an environment where questions can be asked of the respondents and the interviewer is enabled to probe into the answers to gain more in-depth information and meaning. Good one-on-one interviews require trained interviewers and a private setting. Most interviews run about one to two hours in length and provide a wealth of information not normally found with quantitative research techniques, such as surveys.

Like focus groups, however, there are a number of challenges with interviews. First, in many societies, respondents will feel very uncomfortable giving their opinions to total strangers and, in fact, may be stopped by social conventions and mores from even being in the room alone with the interviewer. Second, unless trust is developed between the interviewer and the respondent, the information given and recorded may be construed as an invasion of the respondent's privacy. Third, many respondents feel comfortable being interviewed in familiar environments, such as their homes. However, cultural norms may make home interviews problematic especially with strangers. Finally, it takes time and effort to locate, recruit, and then hire trained interviewers to complete the one-on-one interviews, which can become quite costly. Like focus groups, well-constructed one-on-one interviews can provide the researcher with a wealth of in-depth, well-thought information. But like focus groups, one-on-one interviews cannot be used to predict other's behavior or said to be representative of anyone in that population except the respondent.

While qualitative data aid in identifying and understanding relevant constructs and concepts, quantitative research provides a means of measuring these concepts and projecting them to the larger population in that country. The use of surveys is a widely used quantitative research method. Surveys are usually conducted via questionnaires administered in person, by mail, by telephone, or over the

Internet. Survey research is a quick and efficient way to collect a large amount of relevant data that is amenable to statistical research and generalizable to a larger population.

However, many obstacles exist when conducting surveys in the international context. Contact methods (that is, ways to contact those being surveyed), for example, often pose serious challenges for researchers. In some countries, low levels of literacy or telephone ownership may preclude reaching the sample through mail or the telephone. Surveys using personal interviews can also be perilous. People in many countries are not comfortable being asked questions by a stranger. In some countries entire segments of the population (for example, women) might be totally inaccessible to interviewers.

To improve the effective use of the survey techniques in international marketing research, Michael R. Czinkota and Ilkka A. Ronkainen suggest researchers consider the following areas carefully[21]:

- Sampling: To ensure the validity of an international study, researchers need to establish a representative sample. Representative sampling posts more challenges in places where the population is more culturally diverse (for example, Hong Kong) than in countries with more homogeneous populations (for example, Japan). More diverse populations will require larger samples or more subsamples. For multi-country projects, sampling procedures may vary in reliability and accuracy from one country to another. A mix of different procedures may need to be used in order to obtain comparable samples.

- Research instrument: The research instrument should be adapted to the specific cultural environment and it should not be biased in terms of any one country or culture. Participants' responses may be partially culturally determined. In Latin American countries, for example, products and services routinely achieve high approval ratings because Latin Americans do not like to hurt other peoples' feelings, including marketers. In contrast, a response of "not bad" in France would be almost the equivalent of "extraordinary" elsewhere.[22] To minimize this kind of cultural effect, researchers need to make sure that the research instrument is translated into concepts and terms that have equivalent meaning and relevance in all contexts and cultures studied.

- Question format: Structured questions (for example, multiple choice) cut down the effect of bias. However, open-ended questions are useful in identifying a respondent's frame of reference in the international context. Using a combination of different question formats may produce better research results.

- Question content: In some places, people are unwilling to answer or tend to give inaccurate answers to certain kinds of questions. For example, in countries where taxpayers routinely evade the tax collection system, questions about income level are doomed to fail.

- Question wording: Language and culture differences open up possibilities for misunderstandings and misinterpretations. To reduce problems of question wording, it is helpful to use a back-translation approach.

- The data collector: Many consumers are reluctant to be interviewed for marketing research studies. In some cultures, people who distribute questionnaires are viewed as weird and are not taken seriously. Companies can raise the comfort level of respondents by using native language interviewers who are properly trained to be able to build rapport with respondents.

INTERNATIONAL MARKETING RESEARCH ON THE INTERNET

Over the last decade, the Internet has rapidly penetrated many societies around the world and become an important global marketing tool. According to Commerce.net, there were 490 million online users worldwide by the end of 2002. This number was expected to reach 765 million by the end of 2005.[23] With its fast evolution, wealth of information sources, and global reach, the Internet has opened up many new opportunities for international marketing research.

Secondary Research on the Internet

One of the Internet's major benefits is the ready access to an enormous amount of secondary data across a broad range of topics. As discussed earlier, secondary research plays an important role in the initial stage of market consideration. The Internet enables international marketing researchers to access various secondary data sources virtually from any part of the world at any time. The Internet also makes it easy to update information and thus enhances the timeliness of data.

Secondary research on the Internet is especially beneficial for small and medium-sized companies looking into international business opportunities. Before the Internet, only large companies could afford conducting international marketing research because of the considerable financial investment required. Today, thanks to the vast amount of data from both public and private sources available on the Internet, a small import-export business is able to conduct substantial international marketing research and get the information it needs free or at an affordable price.

To illustrate how to use the Internet for international marketing research, let us consider a hypothetical case in which we are a small U.S. company in Florida wanting to export our concentrated orange juice to China. To start, we may want to learn more about the general business environment in China. A brief analysis of general market variables of China will be helpful. We may need information such as gross national product, economic and social indicators, political analysis, cultural factors, and other summary data for this initial analysis. Many free resources on the Internet can provide us with data for environmental scans. The CIA's *The World Factbook* (available at www.odci.gov/cia/publications/factbook/index.html), for example, provides political, business, trade, and economic fact sheets on all countries around the world. Other good resources that provide consolidated country information include Web sites belonging to government agencies (for example, the Export Portal at www.export.gov) and global organizations (for example, the International Monetary Fund at www.imf.org). One of the best Web portals for international business information is sponsored by Michigan State University (http://globaledge.msu.edu/ibrd/).

Next, a more detailed industry analysis is required to assess the market potential for orange juice in China. Using a search engine is a good start to accomplish this task. First, we choose a search engine (for example, www.google.com) and type in several key words (for example, China "orange juice" market) on the search page. The search yields all the sites that contain the words "China," "market," and "orange juice." We then look into the ones that seem most useful to our study. For example, one of the sites listed is China/FAO Citrus Symposium sponsored by the Food and Agriculture Organization of the United Nations. Click on this link and we find an article entitled "Current Situation and Outlook of Citrus Processing Industry in China." This article summarizes the current situation, market constraints, and future trends of the Chinese citrus juice industry and provides valuable data for our research.

The next task involves evaluating supply and demand patterns in the orange juice industry. Several resources can be useful here. The U.S. Department of Commerce's STAT-USA/Internet service (www.stat-usa.gov) collects business, trade, and economic information from 40 government agencies and is a valuable source for collecting country, industry, and market data. Looking at customs or port records of imports and exports flowing through China is another way to assess the supply and demand patterns of a specific product as well as to identify major buyers and suppliers in the industry. The Port Import Export Reporting Service, available online at the Global Business Intellibase (www.agte.telebase.com), is a useful source for this kind of information.

The Internet can also be used in many other areas of international marketing research such as identifying foreign trade barriers, gaining a better understanding of consumer behavior, identifying local and global competitors, and locating and evaluating potential foreign business partners. In sum, using the Internet for secondary research has become such a common practice that it is a starting place for many international marketing researchers.

Secondary research has been greatly benefited by the pervasive presence of the Internet. However, using the Internet for secondary marketing research in the international context is not without its pitfalls. First, some information available on the Internet may not be of high quality and may not be well structured. It is also often difficult to check the validity of data and authenticity of the source. Second, even though English is the common language used on the Internet, a substantial percentage of the world population accesses the Internet in languages other than English. Collecting data from sites in other languages is often necessary for secondary research in the international context. In addition to language, the content and format may be very different for different countries. Collating and formatting data are often difficult. Even with these limitations, with its easy, fast, and low-cost access, the Internet has become a convenient and powerful tool to conduct secondary research.[24]

Primary Research on the Internet

The Internet also provides a new means of collecting primary data. Using the Internet for primary marketing research is growing rapidly. According to Inside Research, spending on online market research in the United States reached $1.18 billion in 2005, up about 17 percent from 2004.[25] In the following section, we discuss several methods of gathering primary data over the Internet.

Tracking Visitors to a Web Site

The Internet enables companies to collect information about the visitors to their Web sites. Some popular Web sites attract millions of visitors worldwide. Microsoft.com, for example, gets more than 200 million unique visitors a month. Consider an advertisement from Sony Corporation: "Over the last 12 months, www.sony.com has had more visits than the Grand Canyon, the Statue of Liberty, Graceland and Disneyland combined..."

Companies are tracking exposure to Web sites, product, advertising, and company information search patterns. This information can be used for customizing the Web, improving product design, better understanding product usage, forecasting product demand, profiling current customers, identifying new market segments, and evaluating the effectiveness of promotional materials or offers. FedEx Corporation, for example, gathers customer information using electronic networks. Through its Web site, customers can dispatch a courier for package, pickup, locate drop-off points, track shipments, prepare shipping documents, and request a signature proof of delivery in many different languages. All this information can be analyzed by FedEx marketers for planning purposes.[26]

When information is collected from Web site visitors, individuals are often offered some incentive to provide basic demographic data and answer a few simple questions. For example, to receive free services from Travelocity.com (for example, purchasing cheap airline tickets, hotel accommodations, and vacation packages), you will need to become a member. When you join, you are required to submit personal information as well as log-in information, which includes name, address, e-mail address, password, password hint, and your e-mail format. Data can also be collected without the visitor's knowledge through the use of "cookies."

Online Panel

The Internet capacity for interactivity makes it easy to communicate directly with customers and respondents through chat rooms and bulletin boards. Online panels are another popular form of primary research conducted on the Internet. Online panels include groups of people who have agreed to be the subjects of marketing research. Usually they are paid and/or receive free products in return for completing extensive questionnaires. Companies have established large Internet panels such as the Harris Poll Online Panel or American Consumer Opinion. The latter has over 3.5 million members in the United States, Canada, Latin America, and Asia. Greenfield Online has 1.7 million U.S. members and a 2.0 million global panel that include both consumers and businesses. While panel members are sometimes recruited in a nonscientific manner, they are likely to consist of innovators, the segment of greatest interest to marketers who are launching new products.[27]

Online panels have often been used for concept testing, marketing communications testing, and Web site evaluations. For example, Microsoft Corporation launched "Rapid Research," an ongoing research panel, on its Web site at www.microsoft.com. More than 60,000 users on Microsoft.com, including software developers and business and information technology decision makers, have volunteered to be part of the panel. Using the online panel, studies have been conducted on everything from users' media consumption habits to testing the creativity of advertisements. Recently, the panel was used to test different marketing elements for Microsoft's "People Ready" campaign. Over a nine-month period the online panel approach saved Microsoft more than $600,000 in market research costs.[28]

The opportunity to receive immediate feedback and communicate directly with panel members through bulletin boards and chat lines is enormous. A drawback with current online panels is text-based discussion, which means the nonverbal communication of participants, such as facial expression and body language, is not revealed. This drawback should be eliminated as technology matures and the multimedia capacity of the Internet is more fully utilized.

Online Survey

Online survey refers to a survey administered directly over the Internet via e-mail and/or the World Wide Web. Compared with traditional mail surveys, speed, low cost, global reach, and multimedia display are the greatest advantages of online surveys.[29] For example, questionnaires can be sent to respondents via e-mail almost instantaneously. The recipients can then answer the questions and e-mail the completed questionnaire back to the researcher. The results are available immediately, as the responses can be checked and analyzed in real time as they are received. Responses to online surveys can take place quickly. A marketing research firm was reported to be able to complete 1,000 customer satisfaction surveys in only two hours.

Low cost is another significant advantage of online survey. Online surveys have minimal financial resource implications, and the scale of the survey is not associated with finances (that is, large-scale surveys do not require greater financial resources than small surveys). Expenses usually related to mail surveys such as postage, photocopying, clerical support, and data entry are not associated with online surveys. For example, the respective questionnaire can be programmed so that responses can feed automatically into the data analysis software (for example, SPSS, SAS, Excel, and so forth). This adds to the time-saving advantages of online surveys and avoids time spent inputting data. The low cost of online surveys was exemplified by a research firm charging only 15¢ per e-mail survey, a price that is less than one-tenth of typical mailed surveys.[30]

The global reach of the Internet has special implications for international marketing research. Through the Internet, researchers are able to reach individuals with Internet access at relatively low cost no matter where they are located geographically. As more people use the Internet and e-mail around the globe, the Internet population begins to mirror the general population in some countries. Consequently, drawing an international sample becomes feasible. Some researchers predicted that in the future, online surveys will replace mail and phone surveys.

Questionnaires administered via the World Wide Web also have the advantage that product details, picture of products, brands, and the shopping environment can be portrayed with integrated graphics and sound. Other advantages of online surveys that have been identified include, but are not limited to, nonintrusiveness (asynchronous communication), researcher's control of the sample, easy data processing, higher quality responses, lower respondent error, and more complex questionnaire design.

Online survey offers a fast and inexpensive way to collect primary data from respondents worldwide. However, this new method needs to be used with some caution due to several limitations and potential biases associated with it. A serious drawback is the extent to which Internet sampling frames correspond to respondent targeted populations. A sample drawn for an online survey is limited to Internet/e-mail users, which represents a more reduced sampling frame than what might be appropriate for some studies. This is especially problematic in the international context because of the great technology disparity existing among different countries. For example, in high-income countries, Internet access levels average 445 users per 1,000, compared with 60 users per 1,000 in middle-income countries, and 13 users per 1,000 in low-income countries. Due to this limitation, online survey may not be able to deliver meaningful results when conducted in countries with low Internet access. As the Internet becomes more pervasive, this obstacle will become less prevalent.[31]

Another problem of online survey is that versions of Web software available in different countries may not be compatible. Problems may also arise with older browsers, which could fail to properly display HTML (HyperText Markup Language) formatted questionnaires. The appearance of the questionnaires may differ in different browsers (for example, Netscape and Internet Explorer). Technical issues may inhibit respondents, resulting in nonresponse bias. These problems will be resolved in the future with the move toward more user-centered technology and increased software compatibility.

The anonymity of respondents in online surveys is also a debatable issue. Generally speaking, in terms of guarding respondents' anonymity, the Internet is superior to telephone and mall research, but inferiore compared with traditional mail surveys. The candor of respondents is optimized when their anonymity is guaranteed. Depending on the sensitivity of the issues, researchers should carefully weigh the pluses and minuses when deciding the use of online survey or mail survey.

Several factors should be taken into consideration when using online surveys for international marketing research. Those factors include country of interest, Internet access rate, targeted population, type of research, and product type. Online survey is more appropriate for conducting research in developed countries such as the United States, Canada, and some European countries. The method is most suited to surveys among respondent populations that are technology literate. Online survey is more effective for certain types of products such as computers, computer software, or business-to-business research. For large-scale cross-country surveys, an integrative approach (that is, using both online and postal surveys) may deliver the best results.[32]

In addition to the primary research methods discussed above, the Internet also allows various other computer-assisted data collection techniques such as CATI (Computer Assisted Telephone Interviewing) and CAPI (Computer Assisted Personal Interviewing). CATI and CAPI are well established in some developed countries such as the United States and Canada and are beginning to be used elsewhere. They provide faster, more accurate methods of data collection, providing direct input of response and facilitating steering of data collection based on response. As these technologies evolve and advance, they also provide innovative ways to present stimuli and collect data particularly suited to international research issues.[33]

The Internet has the potential to create major advances in international marketing research. As Internet usage continues to climb at astounding rates worldwide, its impact on international marketing research will be more profound. In spite of the debate on the pros and cons of online marketing research, the consensus is that marketing research via the Internet is useful and will be used increasingly in the future.

DIRECT MARKETING RESEARCH

Because direct marketing is for the most part a one-on-one marketing situation in which a consumer is provided with an offer and then decides whether to respond to the offer (seek more information and/or purchase), data mining and marketing analytics become important research tools at the international level. Consumers can be segmented across any number of factors, be they demographic, economic, or social. Because each step in the process is being tracked, data are being collected and can be easily analyzed using a number of statistical and analytical techniques. In doing so, researchers can quickly ascertain which countries, regions, and, more importantly, consumers have responded and how they responded. This enables the marketer to constantly adapt the focus of the project and quickly target the most profitable segments within and across countries. Modern technology centered on the World Wide Web has made this process almost seamless on a global level.

As easy as this process sounds, it too has a number of challenges. First, the data collected normally define only whether or not the consumer responded to the offer and what his or her response was. It does not provide any information on the individual's motivation for doing so. Second, the findings are linear and, unless other information is also available, it is difficult to ascertain high-level predictive modeling with the data. Third, by not understanding the sociocultural context in which the response was made, the outcome may be misleading or inaccurate.

Even with these challenges, marketing analytics is quickly becoming a highly valuable tool for the international marketing researcher. Because marketing researchers are accustomed to performing multivariate statistical analyses and interpretations, marketing analytics is relatively simple to complete. If the protocols are set up properly at the beginning of the project, it is quite possible to analyze data at each step in the process. This will provide marketers with "just-in-time" research that will allow them to change or refocus their plans on a quick, as needed basis.

Ideally, marketing analytics data should be integrated with data from other marketing research to provide a more holistic picture of the consumer and his or her behavior. Whether these data are in the form of secondary data (for example, region or country demographics), qualitative data (for example, focus groups or personal interviews), or quantitative data (for example, surveys), they will provide researchers with a more thorough, triangulated picture of their markets and their clients. With continuing advances in technology, marketing analytics may quickly become the benchmark methodology for marketing research in the 21st century.

FUTURE TRENDS

Given the importance of global markets to many companies, international marketing research needs to be given a more central place in shaping corporate global strategy. The quality of management decisions is soundly based on the quality and quantity of the market information that is fed into the strategic decision-making process. To expand the strategic impact of international marketing research, researchers need to go far beyond mechanically collecting data and presenting raw findings. Instead, they should focus on diagnosing problems and finding solutions. They need to add insights and meaning to the data and make valuable recommendations to management.

A strategic use of marketing research will lead to important insights and directions for companies. In its 1998 annual report, The Coca-Cola Company took a more strategic view of its marketing measurements. Instead of merely reporting its market share of the global soft drink market, it looks at the potential of the total global beverage market, including coffee, tea, and water, and asks how it can increase its share of this broader market. This marketing research decision has important strategic implications. The shift in measures implies a very different focus for the company. Instead of looking at ways to compete with PepsiCo, it now asks how it can replace British "tea time" with a "Coke time" or substitute a "Coke break" for a "coffee break."[34]

Another trend may be a more integrative approach toward international marketing research. Many firms conduct either qualitative research or quantitative research exclusively. European firms, for example, often use focus groups and observation techniques, whereas American marketers prefer "hard" data from surveys. However, companies are likely to get the best results internationally by integrating qualitative and quantitative methods. Interviews with knowledgeable people before a survey can be very helpful in terms of forming questions and structuring questionnaires. In addition, researchers can incorporate open-ended, qualitative questions into large-scale survey studies and analyze them in a quantitative fashion.

Last, international marketing researchers will need to incorporate new technologies in their research designs. With their global reach, instantaneous delivery, multimedia capability, and interactivity, new technologies such as the Internet offer tremendous advantages in terms of speed, efficiency, low cost, and convenience. Researchers should fully incorporate these technologies to help management achieve speed to market.

NOTES

1. V. Kumar, *International Marketing Research* (Upper Saddle River, NJ: Prentice-Hall, 2000), 2–3.

2. Susan P. Douglas and C. Samuel Craig, *International Marketing Research* (Englewood Cliffs, NJ: Prentice-Hall, 1983), 24–25.

3. C. Samuel Craig and Susan P. Douglas, *International Marketing Research*, 3rd ed. (West Sussex, England: John Wiley & Son Ltd., 2005).

4. Kumar, *International Marketing Research*, 5.

5. Subhash C. Jain, *International Marketing*, 6th ed. (Cincinnati, OH: South-Western, 2001), 96–97.

6. Craig and Douglas, *International Marketing Research.*

7. Ibid.

8. Ibid.

9. Ibid.

10. Jean-Claude Usunier and Julie A. Lee, *Marketing across Cultures,* 4th ed. (Essex, England: Pearson Education Limited, 2005), 181–203.

11. Richard L. Sandhusen, *Marketing* (Hauppauge, NY: Barron's Educational Series, 2000), 167–70.

12. Ibid.

13. Ibid.

14. Craig and Douglas, *International Marketing Research,* 47.

15. Sandhusen, *Marketing,* 179.

16. Craig and Douglas, *International Marketing Research,* 26.

17. Ibid., 63–107.

18. Ibid., 109.

19. Kumar, *International Marketing Research,* 89–90.

20. John R. Webb, *Understanding and Designing Marketing Research,* 2nd ed. (London: Thomas Learning, 2002), 215–19.

21. Michael R. Czinkota and Ilkka A. Ronkainen, "The Global Marketing Imperative: Positioning Your Company for the New World of Business," *International Trade Forum* 3 (1994): 22–32.

22. Tim R. V. Davis and Robert B. Young, "International Marketing Research: A Management Briefing," *Business Horizons* 2 (2002): 31–38.

23. Commerce.net, "Industry Statistics: Worldwide Internet Population," http://www.commerce.net/research/stats/ (accessed August 16, 2005).

24. Judy Strauss, Adel El-Ansary, and Raymond Frost, *E-Marketing,* 4th ed. (Upper Saddle River, NJ: Pearson/Prentice Hall, 2006), 142–60.

25. Jon Rubin, "Online Marketing Research Comes of Age," *Brandweek,* 41, no 42 (2000), via Business Source Premier, http://www.findarticles.com/p/articles/mi_m0BDW/is_42_41/ai_66705290 (accessed May 2, 2006).

26. Strauss, El-Ansary, and Frost, *E-Marketing,* 143.

27. Craig and Douglas, *International Marketing Research,* 475.

28. Kate Maddox, Microsoft Research Paves Way for "People Ready," *B to B,* April 3, 2006, http://www.btobonline.com/article.cms?articleId=27581 (accessed June 2, 2006).

29. Janet Ilieva, Steve Baron, and Nigel M. Healey, "Online Surveys in Marketing Research: Pros and Cons," *International Journal of Market Research* 44, no. 3 (2002): 361–76.

30. Ibid.

31. Craig and Douglas, *International Marketing Research,* 9.

32. Ibid., 475.

33. Ilieva, Baron, and Healey, "Online Surveys in Marketing Research," 376.

34. Vijay Mahajan and Jerry Wind, "Rx for Marketing Research: A Diagnosis of and Prescriptions for the Recovery of an Ailing Discipline in the Business World," *Marketing Research* (Fall 1999): 7–13.

CHAPTER 3

Yesterday, Today, Tomorrow: Status of the Teleservices Industry

Tim Searcy

Teleservices at this point and into the foreseeable future provide a high-performance, responsive, and measurable channel for any direct-marketing activity. As a direct-marketing professional, it is incumbent upon you to improve the use of each component channel to accomplish the goals set by yourself or your organization. For this reason, we are constantly looking to best practices and innovative applications for the next great breakthrough. Being mindful of the future helps us to embrace possibilities and prepare for change both internally and externally. Inside the discipline of direct marketing, the teleservices channel has a distinguished but short history. Considering the telephone was recognized as a source for widespread commercial activity for the first time in the 1960s, it is hard to think too far into the future. However, as a communications channel, the telephone is rivaled only by the television for acceptance in the business marketplace. Due to rapid adoption, consumer activism, cost-effectiveness, and disproportionate abuse, many professionals look to teleservices to continue to undergo steady and radical change.

The number of documented accurate predictions in this world is miniscule compared to the multitude of mistaken visions of a utopian future. For that reason, it might be more appropriate to look at the future of teleservices as an astronomer would look at a comet, a bright big ball of leading mass but which is followed by a roughly equal amount of mass spread out over a tremendous distance. It is possible to see a variety of futures for industry leaders, but as has happened historically, an equal number of users of the channel will be running behind, sometimes far behind the leaders, trying to catch up. The future will be a continuum of teleservices usage and sophistication, which will create a disparate group of firms that operate from a high level down to the point in which some practitioners use the channel as it was first introduced over 40 years ago.

Due to the lack of a definitive paradigm in business, many of the solutions presented here may appear to be on the surface contradictory. How can industry focus on expanding the relationship through better-educated representatives and simultaneously eliminate representatives altogether through the use of automation for drastic cost reductions? As teleservices have found out time and again, we are not an industry, but a channel of communication. Like all channels of communication, the tool will be used as makes sense from the user's perspective.

SOME PERSPECTIVE

Change occurs regularly in the teleservices arena in virtually every area. However, from the perspective of the company employing the channel, there are only a few high leverage points in which change makes a material difference:

1. The customer making or receiving the call.
2. The representative making or receiving the call.
3. Technology involved with making or receiving the call.

Other than these three items, the concepts involved in teleservices can be seen only as offshoots.

If you were to turn back the calendar to 1985 or so, some clear patterns would emerge related to the use of the teleservices channel. At that time, consumers and businesses viewed the telephone as a two-way street in which traffic went only one way at any particular time. This focus on a single direction dialog was steeped in the rationale for using the phone. The telephone was supposed to reduce the cost of processing orders or making sales as *compared to* an in-person alternative such as the retail outlet. Cost mitigation drove the channel, and the more cost that was driven out of the sales or service chain the better. For this reason, telephone calls were viewed as strictly transactional. Very little intent existed to use the channel as a means for communicating value or establishing relationships with customers. Candidly, the database and customer relationship management (CRM) systems were not widely available to make use of complicated purchase and demographic information to take advantage of the human contact on the telephone.

Currently, a great deal of investment has been made in pursuit of maximizing the lifetime value of the customer relationship while still keeping costs low for individual transactions in the form of telephone calls. In essence, companies are looking for a solution that balances a need for all of the available revenue in a customer contact at the moment or even into the distant future with a passion for keeping transactional costs extremely low. The attempted management of these two interests has tended to cause companies to lean heavily in one direction or the other. Consequently, most case studies report either a very high level or a very low level of customer satisfaction with the contact center experience. The difference in level has been dictated by the relative focus of the firm setting business rules for the contact center. Firms focused on lifetime value or high customer satisfaction scores ensure performance through investments in technology, personnel, training, and reporting. The alternative is to focus on managerial oversight to drive reductions in the cost metrics that coincide with average hold times, live versus automated speech usage, and reduced staffing levels.

THE FUTURE

The Customer Making or Receiving the Call

It is a well-known maxim that all business begins and ends with a customer. In teleservices, the interaction with the customer is not conceptual; it is very real and operates in real time. For that reason, all decisions concerning investments in the contact center must begin with the customer in mind.

Consumer knowledge has never been greater than right now. Because virtually every company has a toll-free number for service and engages in some level of outbound contact to its customers or prospects, consumers have come to expect this form of interaction. However, as the consumers' knowledge has grown, so have their expectations. Customers would like to be treated well and have their problems resolved quickly, with the least amount of difficulty possible. Unfortunately, because the cost of meeting this set of objectives has grown with the price of labor, companies continue to attempt to get by with less than ideal service. This is not working and will not work in the long run for several reasons.

The transparency to the real differences in company offerings has been created by the Internet. If a customer does not like the price, features, or service of one company, it is only too easy to shift to a better alternative. Many books and articles have been written about the customer-driven economy, but what does it mean to contact center professionals?

The contact center has become the service choice of last resort, not of preference. Customers believe that self-service is highly superior to customer service. ATMs, Google, speech recognition based interactive voice response (IVR), and many other labor-saving technologies have removed the human being from the purchase and service cycle for customers. This will continue far into the future. However, where the company "meets" its customer will change dramatically. Customers' needs will not become more complicated. However, their tolerance for less than perfect service will diminish.

For example, Discover Card recently released some findings concerning current expectations of customers (Business Wire, 2006). Its findings are illuminating, but not surprising.

- Consumers want fast and effective response by phone:

- Reaching knowledgeable customer-service representatives is "extremely important" to 65 percent of respondents
- [This is] followed closely on the heels (64%) of the ease of reaching a "live" person on the phone
- Resolving their issues in a single phone call (61%).
- Don't like being stuck on hold:
  - The survey revealed that most consumers, or 65 percent, consider a wait time "reasonable" as long as it is less than two minutes.
  - Nearly half, or 48 percent, find wait times longer than two minutes unreasonable.
  - When wait times are over three minutes, 80 percent find it unreasonable.
  - Only 26 percent of those surveyed recall connecting with a representative in less than 60 seconds.
- Telephone reigns supreme:
  - Consumers overwhelmingly (73%) prefer to contact customer service using a toll-free number.
  - Only 16 percent prefer to use e-mail, 9 percent prefer using online forms
  - 2 percent prefer online instant messaging.

If we use the Discover findings as a floor instead of a ceiling for customer needs, it becomes clear that customers will want better and more until near perfection becomes the only satisfactory outcome.

In the past, a customer had to "vote with his or her wallet" to express disappointment in a company's performance related to products or service. However, with the rise in consumer activism has come a new level of accountability that state and federal governments are imposing upon contact centers. In recent history, many major issues have been considered for regulation related to consumer interest instead of the traditional consumer protection. For companies this has meant anticipating regulated service levels of performance, demands related to the use of technology, and costs of compliance that were never anticipated in original business planning. For the consumer, having the government as a new-found outlet for anger and frustration has meant that instead of solving a problem with a single company, as a group, they are attempting to solve perceived problems with the channel. As you will see shortly, the consumer directly or indirectly is driving *all* change in call handling and contact technology.

The Representative Making or Receiving the Call

Who is answering the phone? Who is calling prospects and customers? Staffing has been often viewed as a necessary evil. The complexity of the call and the volume of calls operated as the arbiters for the size of center(s) and the type of individual handling the call. No matter how good the technology is, nor how effective you can train people, the raw material of human resource is critical for live operator calls. Companies have found that education, verbal and mental skills, and work ethic must be balanced against available workforce.

Rural centers, urban centers, offshore centers, at-home workers, and every combination of the options have been used to decrease costs. Economic efficiency in the contact center is dictated by average productive call-center minutes per hour spread out across the number of representatives involved in the call handling. Selection of the previously mentioned options or the combination of options is financially driven to maximize productivity.

Likewise, sourcing the labor that is "maximized" has driven the ongoing pursuit of various locations. If a company needs qualified nurses to handle patient inquiries on a variety of simple medical needs, it is likely that it will locate near a nursing school. If a different company expects seasonal calling volumes based on catalog orders, it may choose to have the flexible capacity created by using multiple centers geographically separated to prevent weather interference with the labor pool's ability to staff at peak times. Finally, if the service or sales application is simple, and the language skills are not the foremost concern, a company may choose to use an offshore contact center to save on costs.

Like all elements of the contact center that have to manage the continuum of cutting edge to trailing performer, the future will continue to use all options. However, the choice of location will be completely removed. Building large contact centers with a centralized workforce reporting to a single manager is a thing of the past. The contact center of the future will have true staffing on demand. Imagine a marketplace for contact center skills that is remotely controlled and sourced with little human intervention using available technology. Although we will address the technology that enables situational demand of talented personnel, the fact that a representative will change in role is something to consider.

First, the representative as a source of revenue will grow dramatically. As the Internet "disintermediates" more of the retail market, complex sales and service will still require educated human intervention to complete. Representatives will be trained, tested, managed, rewarded, and sourced remotely. As a matter of fact, a representative will be able to become certified in various types of calls,and operate a reverse auction for his or her standards skills on an as-needed basis by companies needing trained workers to answer calls. The representative will operate as an independent contractor with the ability to shop online for the work that interests him or her, followed by training, and then human resources will interview this individual. No more will a company have to hope that the agent "can cut it"; instead the bidding process for work will force the competitive marketplace to demand that the personnel prepare themselves for the job. Additionally, because telecom, training, management, feedback, and so forth will not require in-person intervention, representatives will be able to be located literally anywhere in the world.

This type of availability of stable, educated, and manageable personnel will remove a great deal of the competitive advantages related to customer service. As intrinsic value is removed from service, and the transparency for purchase available through the Internet takes over, it will be easier for companies to pool their service teams. In essence as consumers are able to more closely associate their individual wants with customized solutions, companies will differentiate based upon product choices. For this reason, service across the range of benefits and features will enable specialists to emerge across product categories instead of simply servicing one or two brands.

Technology Involved with Making or Receiving the Call

If the representative can be accessed anywhere, it is easy to see that the cellular phone customers use to seek assistance is only the first step to ubiquitous access for the buyer as well. Two advances will make access truly amazing. The development of computer chips controlled by RF (radio frequency) and natural speech recognition through microscopic voice interaction units will make immediate contact to service easy. As a customer you will be able to talk to everything from the expensive cup of coffee purchased at a local store to the automobile we drive. This conversation will allow us to get answers to our questions, order more, or report a problem. It will be as simple as voice activating the more highly refined equivalent of our cell phone, referencing the item of concern in front of us, and requesting service. Pressing buttons will be replaced by vocal reference. Although we already interact with many of our technologies by voice, the difference will be that the item we are referencing will also be communicating simultaneously. Your coffee cup will know the preference for the contained beverage you have chosen, its current temperature, your location in relationship to the store of purchase, and by accessing the company's database, the quality of your business to the firm as measured in annual dollars, frequency of purchase, and so forth. You will interact with your products, and consequently their producers will interact with you...in real time.

The unlimited access to service and sales opportunities will be very enabling to the customer, but it will wreak some havoc on companies. Knowledgeable customers are demanding, and the more knowledge they have, the more demanding they will become. This demand translates into an expectation related to the speed and quality of service. First-call resolution will not be something we measure in the large percentages of 80 or 90 percent as we currently do, but rather we will measure it in small percentages such as less than 0.2 percent of all calls are unresolved on the initial call.

Many people have predicted the Internet would decrease the need for customer service. However, like retail and catalog, the consumer uses the Internet as he or she wants, and not as business would like. For this reason a strong attraction to shopping online and buying on the phone will continue. What amount of sales and service will be done by phone instead of Internet is not completely important. Everything we can see as described in the comet analogy earlier applies to consumer purchases as well. An ever-increasing number of options for purchase and service will continue to be presented to customers, and they will query us about all of them at an unidentified level. We can expect that no channel will be completely eliminated. For that reason, all channels will require exploration and improvement.

One of the most exciting developments for the contact center involves real-time translation. The great barrier to a completely open international market for service is the realities of speech communication. Representatives have a difficult time communicating with individuals across the world with unique points of references, backgrounds, idioms, and operating in an entirely different language. As much as ESL (English as a Second Language) speech has enabled offshoring, it has fallen far short of its promise. But if a representative in Shanghai could speak in his or her native Mandarin, with the knowledge that instantly the words were being heard in English in Boston, and the reverse was true as well, the barrier would be eliminated. Real-time translation gives hope for the concept of universal translation becoming a reality. The technology is quickly being developed now, and in the future the universal translation will not involve only two or three languages moving back and forth, but literally every language, everywhere. The keys to this kind of advancement have been identified as follows:

- Truly real-time translation,
- Regional idiomatic adjustment, and
- Feedback loops for ongoing improvement

If the voice skills in technology necessary for advanced translation are present, it is a logical assumption automated natural speech would also operate at a high level. Consumers have been put off concerning natural speech not because of the "computer" feel of it, but because it does not effectively or efficiently solve their problems. Much like the tendency to press "0" to get a live operator, consumers shy away from natural speech and automated speech because of experiences in which the tool has been ineffective. The caution to companies is not to avoid the introduction of these technologies, but use patience to ensure the proper testing has been done to deliver on the promise and expectations set in the consumer's mind.

Another implication of automated speech coupled with instantaneous live operator translation and message comprehension by the computer involves management and coaching. In many call centers, the ability to record all voice interaction is already taking place. Additionally, separate monitoring goes on for most live voice applications. However, live monitoring and feedback is expensive, which causes companies to attempt to cut back on the associated costs by decreasing the monitored call volume or shifting the monitoring technology to more efficient means. However, as technology allows for "concept" distinction during the phone call, it will be easier to manage the feedback loop for improved performance. As a representative the technology could detect a variety of performance issues during a phone call by detecting the variance between the language being used and the preferred script or response being given. At the time of the difficulty, a record of the call, the performance issue, and recommended alternatives could be presented to the representative at the end of the call, or in real time via "whisper technology" in his or her ear, or by note on his or her screen. Additionally, all trend information for the individual, application, team, and so forth will be captured and forwarded to management for design improvement of the program, training, and tools.

Although voice is the most logical extension of current technology, there exists a bright future for video interaction as well. The "TV telephone" has a much-ridiculed history since it was first predicted. However, representatives speaking with customers using a video phone is impractical and in many scenarios undesirable unless there exists a good business reason. However, using video and "flash" formats to augment the value of either automated calls or live voice makes tremendous sense. Combining the benefits of the Internet and the telephone, live chat with "push" capability would allow customers to view demonstrations, self-service technical problems, and interact through technology with their service technicians. Three-dimensional models viewed from the customers' perspectives and holographic representations for better reference and superior service are already becoming available. The more clarity that video can bring to the service or sales experience, the shorter the handling time will be.

All of this technology should be a boon for the companies providing products to the end user. It will be possible for marketers to develop business models in real time. Business decisions will be based on immediate and accurate information. Should the plant manufacture more or less product, which features should be included, and what is the ideal price point will all be managed with a stream of data that can be observed, parsed, and modeled for the manufacturer's benefit.

The ability to manage all aspects of the supply chain from raw materials through end service using this kind of technology will enable virtually all costs to move from fixed to variable. If a company is able to produce "on-demand" solutions that are customized to the specific needs in as close to real time as can be imagined, backlogs and inventory will be unnecessary. Removal of the expenses associated with warehousing and ultimately discounting inventory will increase profitability for manufacturers, while a truly competitive marketplace for products capable of delivering specific performance will be created.

As much control as will be given to the product producer, an equal amount of control will exist for the customer as well. The customer will be able to separate completely the value of the product from the cost of servicing the product. Customers will make decisions about which levels of service to purchase and be able to select plans that meet their needs. As a matter of fact, unlike the current situation in which customers must constantly make decisions with little information about service, the products will provide all reliability and option choices for service on their packaging along with a variety of company specific and nonmanufacturer alternatives for service. By separating the product and the service, new markets will be created for service-only solutions that cut across sectors and business segments.

CONCLUSION

The contact center is one component of sales and service. As each touchpoint grows in popularity, it will be unexpected if the previous favorite shrinks in usage. Rather, the move to provide consumers faster and less-expensive solutions will move the entire industry toward greater one-to-one service by telephone. It is a bright future in which the telephone plays a key role in giving consumers the freedom to purchase what they want, when they want, by whatever means they want, and be serviced in the same way.

Appendix A addresses some key issues facing the teleservices industry. This state of the industry report was prepared for North American by Steve Morrell, Principal Analyst, ContactBabel. Used with Permission. www.contactbabel.com.

APPENDIX A: NORTH AMERICAN CONTACT CENTERS IN 2006: THE STATE OF THE INDUSTRY (1ST EDITION)

Principal Analyst: Steve Morrell

Impact of Offshoring

Despite the talk of a collapse of the contact center industry, there has only been a small decline in the number of contact centers and agent positions. To some extent, offshoring dropped down the industry agenda in 2005, as many of those businesses who would seriously consider it (often large finance, telco and retail operations) have already made decisions one way or the other. We would not say that the offshoring of customer contact has been the unqualified success that many expected—substantial cost savings have failed to materialize in many cases, and the customer perception of offshoring has been broadly negative. However, neither do we expect to see a major movement back to the US—there have been one or two announcements (and rather more quiet informal admissions of a reduction in offshore ambitions)—but generally, those executives whose decision it was to move offshore will not want to be seen to have been wrong. Additionally, as time moves on, working practices offshore will become more closely aligned with those in North American contact centers, as Western managers get their messages across, and the offshore industry matures further. We do not expect any particular dramatic movements either offshore, or back onshore, neither do we expect to see any short-term inroads into the Philippines or Indian contact center industries being made by South Africa, Eastern Europe, the West Indies, etc.: the issues around offshore are just as valid there as elsewhere.

The Impact of Self-Service

Self-service is of much greater importance to the contact center industry over the longer term than is offshoring. The reason for self-service's guaranteed success is two-fold, in that it generally aligns both with what customers want (rapid and accurate interactions) and with what businesses want (a low cost of doing business). This is a simple way of looking at the issue, but in most cases, it holds true. In some cases, a customer will need to talk with a person as the issue they have may be complex, but the main reason for having that type of conversation as far as the customer is concerned is to get the task done in the shortest amount of time. If using self-service is quicker than talking to an agent, then that is what most customers will do. The average technological sophistication level of a customer is steadily increasing, and the latest generation of customers (18–35 year-olds) have always been used to calling a business, rather than writing or physically visiting a business's branch.

From a business's viewpoint, decreasing the cost per interaction through self-service is a positive result, although there will be some discussion of the optimum level of self-service, as many want to learn more about their customers and (more importantly) try to cross-sell and up-sell to them, which is easier in a live agent conversation. ContactBabel believes that one of the key opportunities for vendors in the next few years is to develop the ability to cross-sell and up-sell to customers through the self-service channel. There is some element of personalization through web self-service now, although not as much as has been predicted, but almost nothing through the voice channel, which is a major opportunity.

Changes in Customer Expectation

Although customers still complain about bad service through contact centers, the measurable standard of service has improved almost every year, with improvements in queuing time and call resolution rates occurring most years. Most complaints supposedly about contact centers are actually about the business itself, or the underlying systems or business processes which will not allow the agent to do what the customer requires. Because the contact center is now the main portal into the business, it is this channel that takes the blame when perhaps the agents are not the cause of the problem. Customer expectations of the contact center have in fact increased significantly year-on-year, yet almost unnoticeably. Whereas ten years ago, a queue time of two minutes might just have been part of the customer experience, many customers now consider that to be unacceptable. This constant demand for improvements will continue to drive increasingly sophisticated ways to fulfill customers' requirements for swift and accurate service, in order to get closer to the customers' ultimate goal of zero-queue time and 100% first-call resolution.

Need for Multimedia

Multimedia—usually meaning email—is generally only a small part of most businesses' customer contact realities, although many large businesses had very high hopes for it. Despite predictions (by contact centers themselves) that email volumes would account for over 25% of interactions by now, the UK figure is closer to 5%—a figure from which there has not been much deviation for some years. (A study of North American contact centers later in the year will provide the equivalent US and Canadian figures, but preliminary investigations indicate a figure of less than 10%). Businesses cannot dictate the methods by which their customers wish to contact them—almost all of the "Internet-only" banks eventually decided to offer a phone channel as well, due to the pressure that customers put on them. Customers have become more demanding in the performance that they expect from the companies they choose to do business with, and the ability to change providers who fail them is becoming ever more easy. Email response times, generally, have been appalling, and customers have been put off from using this channel very quickly.

We would question the whole concept behind email as a customer-to-business interaction tool. Customers do not contact businesses for a chat—most interactions are something that needs to be done and/or confirmed, and there is no advantage to the customer to be waiting longer than it would take to pick up a phone. Typing also takes longer than talking, with no opportunity to enter into a conversation—why take a week to have a six-sentence email conversation when you could speak it in a minute? This is why email hasn't taken off—there is little need for it from the customers' perspective. Email is slow to use, takes forever to get a response (if at all), PCs may have to be booted-up and it offers no realistic opportunity of having a real-time conversation. We would expect text chat to have a greater share of overall interactions, as at least it can offer some real-time conclusions, but companies are slow to offer it, and many customers are tentative about trying it. As such, we believe email will never achieve the target rates of 25–50% that many large companies have stated as their aim for this channel.

Changes in Working Practices

The next five years will see the continuing development of working practices and customer expectations which have put so much pressure on the contact center industry, and go some way to explaining occasional poor performance:

- 24/7 culture will become ever more prevalent

- the need for more skilled and highly-trained contact center staff will increase, as the job becomes more demanding
- this will create the need for contact centers to offer more flexible hours and locations, away from the traditional central contact center model
- there will be a greater need for IT-aware business staff to keep knowledge bases, agent decision support systems and website/databases up-to-date
- IP architectures will become mainstream, making virtual contact centers and part-time staff a more important part of the contact center mix
- Independent homeworking will continue to be niche, as management issues and concerns will not go away. However, we believe there is a case for seeing team leaders being based at satellite locations with small teams.

Contract Center in 2025

Although technology moves quickly, the reason that contact centers were set up still remains—customers want to do business quickly, and organisations want to do business profitably. The contact center still gives both parties a reasonable result.

When looking into the far future, we have assumed that:

- Businesses will continue to place profitability above all things, and in particular, will be ruthless in their pursuit of lower costs. Although there has been lots of talk of getting the contact center to increase revenues, in most cases, funding has been granted more easily to projects and initiatives which can prove short-term cost reduction, and we see no reason for this to change
- Customers do not particularly **want** to do business with other people—most lead increasingly busy lives, and see interacting with businesses just as a task to get through. As such, customers will choose the means and time to communicate with businesses which offers them the greatest chance of a swift and successful resolution. Currently, this is through talking to other people, although this may change.

Based on this, we believe that the following have a good chance of occurring:

The customer experience

- Self-service, especially via speech, will be prevalent, and will have taken over from live voice contact as the no. 1 customer-to-business communication method
- A greater number of initial purchases of goods will be done without actually contacting a company. Potential purchasers will use a real or virtual broker to determine the best deal based on their requirements, and purchases will be carried out after reviewing options. The use of a PDA with limited intelligence which interrogates company systems on behalf of a customer seems likely. Actual live calls to a company will be more likely to come from existing customers
- Customer expectations will be so high that there will be no contact center queue. Most large businesses will operate a virtual contact center, using outsourcers or in-house staff not based at the contact center site itself. Customers may still allow the

use of call-back technology—it is unclear to what extent customer impatience will further develop

- Outbound cold calls will have been legislated out of existence, however outbound value-added service will be a strong brand differentiator (e.g. letting customers know about approaching credit limits, late flights, etc.), but this will not necessarily be accomplished using a live voice option
- Inbound security checks will be carried out automatically though voiceprints, reducing call lengths

The agent experience

- There will be fewer agents than today, although there will be many more at the top-end. The average agent will be highly-skilled, technically-competent, and authorized to make decisions immediately. It is possible that they will be based in multiple separate locations in very small teams
- Businesses will need to be careful not to overload agents with data, but will need to present it in a user friendly format. Technology will be used which identifies words in a conversation, picking up key words and pushing possible solutions to an agent's screen
- Much more emphasis will be placed on clearing the agent desktop of unnecessary clutter, while providing the agent with more relevant information dynamically. A speech interface could take over from the use of a keyboard, with structured data being filled in automatically as the conversation occurs naturally
- Training times and salaries for agents will be much higher than today, even in relative terms. Agents will be skilled in sales and marketing, as well as service, and systems will empower them to make decisions
- Voice will continue to be the no. 1 customer-agent communication form, as it is so flexible and quick compared to any text-based interaction type.

The business experience

- Interaction recording solutions and the analytical tools behind it will increase in sophistication so that timely information is provided on a daily and digestible basis to operational and senior people for tactical decisions and feedback on marketing
- How will contact center performance be measured? We do not believe that businesses' aims will change substantially, so first-call resolution and the measurement of revenue against total cost of customer service—customer profitability—will grow in importance even more. We believe that the current fad for improving customer satisfaction is driven by CRM theories (rather than altruism), which link satisfaction with loyalty, and loyalty with profits. As such, this focus will probably wane as new commercial theories emerge, although of course, the profit focus will remain as strong as ever
- A point will be reached when businesses are avoiding so many calls that they realize that they are no longer communicating with their customers, and are losing sales opportunities (even if the customers themselves are quite happy). This means that

automation will reach a point when enough is enough, and businesses actually try to engineer chances to talk to their customers, rather than *vice versa* as is the case today.

REFERENCE

Business Wire, August 7, 2006, "Discover Card Survey Provides Comprehensive Look at Consumer Opinions or Customer Service."

CHAPTER 4

DIGITAL MARKETING: INTERNET DIRECT

Michael Schiller

The Internet poses enormous challenges and presents enormous opportunities to marketers looking to build their brands, increase sales, and capture market share. As marketers approach utilizing the Internet as a marketing tool, they need to be cognizant of the fact that the transformation of the economy by the Internet is really just beginning and that our notions of how we go about creating, delivering, and communicating value to customers will continue to evolve as the Internet evolves. At the present, the dynamic edge of the Internet is creating new tools for the creation of marketing communications and new approaches to the generation and dissemination of brand messages.

THE EVOLUTION OF THE INTERNET AND ITS IMPLICATIONS FOR MARKETING

Management thinker Peter Drucker pointed out in 1999 that the Industrial Age unfolded in waves of transforming technologies beginning with railroads and the telegraph in the 1850s, the internal combustion engine in the 1900s, and the broad implementation of electric power and the radio in the 1920s.[1] Each of these waves of industrial technology transformed the economy by accelerating the flow of materials and information. Railroad and internal combustion vehicles, for example, moved materials over greater distances in less time than previous transportation technologies, broadening the distribution capabilities of producers and distributors. The telegraph and the telephone accelerated the flow of information, broadening people's awareness of events, connecting people across vast distances in real time and even changing the way people structured their very use of language.[2] The internal combustion engine and electricity transformed the urban landscape and changed America from an agricultural nation to a manufacturing nation.

The Digital Age, which began with the invention of the computer, is now in what appears to be its fourth wave, the first being the introduction of computers following World War II, the second being the connection of computers into large networks beginning in the 1960s, the introduction of the personal computer in the 1970s, and the commercialization of the Internet in the 1990s.[3]

Consistent with the experience of the Industrial Age, waves of technology-driven change, the first wave of the Internet—what may now be called the e-commerce wave—was greeted and promoted with a great deal of hype. That hype focused on the transformational aspects of the Internet as it was applied to the transactional relationships of the value chain and the disruption of the flow of money through the supply chains of nearly every material industry in the economy. During the years 1995 through 2001, industry after industry saw their supply chain relationships disrupted as intermediaries and brokers such as travel agents, wholesalers, and distributors were "disintermediated" as the Internet either eliminated or dramatically reduced search and transaction costs. Headlines in leading business publications made claims that the brick-and-mortar businesses were now obsolete, that the business cycle had finally come to an end, and the stock market reached all time highs and valuations. As with previous technology-induced waves and their associated hype, the bubbles crashed and the new technologies were integrated into a changed economic landscape.[4]

In a White Paper prepared in 1999, futurists Kirk Klasson and John Kerr identified six characteristics of the Internet that underlay the changes enabling e-commerce.[5] Those six characteristics include the following:

Scope,

Speed,

Technology,

Customer centricity,

Intellectual capital, and

Trust.

Klasson and Kerr's characteristics appear to define many of the most important qualities of the Internet and have tremendous import for marketers and merit a summary discussion here.

From Scale to Scope

One of the cornerstone characteristics of Industrial Age economics was economies of scale, where industries would become as big as resources would allow in pursuit of lower marginal costs. Vertical integration enabled companies to reduce the cost of search, transaction, and pricing information within their value chain, driving the creation of enormous businesses that sourced their own raw materials, transformed those materials into intermediate and finished products, and delivered finished goods through dedicated distribution networks to consumers. Successful industrial companies made substantial investments in physical assets and plant in order to capture wealth generated through the industrial manufacturing processes.

According to Klasson and Kerr, economies of scale have given way to economies of scope as the nature of resources changes from physical assets to information about assets—knowledge becoming the central focus of firms. As the cost of information falls due to its availability over the Internet, vertical integration and its associated layers of management become more expensive than virtual integration as businesses evolve to specialize in building deep knowledge in specific areas of expertise, linking with other companies in their value chain that have a similar knowledge depth in complimentary areas to deliver the finished product. The health care system, with its ecology of hospitals, specialty service firms such as radiology, ambulatory diagnostic, and other specialist providers work together to deliver a seamless product to health care consumers. In terms of investment, successful companies are now investing heavily in customers, skills, and expertise rather than in physical plants in order to remain competitive.

Speed

The velocity of information has increased significantly as a result of digital technology. This has had two key impacts: First, the speed with which society absorbs and produces new technologies is accelerating. Telephones, for example, required 40 years to get to 30-percent market penetration, television required 17 years to 30-percent market penetration, the personal computer required just 13 years to get to 30-percent market penetration, and the Internet a mere 5 years to reach 30-percent integration. The acceleration of the adoption curve has also resulted in the rise of the Law of Increasing Returns, a phenomenon where once a technology or product establishes itself it tends to dominate the market, shutting out competitors by virtue of the rapid expansion of an installed base of customers.

The second key impact has been the rise of information globalization and 24/7 competition. Financial markets were among the first industries to experience the impact of information globalization as trading financial securities and commodities operates seamlessly across the world. The first experience with globalization of financial markets was the October 1987 market crash, which literally rolled across time zones as market after market fell for days until actions by the U.S. trading community and the Federal Reserve were able to halt the slide in prices. Today, trading across time zones is a given, and the financial markets essentially operate as a seamless, global trading pool. Products that are susceptible to digitization are especially subject to hyperaccelerated competition as infrastructure is quick to assemble and barriers to entry are low.

Technology

Klasson and Kerr identify technologies that enhance content and connectivity as a powerful force shaping the digital economy. These technologies are enabling and driving change through a massive deflation of the cost of managing larger and larger datasets and by reducing barriers to access of remote data sources as proposed by Gordon Moore and Bob Metcalfe. Moore's Law, posited by Intel cofounder Gordon Moore in 1965 states that the capabilities of processing power double every 18 months while the cost of that processing power falls by half in the same time period.[6] In addition, Metcalfe's Law, proposed by Ethernet inventor Robert Metcalfe, states that the power of a network is equal to the number of users squared.[7]

Content and connectivity technology is a powerful commoditizing force. Leveraging universal communication protocols, technology enables the capture, manipulation, and distribution of information about anything of interest, essentially commoditizing any product by making deep information available on a broad basis, eliminating the power of information arbitrage as a source of competitive advantage. For example, computers have allowed us to convert information about products, such as chairs, computers, or other items into digital packages that can be rapidly disseminated to manufacturing sites anywhere in the world in minutes, enabling manufacturing close to the point of use or where the cost of manufacturing, when coupled with transportation costs, is the lowest possible.

Customer Centricity

Klasson and Kerr note that digital technology puts the customer in control of the supply and delivery chain, creating a customer-centric marketing environment. Digital technology puts customers in the driver's seat by reducing search costs to the extent that comparison shopping may be achieved on a global basis, by reducing transactions costs so as to allow for negotiated prices on just about any product or service, changing the economic focus of marketers from achieving the lowest marginal cost to capturing the highest marginal value.

The first industry to take advantage of this ability was the airline industry, which created marginal pricing models to capture the maximum economic value of an airline seat to each individual customer, taking into account a large array of variables such as destination, purchase lead time, duration of stay, and other factors.

Klasson and Kerr additionally note that the nature of digital content—and digital production environments—enables custom product development and delivery, a first step toward the holy grail of marketing—mass customization, the creation of unique product offerings to individual customers with the economics of mass production.

Intellectual Capital

Klasson and Kerr identify that intellectual capital is replacing physical capital as the key driver in productivity and innovation. Companies are now investing heavily in patent research and innovation, both of which are driven by intellectual capital rather than physical capital. That new ideas displace existing ideas at lower costs and faster than capital improvements can reduce costs was observed by Harvard Professor Clayton M. Christiansen in his seminal work *The Innovator's Dilemma,* creating a challenge for any management team seeking to maximize the return on investment in a physical plant in rapidly changing markets.[8]

Markets are responding to this by increasing the valuation of companies that are among the most innovative and which lead in the hiring of the best and brightest minds. The price histories of Microsoft Corporation, Google, and General Motors Corporation over the last three to five years support this contention.

Trust

Klasson and Kerr observe that trust is the key to any relationship, the question being "will the seller deliver on their promise?"[9] They further note that trust is fragile and perishable and is easily weakened by product proliferation, reduced search costs, advertising overload, short attention spans, and expectations of change.

With the Internet giving buyers access to thousands if not millions of alternative suppliers, trust becomes an essential function of brand value, with customers trusting the brands that deliver a consistent experience. That the brand providing the trust is not always the manufacturer is an important aspect of Internet marketing. For example, eBay Inc.'s willingness to guarantee an exchange creates a high-trust environment for both buyers and sellers on the eBay Web site.

Trust evolves through transaction experiences, whether they are information transactions, financial transactions, or delivery transactions: One bad experience poorly handled may destroy built-up trust value.

WEB 2.0

The second wave of the Internet is now sweeping across the economy and appears to be focused on the disruption of the flow of information through the economy. The forces that reshaped commerce are now reshaping the media industries, changing both the commercial relationships between producers of content, distributors of content, and consumers of content, as well as the nature of the content itself. In recent news reports media companies are reporting that readership is falling dramatically for printed products, especially newspapers, while readership for digital offerings, including Web sites, is rising dramatically. The valuation of content businesses such as YouTube, Inc. have reached values similar to those achieved during the height of the e-commerce bubble in the late 1990s and 2000.

In looking at the impact of the Internet on commerce, we can infer that just as the six qualities of the Internet that restructured supply chains and disintermediated brokers, this second wave will disintermediate and transform content brokers. These include ad agencies, media buying firms, and other firms engaged in the creation, production, and dissemination of value signals in the economy.

We believe that the role of these brokers will change, especially that of the advertising agency. Traditionally, agencies created content for their clients, produced that content, and mediated that content, controlling both the message and its dissemination in the marketplace. The changes now impacting the marketing communications arena suggest that the new role of the agency will be to set the context for content creation by brand advocates, customers who are highly connected and highly motivated on behalf of their favorite brands, enable these brand advocates to create content that is of interest to them and their circles of influence, and mediate the message using the tools and distribution mechanisms of their own choice. In this new model, agencies will empower brand advocates to carry the brand message forward, placing constraints on how the message is framed, articulated, and mediated through the rules of the context or events they create. In most cases, these events will coexist in both the virtual space of the Internet and physical space of the consumer, creating a new paradigm and model for marketing that we call digital marketing.

DIGITAL MARKETING

The centerpiece of the digital marketing environment is a Web site. A Web site is essentially a software application that automates a human interaction. Such a site may function as a place where information exchange occurs, where products are browsed and purchased, where customer-service operations are performed, where entertainment is purchased and consumed, or any other human-brand interaction may occur.

Web sites have experienced the following five stages of development:[10]

- *Brochureware*. At its earliest and most simple form, a Web site functions as an online brochure, featuring a home page, description of the company, and other information typically found in brochures.
- *e-catalog*. The second stage of site evolution was the introduction of the e-catalog, a site that presented browsers with data about the products and services available from a company.

- *Interactive*. An interactive site is one that is a transactional site that interacts with the browsing consumer, exchanging information and essentially managing the customer relationship.
- *Multimedia*. Multimedia sites present unlimited presentational and interactive capabilities, providing browsers with rich multimedia brand experiences, including audio, video, and other dynamic content.
- *Platform Expansion*. Sites are now experiencing a migration from the PC to alternative platforms such as mobile devices that can browse the Internet. Mobile devices present significant challenges due to their diversity of capabilities and the nature of their screen and other visual and interactive capabilities.

Today's Web site is more than a medium; it is, in fact, a place where people go to obtain information, find products, and engage in both commercial and social activities. Companies engaged in marketing in this new digital environment need to adapt to the new tools of digital marketing in order to create and manage successful campaigns for acquiring and retaining customers in the pursuit of brand development, sales, and the capture of market share.

THE TOOLS OF DIGITAL MARKETING

The marketing tools for digital marketing draw upon the six characteristics of the Internet in innovative ways that create a new challenge for marketing creativity. The leading tools follow:

- Customization,
- Community,
- ePR,
- e-mail marketing,
- Online advertising, programming
- Viral marketing,
- Blogging,
- Podcasting,
- User-generated video,
- Branded events,
- Search engine marketing, and
- Search engine optimization.

Customization

Web site customization refers to the ability of a site to provide each user with a unique experience. Customization takes the two following forms:[11]

- *Personalization*. Personalization is the function where the site user initiates and manages the customization process.

- *Tailoring.* Tailoring is customization that is initiated by the site and managed by the site as its software dynamically publishes unique versions of the site based on the users' interests, habits, and needs within the context of standardized customer profiles created through data mining and modeling of consumer user data.

Typical tools Web sites use to allow users to personalize their Web site experience included content and layout configuration, data storage, agents such as "bots" that alert users to specific kinds of information, e-mail accounts, chat and bulletin board services, and other tools that enable the user to create a highly individual experience. Tailoring tools typically configure the users' experiences for them based upon their site usage profiles and other information they have provided to the site.

Community

Perhaps the most powerful tool to emerge in digital marketing, digital community is similar to real-world community in that it provides members of a digital community with a sense of belonging, shared interests, personal relationships with others, the development of specialized language and humor that characterizes group membership, and impact on the lives of members.

In the context of brands, digital community enables the sharing brand relevant information. One successful community was developed by a dairy that allowed consumers to share recipes, product experiences, and other brand product usage information, which ultimately enhanced the experience of the consumers with the companies' products.

ePR

Like traditional public relations (PR), the objective of ePR is to create an amplification effect as messages reverberate through the marketplace from both unpaid, highly credible "news" to paid advertising. This is achieved by leveraging the four differences of ePR with PR:[12]

- *Organizational connection.* Unlike most traditional PR respondents, ePR respondents typically have some connection to the brand or company. This may be as a brand advocate or some other relationship.
- *Member connectivity.* Members of the brand community are connected to one another through the digital community, exchanging information and commentary on the brand.
- *Multiple sources.* Most brand advocates and ePR consumers will have multiple sources of information for keeping up-to-date on the brand.
- *Information search.* Most consumers of ePR will seek out information on their brands as part of their membership in the brand community.

Typical ePR activities include press releases, the construction of links to other related sites, corporate blogs that humanize the firm, and online brand management operations.

e-Mail Marketing

The concept underlying opt-in e-mail marketing programs is the capture of e-mail addresses for creating and delivering targeted population marketing communications. Consumers enter into a transaction with the Web site producer whereby they give the Web site their e-mail addresses in exchange for value from the site. The value is typically in the form of content designed specifically to match the interests of the subscriber. The key to successful e-mail marketing programs is to create enough interest in the Web site to drive participation.

When designing e-mail marketing programs, the selling firm should give the users choice over the type of content they receive, assurance of the protection of their privacy, e-mail designs that match the location constraints where the subscriber will normally consume the information such as at work or at home, and give the subscribers control over content, frequency of e-mails, and timing of e-mails. In addition, producers of e-mail marketing programs should be prepared for fake e-mail addresses, junk mail e-mail addresses, and specialty e-mail addresses designed to foil spamming programs.

Online Advertising

Online advertising in the form of banner and tower ads was established early in the development of commercial Web sites as a direct analog to print media advertisements. Later innovations such as pop-up and pop-under windows annoyed users to the point that a flourishing market in ad blocker software emerged in the late 1990s and which was later co-opted by browser software producers who built pop-up and ad blocker software into their browser designs. Currently intercept ads are popular, generally providing a short video on a brand or product as a user moves between Web pages on a site.

The effectiveness of traditional online advertising is being challenged by firms such as Google, which argues that click-through ads such as its AdSense ads are generally more measurable and thus more effective than corporate performance management–based metrics.

Programming

In an innovative break from traditional online advertising, the Mercury unit of Ford Motor Company introduced "Meet the Lucky Ones" in the spring of 2005. This ad campaign consisted of a series of videos and other content structured around a set of characters in the form of an online soap opera. The campaign ran for several weeks and generated a great deal of interest among browsers. The purpose of the campaign appeared to be to attract attention to the Mercury line of vehicles and provided browsers with links to learn more about Mercury's line of automobiles.

Programming campaigns can effectively create online experiences for sharing the brand story and experience by creating compelling online entertainment that attracts consumers to visit a Web site and to learn more about a brand's offerings.

Viral Marketing

Viral marketing is the Internet version of word-of-mouth advertising. It is about getting customers to become advocates for a brand by providing them with video, audio, images, and text that they forward to others. The key to successful viral campaigns is to create irrepressible interesting content that people will forward and thus disseminate brand information.

The first successful viral marketing campaign was the launch of Hotmail in 1996.[13] In each e-mail sent out by a Hotmail user, the bottom of the e-mail contained a link to the Hotmail URL. As more people clicked on the link, more people obtained the free e-mail account and then repeated the marketing process by sending out e-mails of their own with the link.

In many cases companies will also reuse or repurpose content from one advertising method for viral use. In 2003 Honda Motor Company UK ran a two-minute television commercial entitled "The Cog" during the broadcast of the Brazilian Formula 1 Grand Prix.[14] After the airing of the commercial during the program, Honda posted the commercial on its Web site and in 2004 the U.K. dealerships reported record-breaking sales that it attributed, in part, to the advertisement. The viral nature of the ad became apparent in the United States when it showed up on the Internet and was reportedly being viewed 55,000 times per month, resulting in a dramatic increase in both dealership visitation and sales.

Blogging

Blogs, short for Web logs, are a form of public diary or commentary published by an individual or group to share experiences or thoughts with others. They were originally created by people posting their thoughts on current events in their lives and the world for others to see and react to. A typical blog entry has a wide range of embedded links that allow the reader to browse off-site content that the blogger is referencing or reacting to. Most blogs also allow readers to post comments to their posts.

Blogs were lifted to public consciousness by the Howard Dean 2004 presidential campaign, where they were used with great effect to share the campaign message and to mobilize Dean supporters.[15] The leading blog sites include Livejournal.com, blogger.com, and blogspot.com in addition to the social networking sites of MySpace and FaceBook, Inc. The blog market is supported by its own search engines, particularly the Technorati site (www.technorati.com) and Google's blogsearch.google.com site.

Podcasting

Podcasting is the Internet transmission of downloadable MP3 audio and MP4 video files to computers and portable MP3 and MP4 players such as the Apple iPod. Essentially a form of digital radio, podcasting allows people to access audio and video content of interest at their preferred time and place on demand. Podcasting was originally started by individuals who saw the opportunity to create their own "radio shows" much like people did in the 1960s and 1970s after the introduction of the audio cassette.

Podcasting became widespread following the issuance of Apple's iTunes software release 4.5 in July 2005. In that release, the iTunes Music Store contained a section for podcasts containing downloadable content from professional content producers such as National Public Radio and Major League Baseball. Amateurs, professional content producers, and others were able to make their podcasts available through the iTunes Music Store and by allowing for direct links to the producer's Web site using the iTunes software. Since then, podcasting has become popular, especially among producers of professional content.[16] Podcasting has become so popular that even churches are using it to spread the word through "Godcasting" or "Godpodding!"[17]

User-Generated Video

The most recent innovation in digital marketing has been the development of User Generated Video content, or UGV. The Web site YouTube, launched in late 2005 and which began to take off in 2006, has popularized homemade video content as people began to use the site to post and share their own work with others as well as clips of content from professional content providers such as entertainment producers.[18]

Branded Events

The most important movement in digital marketing is the rise of the Branded Event. The goal of the Branded Event is to feed target consumers deemed "brand advocates" with opportunities for the creation of viral content. Events may consist of promotional campaigns, real-world events, competitions, and other events that mobilize and energize brand advocates to "evangelize" on the benefits of the brand

and its products. Each event should establish a set of rules for participation and a goal or outcome that rewards compliance. An example may be a competition in which brand advocates take pictures of the product in use in a positive way and then have the overall audience or a panel of judges rate the entries based on voting. The winner may receive a prize.

In addition to serving as content creation vehicles that frame the brand in desired ways, branded events also create a platform for integrating multiple digital marketing initiatives into a cohesive campaign. A car show, for example, can engage participants in video creation, still image creation, podcasts, blogging, ePR, and other vehicles that ripple across the market creating buzz and building the image of the brand.

Search Engine Marketing and Optimization

Search engines produce customized yellow pages for customers that are tailored to their specific search needs. There are two strategies for approaching search engines: optimization of your Web site so as to achieve higher rankings in search results tables and purchasing of search result placement.

Optimization involves the arcane art of trying to estimate how search engines rank sites. Key aspects typically involve the use of keywords on a Web site, having other pages link to the target page, and other criteria. The biggest challenge for those building optimization strategies is the difference in the methods used by the search engines. Google, for example, is focused on using an algorithm that ranks sites based on a proprietary formula. Yahoo! in contrast, also uses editorial review of rankings to ensure that the page links served up in searches are accurate in terms of the needs of the searcher.

Search Engine Marketing involves the purchase of placements on search pages tied to the use of specific keywords used by customers conducting searches. Firms typically identify the words they want to be associated with in the customer search process and then bid on those words in order to purchase a highlighted link on the resulting search page. The different search firms will work with clients to define the best keywords and to search criteria for the company drawing upon their analytical analysis of customer search behaviors.

THE FUTURE OF MARKETING

As we have seen, the impacts of the Internet and digital technology on marketing are just now beginning to be seen as the second wave of technology innovation, Web 2.0, unfolds in the wake of the first wave, e-commerce. Future technology waves yet unforeseen will continue to add to and modify the business and social environments in which marketers operate as they seek to build their brands, increase sales, and capture market share. Digital marketing as it is now evolving will become the critical foundation for marketing in the future.

NOTES

1. Peter Drucker, "Beyond the Information Revolution," *Atlantic Monthly,* October 1999.

2. Garry Wills, *Lincoln at Gettysburg: The Words That Remade America* (New York: Touchstone, 1992).

3. Alfred D. Chandler, Jr., *Inventing the Electronic Century: The Epic Story of the Consumer Electronics and Computer Industries* (New York: Free Press, 2001).

4. Edward Chancellor, *Devil Take the Hindmost: A History of Financial Speculation* (New York: Penguin Group, 1999).

5. Kirk Klasson and John Kerr, *New Economy Primer* (Cambridge, MA: Cambridge Technology Partners, 1999).

6. "Moore's Law," http://en.wikipedia.org/wiki/Moore's_law.

7. Bob Briscoe, Andrew Odlyzko, and Benjamin Tilly, "Metcalfe's Law Is Wrong," *IEEE Spectrum,* 43, no. 7 (2006): 34–39.

8. Clayton M. Christiansen, *The Innovator's Dilemma* (Boston: Harvard Business School Press, 1997).

9. Klasson and Kerr, *New Economy Primer.*

10. Kevin Coleman, "Make your Web Site a Business Success," *e-Business Advisor,* September 1998.

11. Jeffrey Rayport et al., *Introduction to e-Business* (New York: McGraw-Hill, 2003).

12. Dave Chaffey and P. R. Smith, *eMarketing eXcellence* (Burlington, MA: Elsevier, 2005).

13. Steve Jurveston, "What is Viral Marketing?" *Red Herring,* May 1, 2000.

14. Angela Dobele, David Toleman, and Michael Beverland, "Controlled Infection! Spreading the Brand Message through Viral Marketing," *Business Horizons* 48 (2005): 143–49.

15. Joe Trippi, *The Revolution Will Not Be Televised* (New York: Harper Collins, 2004).

16. "As Podcasts Boom, Big Media Rushes to Stake a Claim," *Wall Street Journal,* October 10, 2005, p. 1.

17. "Missed Church? No Worries. Download It to Your iPod," *New York Times,* August 29, 2005.

18. Rachel Rosmarin, "Web Users Eat Up Video," *Forbes.com,* May 24, 2006, http://www.forbes.com/2006/05/24/youtube-myspace-video_cx_rr_0524video.

CHAPTER 5

CHARACTERISTICS OF ONLINE SHOPPERS IN THE EUROPEAN UNION

Mario Martinez Guerrero, Jose Manuel Ortega Egea, and
Maria Victoria Roman Gonzalez

E-commerce is growing rapidly because it is offering consumers the opportunity to save time and money and to access better products or services by not going to a shop. However, it does not yet pose a threat to brick-and-mortar shops. Despite the enormous potential of e-commerce, its share of the total economy remains small: less than 2.5 percent in the United States (U.S. Census Bureau, 2006). The lack of consumer confidence in online security and privacy has been identified as a major problem hampering the growth of e-commerce. This issue has drawn considerable attention among researchers (Park, Lee, and Ahn, 2004; Pavlou, 2003; Featherman and Pavlou, 2003; Featherman and Wells, 2004). Nevertheless, as individuals become more familiar with online consuming, and more effective protection mechanisms are put in place, other barriers to e-commerce will come to the forefront.

One of the issues that has been overlooked of late relates to customers' navigation activities while visiting e-commerce Web pages. It is increasingly being recognized that the ability of the consumer to navigate through a given site dictates the extent to which he or she is willing to engage in a transaction. When navigation difficulties arise, potential customers are often not able to access information, make purchases, or obtain service resulting in lower levels of satisfaction. The result is that companies fail to maximize the potential of their Web site to establish a direct, ongoing relationship with their current and potential customers.

In order to maximize the potential of e-commerce, it is critical to accurately understand consumers' navigation problems while shopping online.

Unfortunately, there is a marked lack of research concerning this issue. In this chapter we profile Internet users using previously experienced navigation problems on shopping Web sites as a foundation. The application of usability is proposed as a solution to Web site navigation issues.

Initially, the application of usability is clarified and discussed in the context of its importance for Web sites' development and maintenance. As part of this discussion, the key techniques for analyzing Web site usability are explored. From there, Internet users experiencing navigation problems while shopping are profiled. In creating these profiles, hierarchical segmentation and latent class regression analysis are applied to a sample of online shoppers with navigation problems, drawn from the database "Flash Eurobarometer 125: Internet and the Public at Large." These statistical analyses examine the relationships between customers' demographic traits and the likelihood they will experience navigation problems. Recommendations are then provided to firms and organizations for the improved effective application of usability techniques on their Web sites.

NAVIGATION PROBLEMS FOR ONLINE CUSTOMERS

E-commerce offers speed, convenience, and often better prices, but many e-commerce sites are still cumbersome to navigate resulting in many consumers failing to purchase products from e-commerce sites (Liu et al., 2003). Interface limitations, search problems, and the lack of Internet standards have been identified as barriers specific to e-commerce (Rose, Khoo, and Straub, 1999). The Technology Acceptance Model (TAM), developed by Davis (1989), has shown the influence of consumers' perceived ease of use of e-commerce Web sites on their decision to shop online (Chen, Gillenson, and Sherrell, 2002; Klopping and McKinney, 2004; Pavlou, 2003).

When consumers do not know how to find and buy products on e-commerce Web sites, the difficulty may be attributed to a Web site design that does not fit either the expectations or ability level of the users. Such problems are growing as Internet usage spreads to less-experienced users (Manchón, 2002) with low computer literacy (that is, users who do not know how to use some of the most basic Web site interactivity elements). Due to new users' lack of computer experience, each Web site visit frequently involves a trial-and-error learning process, contrary to the more sophisticated Internet user. Web designers often assume that all visitors to a site have the needed knowledge to navigate through Web pages, an assumption that may lead to the creation of usage barriers for novice users. The situation becomes more complex as the typical Internet user becomes dependent upon different communication tools (e-mail, www, chats/forums, and so forth), hundreds of content formats (such as commercial programs and different file extensions), and many technological formats (Cañada Crespi, 2002).

According to one recent study, "Online stores need to endeavour to enhance customer satisfaction to maintain a positive relationship with customers" (Kim and Eom, 2002). Customer satisfaction is related to the level of customer loyalty (Cho and Park, 2001; Kim and Eom, 2002) and is also associated with intentions regarding repeated purchases (Jones and Sasser, 1995; Patterson, Johnson, and Spreng, 1997). Several factors (quality of products, prices, delivery time, payment methods, and so forth) determine customer satisfaction, including the purchasing process on shopping Web sites.

At the same time, consumers reject e-commerce Web sites where they have suffered navigation problems, due to Web designs not based on users' needs. Customers who experience such problems have a high probability of not purchasing a product from online sources if they have a readily available choice of shopping elsewhere. In the end, from a behavioral point of view (even considering the specific features of any information technology system) the quality of the experience affects user acceptance (Morris and Turner, 2001). The value experienced, perceived or actual, after visiting a site is essential in order to retain users (Dellaert and Kahn, 1999). The existing evidence supports the notion that the user experience in a Web site visit is crucial to the point where ease of use can determine if a user will become an actual purchasing customer. While satisfaction with the Web site interface does not guarantee customer loyalty to any given site, it is certainly important to keep customers both satisfied and motivated to return (Kim and Eom, 2002).

USABILITY ON E-COMMERCE WEB SITES

The goal of usability on a Web site should be to facilitate the design of Web pages which, in turn, facilitates the user's ability to maximize the site's specific value to the individual user. There are two official definitions of usability according to the International Organization for Standardization (ISO): (1) according to ISO/IEC 9126, "usability is the capability of the software product to be understood, learned, used, and attractive to the user, when used under specified conditions," and (2) in ISO 9241, usability is defined as "the extent to which a product can be used by specified users to achieve specified goals with effectiveness, efficiency, and satisfaction in a specified context of use" (International Standards Organization, 1991).

Applying the second, most recent, definition, usability helps users accomplish their tasks in accordance with the following requirements:

- Effectiveness (that is, to reach their goals),
- Efficiency (that is, to fulfil the task with adequate effort or resources), and
- User satisfaction.

Usability includes several factors involved in the user experience including information, organization, interactivity, and personalization, which were all identified as significant factors in Web site effectiveness (Chakraborty, Lala, and

Warren, 2002). The overarching concept is that companies may apply these usability criteria in the process of designing and development of their Web sites, in order to ensure an easy accessibility to Web contents. Usability plays a role in adapting the user interface to customers' online behavior. Therefore, it is key for companies to understand their consumers' Web site navigation patterns (Constantine, 2000).

In addition to the interface, a complex set of decisions gives users the possibility of performing their tasks in an easy, efficient, and satisfactory way with few errors. Web applications should be developed to satisfy user needs while incorporating these decisions into an "invisible" interface in order to reduce potential confusion on the part of users (Olsina, Lafuente, and Rossi, 2000). Investments in usability can quickly lead to quality and higher levels of competitiveness. If visitors are satisfied, they will be more prone to interact on a number of levels with companies on their Web sites.

Usability can also lower the negative impact of one of the main barriers to e-commerce: lack of consumer trust. The interface design of a Web site has an impact on users' level of confidence (Flavián Blanco, Guinalí Blasco, and Gurrea Sarasa, 2004; Jinwoo and Moon, 1998; Nielsen, 1999; Patton and Jøsang, 2004). Users have the ability to complete their tasks efficiently and effectively. As an added bonus, usability contributes to a favorable perception of the site, which builds customer confidence (Roy, Dewit, and Aubert, 2001). "Trusting" users will not only purchase products, they will also feel satisfied and their loyalty to the site will increase (Flavián Blanco, Guinalí Blasco, and Gurrea Sarasa, 2004). Unfortunately, Web site developers frequently do not take into account potential visitors to the site. Thus, it is not uncommon to find usability problems in any test navigation session (Fidalgo, 2000; Nielsen, 2005; Tognazzini, 2004). Therefore, a characterization of current users and consumers with common navigation and usability problems would be valuable for the design of an efficient commercial Web site.

METHODOLOGY

The analyses for this chapter are based on survey data included in the cross-national database "Flash Eurobarometer 125: Internet and the Public at Large." This survey is carried out every six months by the European Commission in all European Union (EU) countries. See Table 5.1.

Based on a total sample of 30,336 individuals, 17,000 are currently using the Internet and 6,098 have previously shopped online. Participants with experience in Internet purchases were asked about their shopping problems: 1,726 of them have encountered navigation troubles in the past. According to the data shown in Figure 5.1, 28 percent of surveyed online shoppers have experienced navigation

Table 5.1
Sample Characteristics—Flash Eurobarometer 125

Data collection method	Telephone survey
Selection method	Random
Total participants	30,336 respondents (approximately 2,000 per country)
Sampling error	±0.6% (p = q = 0.5)
Confidence interval	95%
Collected information	Sociodemographic indicators (age, country, sex, occupation, and so forth) and other variables related to place of access, frequency, and purposes of Internet use.

problems, which represent the most common barrier to successful online purchases.

Initially, descriptive statistics are examined in order to clarify the sociodemographic characteristics of the participants in the study. Next, two different statistical methodologies are applied to the data from individuals who had experienced navigational problems while shopping online.

- Hierarchical segmentation. The Exhaustive CHAID (chi-squared automatic interation detector) algorithm is employed. Methodologically, this approach identifies hierarchical interactions between a dependent variable and a set of independent indicators. This tree-like statistical analysis is useful as a comprehensive data exploration tool.

Figure 5.1
Problems When Shopping Online

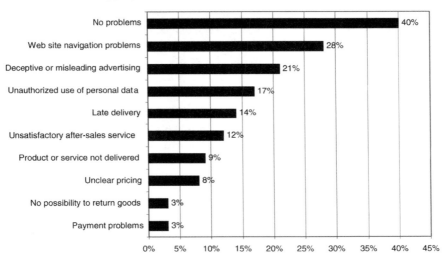

- Latent class regression analysis (Latent GOLD v2.0 software) is applied to test several regression models with different sociodemographic explanatory indicators. The aim is to explain the existence of navigation problems (dependent variable) through sociodemographic variables (independent variables). Latent class regression analysis is especially useful and flexible for dealing with categorical and mixed types of indicators.

The goal of the analyses is to identify respondents' sociodemographic traits significantly related to such navigation problems. Both statistical analyses include the following as sociodemographic indicators: country, sex, age, occupation, locality type, education completion age, and age cohort difference within the household.

PROFILE OF INTERNET USERS WITH NAVIGATION PROBLEMS

The sociodemographic features of all surveyed individuals, Internet users, online shoppers, and those who have experienced navigation problems are shown separately in Table 5.2.

The following trends are observed with regard to such characteristics:

- Country: The use of the Internet and electronic commerce is more widespread in Denmark, Germany, Luxembourg, Holland, Austria, Finland, Sweden, and the United Kingdom. In these countries, except for Austria, there is a higher share of online shoppers experiencing navigation problems.
- Gender: Male respondents account for most users of the Internet (52.20 percent), electronic commerce (57.99 percent), and individuals with navigation problems (60.95 percent).
- Age: Individuals from 14 to 24 and from 25 to 39 years of age are the main Internet users. However, there is a lower presence of online shoppers in the first age group. The segment between 25 and 39 years of age shows the highest rate of Internet purchasers with navigation problems (46.41 percent).
- Education Completion Age: The results point to a positive relationship between respondents' age when completing their full-time education and Internet use.
- Locality Type: The relative distribution of individuals in metropolitan, urban, and rural zones remains stable for the analysis of Internet use and e-commerce services.
- Occupation: Unemployed people show the lowest rates of Internet use and online shopping. Conversely, employees account for most users of the Internet (44.30 percent) and e-commerce (50.44 percent).

Table 5.3 shows how surveyed people access the Internet and their purposes.

There appears to be only a slight difference between users with navigation problems and those who do not experience any problems. The data show that

Table 5.2
Sociodemographic Characteristics

	Total Sample	Internet Users	Online Shoppers	Shoppers with Problems
Country				
Belgium	6.56%	5.43%	3.16%	2.72%
Denmark	6.64%	8.76%	9.41%	9.10%
Germany	6.59%	7.18%	9.84%	10.78%
Greece	6.59%	2.14%	0.57%	0.41%
Spain	6.61%	4.63%	1.95%	2.09%
France	6.62%	5.84%	5.31%	4.58%
Ireland	6.59%	6.68%	5.95%	4.58%
Italy	6.60%	4.95%	2.49%	2.72%
Luxembourg	6.59%	7.68%	8.56%	5.56%
Holland	6.61%	8.35%	8.30%	8.00%
Austria	6.59%	7.32%	7.10%	2.20%
Portugal	6.59%	3.78%	1.44%	1.91%
Finland	6.59%	7.45%	6.82%	11.94%
Sweden	6.59%	8.04%	9.74%	13.50%
United Kingdom	7.62%	11.79%	19.33%	19.93%
Gender				
Men	46.09%	52.20%	57.99%	60.95%
Women	53.91%	47.80%	42.01%	39.05%
Age				
15–24	15.54%	24.14%	19.29%	16.74%
25–39	28.80%	36.56%	42.62%	46.41%
40–54	24.51%	26.31%	27.71%	28.10%
>55	30.99%	12.89%	10.28%	8.63%
Education Completion Age				
No Education	1.78%	0.39%	0.33%	0.35%
<16	22.56%	8.65%	5.58%	4.58%
16–20	44.74%	48.79%	46.05%	40.61%
>20	29.18%	41.20%	47.05%	53.42%

(continued)

Table 5.2 (continued)

	Total Sample	Internet Users	Online Shoppers	Shoppers with Problems
LOCALITY TYPE				
Metropolitan zone	25.86%	27.52%	27.21%	31.00%
Urban zone	39.25%	41.30%	42.47%	40.96%
Rural zone	34.85%	31.15%	30.31%	28.04%
EMPLOYMENT				
Self-employed	8.58%	9.34%	10.50%	11.99%
Employee	31.08%	44.30%	50.44%	51.74%
Manual worker	13.67%	13.22%	12.81%	12.63%
Without professional activity	46.11%	32.53%	25.66%	22.71%

Source: Self-elaboration based on Gallup-Europe, 2002.

online shoppers can be regarded as advanced users compared to the total of Internet users:

- Higher percentage of people having Internet access at home.
- High-speed connections.
- Better security elements.
- More frequent connections from different places.
- Higher rate of Internet use to make contact with the public administration.
- Higher rate of private Internet use: e-banking, information searches, job seeking, health and tourism advice, and education activities.

It may seem contradictory to identify online shoppers with navigation problems as advanced users. Nevertheless, experienced Internet users may find more problems because of more frequent Internet uses. In addition, less-experienced users may not notice navigation problems and attribute errors to their lack of knowledge rather than Web-design deficiencies.

In addition to descriptive statistics, hierarchical segmentation and latent class regression analyses are also applied to determine which sociodemographic variables are significantly related to online shoppers' navigation problems. Hierarchical segmentation, applied to a total of 6,098 Internet users who answered the question related to navigation problems while shopping online, suggests that country is the most significant variable in differentiating between users with and without navigation problems (Chi-square: 330.53; Risk estimate: 0.29).

Figure 5.2 clearly shows that the share of online shoppers with navigation problems differs across countries. More navigation problems are experienced by

Table 5.3
Internet Features

	Internet Users	Online Shoppers	Shoppers with Problems
Internet access at home			
Yes	76.58%	89.47%	89.75%
No	23.36%	10.51%	10.20%
Internet access type			
Standard telephone line	51.35%	55.64%	55.45%
ISDN (integrated services digital network) line	12.33%	17.42%	15.99%
ADSL (asymmetric digital subscriber line) connection	7.42%	11.97%	14.25%
Cable	6.40%	7.39%	7.30%
Mobile connection	1.28%	1.97%	2.20%
Security elements			
Antivirus	62.39%	76.50%	78.27%
Smart card reader	10.57%	13.07%	13.09%
Encryption software	13.11%	18.53%	20.80%
Firewall	19.72%	29.27%	31.63%
Electronic signature	9.32%	12.84%	14.77%
Connection place			
At home	74.54%	87.96%	89.28%
At work	45.02%	54.28%	61.76%
At a friend's, a relative's place	25.64%	27.37%	30.59%
Other	52.99%	60.77%	71.85%
Internet frequency use			
Every day or nearly every day	44.94%	62.51%	69.35%
Several times a week	24.89%	22.60%	20.34%
Approx. once a week	15.46%	9.71%	7.07%
Approx. once a month	8.15%	3.39%	2.14%
Less often	6.22%	1.66%	0.93%
Security problems			
Fraudulent use of your credit card number	1.39%	2.57%	3.13%
Unsolicited e-mail	35.98%	51.31%	63.44%

(continued)

Table 5.3 (continued)

	Internet Users	Online Shoppers	Shoppers with Problems
Contact a public administration via the Internet			
Find administrative information	38.84%	51.75%	61.99%
Send an e-mail	26.32%	37.06%	45.08%
Fill in forms or carry out procedures online	28.28%	42.57%	52.61%
Other reasons	1.62%	3.05%	4.40%
Never contacted an administration	47.25%	32.13%	23.70%
Other Internet private uses			
Banking operations	35.96%	53.77%	62.80%
Look for topical items	73.58%	81.55%	85.23%
Find job ads	29.68%	38.13%	43.86%
Improve training/education	40.40%	43.42%	49.19%
Seek travel	63.36%	78.93%	84.53%
Seek health-related advice	38.78%	46.79%	52.78%
Event tickets	29.93%	46.84%	53.24%

Source: Self-elaboration based on Gallup-Europe, 2002.

e-shoppers from countries with higher Internet usage rates, such as Finland and Sweden. These countries have been characterized as advanced in a previous segmentation study based on Europeans' Internet usage patterns (Recio Menéndez and Ortega Egea, 2003). The highest share of online shoppers with navigation problems in Portugal (37.50 percent) represents an exception to this trend, largely because it was not regarded as an "advanced" country in terms of Internet use.

The statistical significance of other sociodemographic variables, which were identified as discriminant indicators in the first hierarchical segmentation stage, is included in Table 5.4.

Several latent class regression models were also tested, including different sociodemographic variables and number of classes. Nonsignificant variables were progressively removed from the regression model in order to identify an optimal model including solely statistically significant indicators. The regression analyses identify a one-class model as the optimal result. Evaluation of fit indices indicates that the final model provides a statistically significant fit to the data (p-value = 0.99).

Figure 5.2
User Groups per Country

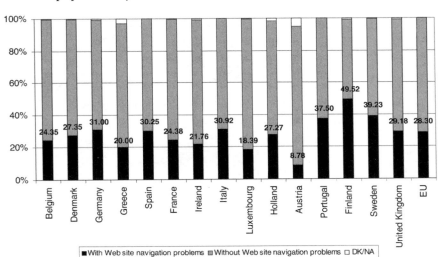

According to the final regression model, the following sociodemographic variables are significantly related to the navigation problems experienced by Internet
users while shopping for products or services online: country, sex, age, and occupation (see Table 5.5).

The country variable provides significant effects on online shoppers' navigation
problems, which points to the existence of substantial national contrasts.
Respondents from Spain, Italy, and Portugal appear to exhibit the highest tendency to experience navigation problems in the European Union. Conversely, online purchasers from Austria, Greece, Holland, Ireland, and Luxembourg are the
users with the lowest tendency to experience such troubles. Surveyed e-shoppers
from other EU countries reveal somewhat more moderate (positive or negative)

Table 5.4
Significant Parameters of the Hierarchical Segmentation Model

Variable	Segment Results	Chi-square	g.l.	Adjusted Probability
Country	14	330.5326	26	0.0000
Education Completion Age	3	56.0530	4	0.0000
Occupation	4	62.3495	6	0.0000
Age	13	85.6910	24	0.0000
Gender	3	27.7139	4	0.0003

Table 5.5
Significant Variables in the Latent Class Regression Model

Predictors	Beta	Wald Statistic	p-value	z-value
Country		292.135	8.9*E-46	
Belgium	−0.3786			−0.2452
Denmark	−0.2240			−0.1472
Germany	−0.3050			−0.2011
Greece	−1.2227			−0.7832
Spain	2.0168			0.1647
France	−0.2063			−0.1337
Ireland	−0.6448			−0.4237
Italy	2.0513			0.1721
Luxembourg	−0.6315			−0.4150
Holland	−0.7029			−0.4642
Austria	−1.8790			−12.407
Portugal	2.1468			0.1705
Finland	0.0758			0.0499
Sweden	0.2547			0.1669
United Kingdom	−0.3506			−0.2317
Gender		18.8665	8.0*E-5	
Men	0.1594			34.005
Women	−0.1594			−34.005
Age		31.5647	0.00011	
15–25	−0.0808			−0.8019
26–33	0.4498			31.225
34–39	−0.0669			−0.6966
40–48	0.0415			0.4011
>48	−0.3437			−41.147
Occupation		13.6742	0.0011	
Self-employed, qualified	0.1809			36.075
Manual workers, unemployed	−0.1809			−36.075

relationships with regard to navigation problems. Gender also exerts significant effects, as male e-shoppers experience relatively more navigation problems than women. With regard to age, respondents aged between 26 and 33 have a high tendency to suffer navigation problems. Finally, according to respondents' occupation, self-employed and skilled employees tend to have more navigation problems than manual workers or unemployed people.

IMPLICATIONS FOR FIRMS

Usability is increasingly required for the development of e-commerce Web sites, as the Internet spreads to user groups with less computer experience. These individuals are typically comprised of heterogeneous segments with regards to sociodemographic characteristics and Internet usage patterns. Shopping Web sites, in particular, need to be customer oriented if companies want customers to utilize the site for commercial communications or transactions. In this regard, usability is an essential component for increasing Web site reliability and user satisfaction.

Improved Web site usability is not just helpful for less-experienced users. It also makes Web site navigation much easier for advanced users, who suffer most frequently from Web-design failures because of a higher Internet use. Overall, the conclusions that can be drawn from this study with respect to online shoppers' navigation problems can be summarized as follows:

- Web site navigation problems represent the most common inconvenience for Internet purchases.
- Web-design problems affect all kinds of users, not just those less experienced with Internet usage.
- Internet behavior patterns associated with navigation problems evidenced by online shoppers across all groups resemble those of advanced users.
- As advanced users experience more navigation problems because of the time spent on the Internet, longer navigation time likely leads to additional problems.
- Less-experienced Internet shoppers may not recognize usability deficiencies and attribute errors to their lack of computer or Internet literacy, resulting in a reluctance to engage in Internet usage.

Given that certain sociodemographic variables are significantly related to customers' profiles with more navigation problems, e-commerce companies should study the characteristics of their online customers in order to provide stronger support to the user segments experiencing the highest level of difficulties.

This study has identified that the following sociodemographic indicators are significant in terms of dealing with Web site navigation problems:

- Country is the variable showing the highest influence on respondents' navigation problems.

- Age. The latent class regression model shows that online shoppers between 26 and 33 years of age tend to experience relatively more navigation problems.
- Occupation. Both statistical analyses confirmed the relevance of this variable.

Other tested sociodemographic variables have also been shown to be significant under specific circumstances: gender (latent class regression) and education completion age (hierarchical segmentation).

This chapter has focused only on the effects of customers' sociodemographic traits. The main limitation relates to the noninclusion of other kinds of potentially relevant indicators, such as customer attitudes or behavior. This limitation represents an opportunity for future research focused on the type(s) of products purchased by consumers through the Internet, as well as on their perceptions and attitudes toward the Internet as a shopping channel.

REFERENCES

Cañada Crespi, J. (2002) In La experiencia del usuario (Ed, Knapp Bjerén, A.) Ediciones Anaya Multimedia, S.A., Madrid, pp. 133–174.

Chakraborty, G., Lala, V., and Warren, D. (2002) Journal of Interactive Marketing, 16, 51–72.

Chen, L.D., Gillenson, M.L., and Sherrell, D.L. (2002) Information & Management, 39, 705–719.

Cho, N., and Park, S. (2001) Industrial Management & Data Systems, 101, 400–405.

Constantine, L.L. (2000) "What do users want? Engineering usability into software," www.foruse.com/articles/whatusers.htm.

Davis, F.D. (1989) "Perceived usefulness, perceived ease of use and user acceptance of information technology," MIS Quarterly, 13(3), pp. 319–340.

Dellaert, B.G.C., and Kahn, B.E. (1999) Journal of Interactive Marketing, 13, 41–54.

Featherman, M.S., and Pavlou, P.A. (2003) International Journal of Human-Computer Studies, 59, 451–474.

Featherman, M.S., and Wells, J.D. (2004) In Proceedings of the 37th Annual Hawaii International Conference on System Sciences (HICSS'04) Hawaii.

Fidalgo, A. (2000) "Usabilidad: La gram desconcada," http://www.ainda.info/saben_usuaries.html.

Flavián Blanco, C., Guinalí Blasco, M., and Gurrea Sarasa, R. (2004) In XVI Encuentro de profesores universitarios de marketing, Alicante, pp. 210–216.

International Standards Organization (1991) ISO 9125 Information Technology—Software Product Evaluation—Quality Characteristics and Guidelines for Their Use.

Jinwoo, K., and Moon, J.Y. (1998) Interacting with computers, 1–29.

Jones, T.O., and Sasser, W.E. (1995) Harvard Business Review, 73, 2–13.

Kim, E.B., and Eom, S.B. (2002) Industrial Management & Data Systems, 102, 241–251.

Klopping, I.M., and McKinney, E. (2004) Information Technology, Learning, and Performance Journal, 22, 35–48.

Liu, S.-P., Tucker, D., Koh, C.E., and Kappelman, L. (2003) Industrial Management & Data Systems, 103, 600–610.

Manchón, E. (2002) "Qué no saben los usuarios?" http://www.ainda.info/saben_ usuarios.html.

Morris, M.G., and Turner, J.M. (2001) International Journal Human-Computer Studies, 877–901.

Nielsen, J. (1999) "Trust or bust: Communicating trustworthiness in web design," http:// www.useit.com/alertbox/990307.html.

Nielsen, J. (2005) "Top ten web design mistakes of 2005," http://www.useit.com/alert-box/designmistakes.html.

Olsina, L., Lafuente, G., and Rossi, G. (2000) In 1st International Conference on Electronic Commerce and Web Technology, Vol. EC-Web 2000 (Ed, Springer-Verlag) Londres, pp. 239–252.

Park, J., Lee, D., and Ahn, J. (2004) Journal of Global Information Technology Management, 7, 6–30.

Patterson, P.G., Johnson, L.W., and Spreng, R.A. (1997) Journal of the Academy of Marketing Science, 25, 4–17.

Patton, M.A., and Jøsang, A. (2004) Electronic Commerce Research, 9–21.

Pavlou, P.A. (2003) International Journal of Electronic Commerce, 7, 101–134.

Recio Menéndez, M., and Ortega Egea, J.M. (2003) In Forum Internacional Sobre las Ciencias, las Técnicas y el Arte Aplicadas al Marketing. Academia y Profesión. Madrid.

Rose, G., Khoo, H., and Straub, D.W. (1999) In Communications of the AIS, Vol. 1, pp. 1–74.

Roy, M.C., Dewit, O., and Aubert, B.A. (2001) Internet Research: Electronic Networking Applications and Policy, 11, 388–398.

Tognazzini, B. (2004) "Top 10 reasons to not shop on line," http://www.asktog.com/columns/062top10ReasonsToNotShop.html.

U.S. Census Bureau, U. (2006), Vol. 2006, U.S. Census Bureau.

CHAPTER 6

GUERILLA DIRECT: THE CASE FOR
MENTAL_FLOSS

Toby Maloney and Melanie Maloney

> Once upon a time there was a great story. Too bad no one heard it.
> —Edward Howard, Public Relations Guru

That all-too-frequent occurrence referenced in the quote above has not been the case for Mental Floss LLC, a rapidly growing media company, known for its quirky, offbeat products that blur the line between education and entertainment.

How did a late-night dorm room idea for a magazine quickly morph into a multimillion-dollar business? Why is this magazine (and its numerous product-line extensions) taking off? Is *mental_floss* magazine just the beneficiary of an eye-popping marketing budget? Or is it that rare bird—a unique product that is filling an unmet need in the marketplace?

People love to feel smart, but there is just one problem: Whether you are a busy young mom, an overworked college student, or an active retiree, there just is not enough time to do everything you want, including learning about the things that interest you. Who can keep up with it all?

Starting with its name, *mental_floss* has created a unique brand that solves the problem. Our products take the chore out of learning by presenting information in a way that is quick, simple, and fun. People seem to love what we create. Our challenge: How do we best market our products to an unsuspecting world?

As Mr. Howard observed so well, even if you have a great product and a great story to tell, unless someone hears it, it really does not matter. In this chapter, we share some of what we have learned over the past five years as we have introduced people to *mental_floss*.

And no, we have not done it through massive marketing budgets or deep corporate pockets; we have done it through hard work, a willingness to take measured risks, and a close eye on cash flow. We have also been as single-minded and persistent about it as our office Airedale is when he is eying a treat.

While talking about one's success is always risky business, we are going to tempt fate and share some things that might help you as you launch or grow your enterprise.

YOU MUST HAVE AN IRRATIONAL, 24/7 COMMITMENT TO YOUR BUSINESS AND HIRE PEOPLE WHO SHARE YOUR PASSION

Let us be brutally honest about it: Starting a magazine requires an incredible leap of faith, even in the best of times. Every year 800–1,000 magazines are launched in the United States. Most of them fail, often in the first or second year. And this Darwinian process does not play favorites—whether you are the baby of a media giant or the idea of a bunch of kids in a dorm room at Duke, the odds are definitely against you.

Add to these sobering statistics the fact that in 2001 (when *mental_floss* was launched), it was not exactly a boom period in the magazine industry. Ad revenues were down, other household name publications were folding at a dizzying rate, the economy was tanking, and the real journalistic experience of the founders of *mental_floss* would not fill two lines on a resume.

So why is *mental_floss* taking off when so many publications have folded? Simple question, complicated answer. While there are many reasons why our business is growing, there is one basic reason that *must* be mentioned: Every member of the original crew—the co-founders, the editor, our incredible researchers, and our investors had and continue to have an unshakable belief in what we are doing. That commitment and matching work ethic have enabled a handful of people to transform a great idea into a multimillion dollar success story in less than five years.

This irrational, 24/7 commitment continues to manifest itself in multiple ways. What we are talking about here are the basics: the blocking and tackling that any truly successful business *never* forgets. It is making the extra effort; it is working until the task at hand is completed; it is returning phone calls and e-mails as quickly as possible. This drive to create superior products and delight our loyal fans is a core part of our success. Everyone in our small, virtual company shares that same passion for getting it right the first time and fixing it ASAP, if we do not.

We are proud of the products we are creating. That sense of personal pride and belief in something bigger than ourselves has enabled us to overcome hurdles that might otherwise seem insurmountable. Of course, we also quickly realized that a tremendous commitment alone is not enough. Zealots with "me-too" products or slight variations on a theme often do not get too far in the marketplace.

We started with a great name and a truly original idea for the magazine's content. But that alone is not enough to build a business these days. From the very beginning, Will Pearson and Mangesh Hattikudur, the co-founders of *mental_floss,* have reached out to form alliances. Their ability to reach out (even as underclassmen at Duke) has been an integral part of our success.

PARTNERSHIPS AND JOINT ALLIANCES ARE A GREAT WAY TO GROW YOUR BUSINESS

Whether it was seeking counsel from the faculty and staff at Duke, choosing an advisory board, seeking angel investors, or learning the basics of the magazine industry, we have reached out to build relationships and form alliances across a broad spectrum of publishing and media experts.

The *mental_floss* advisory board is a good example of this skill at forming alliances. Members of the board include nationally recognized corporate leaders who are at the top of their game: Samir Husni (Mr. Magazine), Jackie Leo (editor-in-chief of *Reader's Digest*), Jerry Footlick (former senior editor of *Newsweek*), and George Hirsch (former publisher of *Runner's World*), among others.

It is interesting to note that these highly acclaimed, busy people have happily contributed their keen insights and drawn on their years of experience to assist the fledgling team at *mental_floss.* Their compensation? Sincere thank-you notes and samples of our latest products. Why have they done it? To help some young people follow their dream? Because they love David versus Goliath stories? Or perhaps because they were struck by the fresh thinking behind *mental_floss* and the enthusiasm of the co-founders? The answer is probably "all of the above." Whatever the reasons for their involvement, the editorial advisory board has been a key element of the magazine's continuing growth.

It was only natural, then, that *mental_floss* would continue this pattern of reaching out to potential *Fortune* 500 partners. This emphasis on an aggressive, opportunistic approach to forming partnerships has been a constant throughout the magazine's history and has been a critical element of the company's impressive results. A small company with big ideas and limited resources + a big company with lots of resources = growth opportunity for *mental_floss.* A few examples follow:

A highly successful, collaborative effort between *mental_floss* and HarperCollins Publishers has enabled *mental_floss* to create and get national and international distribution for a series of seven popular books (*Condensed Knowledge, Forbidden Knowledge, Instant Knowledge, Cocktail Party Cheat Sheets, What's the Difference? Scatterbrained, and Genius Instruction Manual*), and 2007 will see two more books in the series.

In the past five years, **mental_floss** has syndicated content and partnered with *Reader's Digest,* AOL's Research & Learn, Discovery Communications' network sites (Travel Channel, TLC, and Animal Planet), *Star-Ledger (Newark),* and other leading online and print publications.

The common thread running through each of our partnerships has been our aggressive efforts to seek out situations where both parties can benefit from the relationship. What we do not have in cash and resources, we can make up for with the quality of our product. This ability to create content with an edgy, hip, quirky feel has enabled us to build an impressive list of major companies that are giants in their fields, but seem happy to work with us.

We are constantly seeking out new partners who can help us further build our brand and introduce more consumers to our products. It is not a particularly glamorous process—we are forever gathering information, looking for opportunities, and talking with people who might be a fit with us. We do not approach only *Fortune* 500 giants; we also seek out smaller entrepreneurial companies who share our passion and vision for growing a business and are always on the prowl for cross-promotional and trade opportunities.

MOVE QUICKLY AND SEIZE OPPORTUNITIES, BUT RECOGNIZE WHAT YOU DO NOT KNOW

Speed might kill on the highway, but it has been an incredible asset for our business. One of our saving graces over the past five years has been our ability to move quickly when opportunity presents itself. A case in point would be our relationship with *CNN Headline News.* We got a call one day from a producer asking if we would be interested in appearing the following day. We immediately rearranged our schedules, created appropriate content for the segment, and the next day had Will Pearson, co-founder of **mental_floss,** ready to go. This original "one-off" appearance quickly led to a regular segment, and Will has since appeared more than 125 times on *CNN Headline News.* A major reason why Will has been invited back so many times is that he is very articulate, quick on his feet, and he has outstanding content that our crack research team develops for him.

This ability to move quickly and take advantage of opportunities has been an essential element of our success. As a virtual company, with employees spread across the country (Atlanta; Birmingham, Alabama; Birmingham, Michigan; Boston; Cleveland; and Cary, North Carolina), the Internet has been our lifeline not only because of the obvious advantages of having a Web site (www.mentalfloss.com), but also because it is a primary tool for us in researching and reaching out for new opportunities.

While we are still trying to avoid being the dog that chases every car down the street, we continue to investigate carefully just about every opportunity that appears to have any merit. The number of deals, new products, and press placements that have started with a simple exchange of e-mails is beyond belief. We continue to be amazed at how easy it can be to reach people and get a conversation going through e-mail and follow-up phone calls.

Of course, the exchange of e-mails is only the beginning of a process that might sometimes take six months, a year, or even longer to reach closure for a strategic alliance or story placement.

We aggressively seek opportunity, but we take a much more conservative approach when it comes to spending company funds and have stayed away from "bet the farm" strategies. In a start-up/early-stages business, it is truly amazing how many people want to help you spend money—from real-estate agents working to convince you of the need for lavish offices to direct-mail marketers who are eager to assist in a megadollar campaign to brand consultants or public relations (PR) gurus who have the "perfect" solution and want to be on retainer. We have met them all during the past five years. We decided early on that we would not put the enterprise at risk through a foolish big bet no matter how alluring the sales pitch.

At the other end of that spectrum, we have also been blessed by having such a limited knowledge of the publishing industry. Our lack of knowledge has forced us to look at things with a fresh eye and to sometimes defy conventional thinking.

A case in point follows: We have not relied on traditional pricing/advertising models to build our business. At $21.97 for a one-year subscription (six issues), we priced our magazine with the thought that our customers are getting a lot of entertainment and value for their money. We believe that our content is worth paying for—and so far, the marketplace appears to be agreeing with us. We also needed the subscription revenue, particularly in our early days, to keep the magazine going.

A more traditional publisher might have followed more conventional wisdom by pouring lots of money into market testing, direct-mail pieces, and so forth rather than going against the tide for its pricing model. Likewise on the advertising front, we are building a solid core of national advertisers as we continue to grow our paid circulation base. In this instance, we have also taken a different path by having a business model built on building the brand through multiple distribution channels (online, books, board game, content syndication, calendars, *Law School in a Box,* and *Medical School in a Box*).

We like to think we have not stumbled into two other traps that frequently trip up new businesses: first, the trap of thinking we know it all because we have had some success. In addition to aggressively seeking alliances and partnerships, we routinely seek counsel in those areas we really do not know much about—whether it is seeking legal counsel on trademarks and copyrights or getting help on how we can better distribute the magazine—rather than adding more staff or expense.

Second, we have not been hampered by that deadly phrase that infects so many organizations—"Oh, we tried that before and it didn't work." Unencumbered by past failures, we have been able to try new approaches and defy conventional wisdom in ways that a more established organization might reject out of hand.

Of course, it would be a mistake to suggest that every decision we have made has been brilliant and immediately successful. With the value of hindsight, one area that we clearly were late out of the starting gate was the Internet. Even though we had a site from the get-go, it took us awhile to fully realize the commercial potential of an online presence.

GUERRILLA MARKETING AND THE INTERNET ARE THE WAY TO GO

For us, our guerrilla marketing efforts and the Internet have been a match made in heaven. Through our online presence, we have been able to leverage our modest guerrilla marketing budget far beyond what we could have ever imagined. Some facts follow that illustrate what happens when you use creative marketing ideas and harness them to the power of the online world:

- Since its launch in a dorm room in 2001, *mental_floss*'s paid circulation has grown to over 100,000 (with subscribers in 17 countries).
- Our Web site is routinely included in Alexa Internet, Inc.'s list of the top 50,000 most-visited sites.
- *mental_floss*, in partnership with HarperCollins, will have 300,000 books in print by year-end 2006.

Our guerrilla marketing efforts have been a team effort that has yielded great results at the national and local levels. Through an all-out team effort, we have received extensive national media attention in major newspapers (*Washington Post, Chicago Tribune,* and *LA Times*), in magazines (*Newsweek, Entertainment Weekly,* and *Reader's Digest*), on TV (more than 125 appearances on *CNN Headline News*), and in more than 150 radio interviews.

This has been accomplished without relying on the usual tools of the trade such as high-priced PR firms on retainer, lavish launch parties, or pricey marketing campaigns.

It has been done the old-fashioned way; we have reached out to friends, family, former classmates, business colleagues, educational institutions, and anywhere else we think might help us tell our story. We have done middle of the night radio interviews in Chicago and New York, morning drive-time in Cleveland, and mid-day in St. Louis and just about everywhere else we can talk our way into. We have called and e-mailed hundreds of reporters whom we think might have an interest. We have had relatives who own dairies run *mental_floss* trivia on their milk cartons.

All of these efforts have had a common goal: to introduce people to *mental_ floss*. And it appears it is working as every opportunity seems to yield yet another opportunity. Old-fashioned word of mouth (and today's blogger version) has really helped us build our brand. Mention of our site on a popular blog sends thousands of visitors to our site. Old media have also played an important part. There is the TV producer who read a story about us in the *LA Times* and who is interested in talking with us about a possible TV show, or the toy/game inventor who saw Will on *CNN Headline News,* bought the magazine, and then approached us about developing a board game.

Guerrilla marketing efforts and the Internet both offer countless opportunities to build and grow a business without spending a lot of money. It just takes tenacity, time, and the ability to constantly seek out ways to get your message in front of people.

In our online efforts, we have repeatedly used contests and discounts to sell more of our products. Whether it is teaming up with a major bookstore chain (Books-A-Million, Inc.) for the Great Gasoline Giveaway or a more straightforward contest in our e-mail newsletter or blog, our goal always is to bring more people to our site. Our online presence has evolved from a fairly simple, straightforward site with a popular daily fact/quiz and the opportunity to buy a subscription, back issues, and T-shirts to more of a destination where people can still buy our products, but they also enjoy our blog, vocab rehab, and much more.

Going forward, we believe the importance of an online site will only continue to grow as we add more features and make it a daily "must-see" site. We have been able to lure a *Newsweek* writer to help us further transform this all-important element of our long-term success.

Successful guerrilla marketing and Internet success are built on constant innovation, a willingness to take measured risks, and the ability to move very quickly. One of our more recent examples best illustrates this point. When the recent sad news about the demise of Pluto broke, it gave us a great business opportunity.

We, like the rest of the world, were saddened to hear of the planet's untimely demise, but we managed our grief and turned the news into a wonderful business opportunity. We created T-shirts reading "Pluto—1936–2006—Revolve in Peace" and sold out in the first 48 hours. Countless reorders followed and we introduced that many more customers to the world of *mental_floss*.

KEEP AN EYE ON THE CASH REGISTER AND DO NOT POLISH YOUR SNEAKERS!

Managing cash flow is almost always one of the most obvious and biggest challenges for any start-up or young business. We are happily celebrating our fifth anniversary because we have not lost sight of this fundamental business reality: You have to really keep an eye on your expenses. It seems just about everyone wants to help you spend your money. Do not let them. Take a really hard look at every expense and when you do spend money, make sure it is on things that can grow your business. It is so easy, particularly as you watch your business grow, to get seduced into thinking that you really do need to have all the trappings of success. Do not fall into that trap. So far, we appear to be successful in not going crazy on the spend side—whether it is adding new full-time staff, fancy office space, or plunging ahead into new expenses that put the overall enterprise at risk. Admittedly it is a more conservative approach than many might advise, but it appears to be working for us as we celebrate our fifth anniversary and continue to grow.

Another important learning for us is that we have not fallen into the trap of "polishing our sneakers." This phrase, which the chief executive at Raytheon popularized when he included it in his inspirational book[1] (much of which was lifted from other sources), is worth remembering. It simply means "don't fall so in love with an idea that you can't give it up."

Companies often expend large amounts of precious resources because everyone is afraid to say something is a dumb idea or it is not working. We have certainly done some dumb things over the past five years, but we have had the good sense to realize when something really is not working and to move on to the next opportunity. Some of our earliest joint alliance efforts looked good on paper, but in the real world they did not work. Rather than going back endlessly to attempt to revive or revisit the idea, we took our lumps, learned from the experience, and moved on.

GO WITH YOUR GUT, BUT LISTEN TO YOUR CUSTOMERS

One of the trickiest challenges for any entrepreneur or business is learning how to get the right balance between going with your gut while also having the ability to listen to your customers and the marketplace. As a small company, we cannot compete with large organizations in terms of resources for extensive research and prelaunch testing of our products; we compensate for this with our ability to move quickly when we see an opportunity.

Even Hollywood, with all of its resources, struggles with this dilemma of being able to predict what the customer will respond to and getting the balance right between research and going with the gut. There is no magic formula for creating a blockbuster hit, nor is there any guarantee that all the research in the world will create a popular movie.

While there is no easy answer on gut versus customer research, it is important to be aware of this challenge and to try to manage it intelligently. We feel we take some of the risk out of the equation by not betting the farm on any one product and by paying careful attention to what we hear back from our customers—in terms of revenue, complaints, and suggestions. Online communication enables us to do more research at a reasonable cost and, even more importantly, to get back to our customers with a response quicker than ever. This more balanced approach has served us well as we celebrate our fifth anniversary and continue to grow.

NOTE

1. William H. Swanson, Swanson's Unwritten Rules of Management (Waltham, MA: Raytheon Company, 2005).

CHAPTER 7

BUSINESS-TO-BUSINESS INTEGRATED MARKETING

Nadji Tehrani

Every so often, marketing reinvents itself. I love marketing because it changes all the time and keeps you on your toes. A French philosopher once said, "The more things change, the more they stay the same." However, when it comes to marketing, that is only 50 percent true. Namely, the methods of marketing change, but the marketing principles stay the same. I feel that because of the ever-changing nature of marketing, there will always be a great challenge in figuring out what the formula for success is today versus yesterday.

Putting all of the above together, it becomes clear that marketing is often like shooting at a moving target; that is why it is the most challenging and most complex part of any corporation. Ironically, to make matters worse, very few, if any, companies pay enough attention to this vital art and science.

As I travel around the United States visiting companies, I continuously find that a certain amount of blunders continues in many companies. Here are a few examples:

- Some companies hire a complete marketing staff, but they give them no budget to market anything! I hope this makes sense to somebody.
- Other companies want to get by with public relations (PR) only. In other words, they give only lip service to marketing by trying to get something for nothing. Obviously, that kind of marketing will never succeed, and the companies that believe in that philosophy will flounder until they lose their competitive advantage.
- Other companies commit even greater sins by spending millions of dollars developing a product or group of products, and then they say there is no money left for marketing! To me, this is completely backwards! Many companies successfully do it the

other way around. They do not have much of a product, but they market the hell out of it, and, as unlikely as it may seem, those are the companies that come up with the biggest market share!

Not long ago, I visited a company that offers one of the best, if not the best, speech product for our industry. We met with the CEO and asked about his company and his marketing plans. The answer was something like this: "We have invested 35 years in building this product line and we have no money to market it." I will never understand this kind of logic. This company will also flounder until someone else comes along with an inferior product and markets the hell out of it and eats his lunch. Having said all of the above, it seems to me as if many companies somehow prefer to ignore marketing. These companies fail to realize that companies exist for two and only two reasons: namely, marketing and innovation. Without these, no company would get anywhere.

WHAT IS INTEGRATED MARKETING?

When newspapers were invented, they gradually became an important tool for marketers. When radio was invented, some uninformed marketers said, "Well, that's the end of newspapers." That was 60-plus years ago. When TV was invented, the same people said, "That's the end of newspapers and radio and so on!" Today, we know that those misguided comments were nothing more than hogwash. Yes, newspapers, radio, TV, and the Web are still around, and they are all serving an important function in marketing. To the extent that people have different tastes, some prefer print, some prefer the Web, some prefer the mail, and so forth, conventional wisdom dictates that if you want to reach your total market, you have one and only one solution, and that is integrated marketing, encompassing all of the above components. As Reed Business Information states, "Understand that one advertising medium can't do it all. An integrated approach of print and online initiatives will allow you to better accomplish your goals and objectives. To reach their goals, marketers need to piece together their own custom Integrated Marketing Solution."[1]

Likewise, Ed Abram, vice president, Integrated Marketing Communications, IBM Global Sales and Distribution states, "Our research proves that effective marketing campaigns require end-to-end, multi-touch campaigns. You can't drive business with a single touch."[2]

Today's business-to-business (b-to-b) marketer has a plethora of tools to use in his or her toolbox. Among these are newspaper, radio, TV, Internet, direct mail, target marketing, database marketing, public relations, custom portals, telemarketing, print advertising, trade-show marketing, relationship marketing, e-mail marketing, and search engine marketing. What is important to remember here is that you must identify the right combination of these tools and decide how to use them in your campaign. In some cases a number of these tools will be used simultaneously, while in others the tools will be sequenced so that one directly enhances the other. For the b-to-b marketer, the science is understanding how these tools work independently and together, and the art is being able to extract the best from the tools to have a successful campaign.

The business universe gets more competitive and more demanding every minute. Both the pace of business as well as the number of participants are continuously increasing. What does that mean for marketers? It means that they are battling for attention against an ever-shrinking time frame in an ever-more-crowded arena. Business-to-business advertising eliminates many of the obstacles. In a high-attention venue, with an involved and deeply interested audience, advertisers have the time, the attention, and most of all, the interest of audience members. That is why it makes good business sense to extend the advertising impact by taking advantage of the multiplicity of media platforms b-to-b vehicles offer. A combination of print advertising, Web site presence, trade show appearances, and conference sponsorships means an advertiser's impact on the audience is magnified geometrically.

Hopefully by now, it is abundantly clear that to succeed in today's ultracompetitive business world, marketers must develop a cutting-edge marketing strategy by effectively using every component of integrated marketing. Remember that marketing is NOT a part-time job, there is NO shortcut in marketing, and if you do not market, you do not exist! Oh, yes, always remember effective positioning and differentiation.

THE MISSING LINK IN MARKETING: DIFFERENTIATION AND POSITIONING

Your customers must have a reason to buy from you and that reasoning comes from positioning and differentiation. In order to better understand the purpose of positioning and differentiation, which, in my opinion, are the most crucial parts of marketing strategy, let us refer to *The American Heritage Dictionary, Second College Edition,* for the definitions of differentiation and positioning. Although there is not a direct definition for differentiation and positioning in marketing, if you look at the definitions for differentiate and position, you can arrive at the same conclusion, as follows. American Heritage defines "differentiate" as follows: "(1) To constitute the distinction between or (2) To perceive or show difference in or between; and discriminate."

It describes "position" as follows:

- The right or appropriate place.
- The way in which something or someone is placed.
- The act or process of positioning.
- To place in proper position.

• Last but not least, An advantageous place or location.

Looking at the above definitions, one can conclude that to effectively market, any product or service must be differentiated from its competition, thereby giving the potential buyer a reason to purchase the product or service in question. As for positioning, the definition clearly points out that it is crucial for any product to be positioned in an appropriate place or, preferably, advantageous location.

Over the years, I have learned that if you do not position yourself advantageously, your competition will position you and your product in the most disadvantageous way. Having said that, one must clearly explain that positioning is not a part-time job by any stretch of the imagination. Positioning and differentiation, like marketing itself, are not part-time jobs. In fact, to do them properly, they are more than full-time jobs. That means you must market every day, you must position every day, and you must differentiate every day, 365 days a year, 24 hours a day, 7 days a week. In short, marketing, positioning, and differentiation are 24/7 jobs, period, end of story.

An example can be cited by describing the success and failure of Company X and the ultimate success of Company Y. In the mid to late 1980s, Company X took advantage of the inbound telemarketing boom by using a toll-free number and advertised it heavily as the preferred source to buy its products around the clock. In the early development stages of the company, the firm marketed heavily and practically all day long, every day, until it positioned itself as THE source for the product in question and thus enjoyed the number 1 position in market share. A few years later, the company was sold. All advertising, positioning, and differentiation were stopped by the new owners. Company Y came along and did what Company X used to do and started to heavily market, advertise, differentiate, and position itself as the new leader. Guess what? Company Y is the unquestionable leader in the marketplace and next to nothing is heard about Company X. This is a true story. The idea is not to bad-mouth any company, but to simply point out that great marketing, positioning, and differentiating made Company X successful, but when all of these marketing activities stopped, it lost market share and its leadership position to another company that did a better job of marketing, advertising, positioning, and differentiating.

POSITIONING AND DIFFERENTIATING ARE VITAL TO THE SUCCESS OF ANY MARKETING CAMPAIGN

With so much global competition, customers need a reason to buy from you and that reason comes from your positioning and differentiation, which explains to your customer or potential customer what sets you apart or what sets your product or service apart. Without that, no one has any reason to buy your product or service as opposed to your competitors. In their book, *The New Positioning:*

The Latest on the World's #1 Business Strategy, Jack Trout and Steve Rivkin define positioning as "not what you do to the product, but what you do to the mind."[3] Trout further believes that the ultimate marketing battleground is the mind, and the better you understand how the mind works, the better you will understand how positioning works.

In an ultra-fast-moving and rapidly changing environment, one can practically assume that market conditions also change month to month, maybe even day to day as opposed to 25 years ago when things changed more slowly. Consequently, one must always remain 100 percent focused on the marketplace, as well as on the validity of positioning vis-à-vis the current conditions of the marketplace. It would be a disaster if one were to lose sight of adjusting one's positioning to reflect the changing marketplace requirements. The next important item is that when companies fail to change their positioning, they lose market share and lose considerable revenue. In fact, such companies may not even survive when markets change so rapidly.

In today's extremely complex, information-jammed world, we are exposed to thousands of advertisements and promotions of various kinds and, in short, are inundated with information explosion. It has been said that in the last 30 years, more information has been produced than in the previous 5,000 years. The emergence of the Internet has added ultrasonic speed to the growth of information available. Therefore, to make your products and services stand out in the marketplace, you must do a superb job of positioning, differentiation, marketing, and advertising. You do not want to be a penguin; you want to position yourself as a peacock.

Take a look at a peacock and a penguin. What stands out? Obviously it is the peacock with its magnificently colorful feathers and its artistic design. If you were to buy one of them, which one would you buy, the peacock or the penguin? Those who would buy the penguin would need to see a psychiatrist. The bottom line is, the peacock is different from the rest of the crowd; it stands above the rest with magnificent and attractive colors in the bland land of the penguins. If you truly want success in your positioning or the position of your company or product, you do not want to be a me-too or a penguin. You want to be unique and position yourself as such. In short, you want to position yourself as a peacock in the land of penguins. That is how you gain market share, penetrate the minds of the buyers, and become a leader.

The first law of positioning states that it is better to be first than to be better. Who was the first man who flew over the Atlantic? Obviously, it was Charles Lindbergh. Who was the second person to fly over the Atlantic? Answer: nobody knows and nobody cares. What was the name of the horse that won the Triple Crown in 1973 and broke practically all racetrack speed records? The answer: Secretariat. What was the name of the horse that always came in at the number 2 position right behind Secretariat in all three races? The answer: no one remembers and no one cares about number 2. Only horse-racing fans would remember that the name of the second-place horse was Sham. The bottom line: the first law is true and if you really want to be a market leader, you must position yourself as such every minute, every hour, every day, every month, 365 days a year, and 24/7.

ONLINE MARKETING COMES OF AGE

Everyone knows that the latest evolution in marketing focuses on online marketing. Every time a new marketing concept comes along, people say, "This is the answer to all marketing needs. We are going to cancel everything else and jump on the online bandwagon!" Back in 1982, when we launched *Telemarketing* magazine in a pioneering act to lay the foundation for what is now the multibillion-dollar contact center/customer relationship management (CRM) and call-center industry, most people said the same thing about telemarketing. I heard people dropping direct mail or print advertising in favor of telemarketing.

This was not the right thing to do, because no one buys anything from a company he or she has never heard of. When the marketers came to their senses in the early 1980s, they learned that in order to get the best results from telemarketing, they must combine it with direct mail, trade-show marketing, and personal visits (for high-value products) in order to get maximum results. In other words, we learned back then that the only way to market effectively is through integrated marketing. Stated differently, the more things change, the more they stay the same. Today, integrated marketing is also the only way to go. One cannot cancel all other marketing plans in favor of online marketing only. There is no disputing the fact that a well-designed print ad will stand out in a publication just as a well-designed online ad will be noticed on a Web site. And standing out in a crowd ensures that your brand is recognized and your marketing message is conveyed.

More and more companies today are leaning toward online marketing. Many are making the mistake of stopping everything else and putting all of their marketing eggs in the online basket. This is, in my opinion, completely unwise because other forms of marketing such as print, trade shows, exhibition, and so forth create the perception of stability, dedication, longevity, awareness, and commitment of the company, not to mention brand recognition and marketing through education, which are vital in the marketing process.

As stated above, no one buys anything significant from a company he or she has never heard of. Here are some guidelines for online marketing and beyond:

1. When thinking of doing online marketing, do not forget other forms of marketing.
2. Check the reputation of the company behind the Web site on which you would like to do your online marketing.

3. More importantly, check the Alexa Internet, Inc. (www.alexa.com) ranking of the Web site on which you plan to advertise. This step is by far the most important part of selecting a suitable online marketing vehicle that has proper Web traffic. Alexa.com is a division of Amazon.com, and it specializes in auditing Web traffic of ALL Web sites regardless of the type of Web site. When looking at Alexa.com rankings, it is vital to remember that the lower the ranking number, the greater the Web site traffic in terms of bringing the necessary eyeballs to that Web site. In other words, you do not want to choose Web sites that have higher ranking numbers than 4,000 on Alexa.com. As an example, the Alexa ranking of TMCnet.com is approximately 3,000, plus or minus. As such, TMCnet.com is ranked by Alexa.com as being in the top 3,000 Web sites in the world! Web sites with much higher numbers simply do not have the traffic, and it could lead to a waste of your marketing dollars.

4. Compare the Alexa ranking charts directly with competing Web sites by superimposing all of the competing Web sites along with your preferred Web site on which you would like to advertise. This will give you an idea of the suitability of your chosen Web site. Once again, these charts are vitally important to help you judiciously select and eliminate the sites with extremely poor traffic.

5. Check the quality of the content. Quality editorial matter brings quality readers, and quality readers become quality sales leads for your products and services.

6. Investigate the WebTrends rankings of your chosen site versus the competition.

7. Check the relevant term ranking on the leading search engine sites before you select your final Web site for your marketing purposes. For example, TMCnet.com ranks as number 1 in over 40 relevant terms on Google. We are not aware of any other site in the telecom industry that even comes close. If your chosen site cannot match this type of prominence, it simply does not deserve your advertisement.

8. ALWAYS remember that on Alexa.com, the lower the number, the better the traffic.

9. Look at your chosen site's value proposition. How does it compare your value proposition with competing sites?

10. Investigate the "Renewal Rate" of other online advertisers on your chosen Web site. If the Renewal Rate is less than 90 percent, do not waste your money advertising on that Web site. As a point of reference, the marketing channel renewal rate on TMCnet.com is 99 percent.

11. Does your chosen Web site offer guaranteed lead generation? If not, forget it.

12. Remember that only outstanding content delivers quality sales leads. Therefore, place maximum emphasis on the integrity and longevity and reputation of your chosen Web site.

THE MOST EFFECTIVE WAY TO GENERATE LEADS

Integrated marketing and/or multimedia programs are effective ways to market and generate sales leads. In today's world, customers tend to react to advertising and marketing materials in different ways. In other words, some prefer voice (radio or telephone), others television, others magazine, others print advertising, others channel marketing, and others Internet advertising of several forms. To conduct full-court marketing or a winning marketing program, you must consider integrated marketing as the vital point of your marketing program. Indeed, nearly ten years ago, the tagline of *Customer Inter@ction Solutions* was "The Magazine of Integrated Marketing." That was a decade ago when we came to the realization that someday we must all consider integrated marketing because "one-size-fits-all" does not work in marketing.

There has been an evolution in the nature of incoming leads. Having gone through direct mail via coupons, postcards, regular mail, and bingo cards, the nature of incoming leads upgraded to telephone plus mail, then to 80 percent via toll-free 800 numbers in the 1980s and 1990s. No matter where you advertise, nowadays over 90 percent of the leads are coming via your Web site and the rest via toll-free inbound 800 numbers or regular phone.

Even if you conduct integrated marketing and generate the most qualified sales leads, placed in the hands of an unproven salesperson, no sales will result. In other words, if you do not keep in mind all of the above guidelines, such as appropriate integrated marketing, and so forth, you still may hit a point where your marketing campaign is not producing desired results. In that case, we suggest you keep in mind all of the above guidelines and develop a checklist to determine where there is a shortfall and misconnection in your marketing campaign and fix it.

If you follow the anatomy of a healthy organization, you will find that without exception, no company can exist without new business, and simply stated, no company can remain in business without sales. It follows, therefore, that to generate sales, one must have sales leads because "all sales begin with sales leads." As vital as lead generation is, it is mind-boggling that so many companies ignore this phenomenally important part of business and simply give it casual attention, if any at all.

Leads can be generated from any or all of the following:

- Trade shows,
- Print advertising,
- Telemarketing,
- Channel marketing,
- Web advertising,
- Direct mail,
- Integrated marketing (which is regarded as the most powerful method),
- Effective response-driven campaigns (which begin with response-driven advertising),
- Effective positioning (no marketing campaign could be functional without it),
- Differentiation (again, no marketing campaign could be functional without it), and
- Public relations.

THE ROLE OF CRM

Next comes the job of CRM, the objective of which is to keep the customer satisfied by developing a strong relationship with the customer. In short, the job of advertising is to generate sales leads, and the job of salespeople is to close the sales and turn the leads into customers. The job of CRM is to keep the customers.

One of the original purposes of CRM has been to develop a technique that will help companies improve customer retention, customer satisfaction, and customer loyalty. However, if you truly analyze your relationship with your vendors, or many companies' relationships with their vendors, you will find that in most cases, customers are taken for granted and therein lies the root of the problem. I learned a long time ago that if you do not nurture your relationship with your customer on a weekly or monthly basis, it is only a matter of time before you will lose that customer. And yet, many companies totally ignore their major customers, and that is a violation of all the commandments of good CRM!

For example, how many of you have heard from your car manufacturers after you have purchased a car? Did anyone call to see if you were satisfied? Do they call you every month or every six months or every year? Most importantly, did anyone call you a month or two prior to when your lease terminated to try to sell you a new car? In my experience, the answer to all of the above is a resounding no!

I chose car manufacturers as an example because a car is a very expensive item, and it could range anywhere from $20,000 to $60,000 or more per customer. To me, that is a significant purchase and manufacturers must communicate regularly with customers, not only to find out if they are satisfied, but also to encourage them to buy their next car from that particular company. At the moment, none of the above is taking place and that is why practically all of the car manufacturers are losing customers left and right to their competitors!

When a vendor fails to contact its customers frequently, no relationship is built. As a result, the customer has no reason to be loyal to that vendor. If you ignore your customers and do not show appreciation and care, the customer has no reason to remain loyal to you. I realize that most companies are unintentionally committing the above mistakes, but in this day and age when the customers have many choices, it is the violation of all the commandments of business, not to mention CRM, to ignore customers and not try to show appreciation and care in order to keep that customer loyal!

On the other hand, to go to the next level in building customer loyalty and conducting true CRM, you need to find out what it takes to help your customers acquire new customers and keep them. If you can achieve this, then you will have a customer for life. But then again, how many companies are doing this? I would guess, less than 1 percent and, therefore, there is no customer loyalty and retention, and billions of dollars of losses in business are the result every year because of the above problems.

If you are really and truly committed to positioning your company for maximum market share and profitability, here are a few suggested steps for you to take:

1. The Role of CRM: You must genuinely try to keep most, if not all, of your existing customers through implementation of a truly functional and sensible CRM and e-CRM program.

2. The Case For Marketing Frequency: Position and differentiate your company 24/7/365 in an advantageous way and remember that aggressive marketing, advertising, and promotion are NOT part-time jobs. A true leader does not claim leadership for one week, disappear for six weeks, place a couple of ads, and then disappear again for six months. Those types of leaders will not be leaders for long. In fact, they will become followers and in some cases go out of business.

3. On Positioning and Differentiation: Through your clever positioning and differentiation tactics, be very specific communicating to the marketplace what sets your product or service apart from your competition. This is vitally important because it gives your customers and your prospects a reason to buy from you rather than from your competition. Remember, if you do not position yourself 24/7/365, your competition will position you in the most disadvantageous way.

4. Market Aggressively: Maintain the most powerful, aggressive marketing campaign that includes a clever marketing strategy, truly effective advertising, and targeted vertical trade-show participation. Remember that there is no shortcut to marketing domination, the greatest market share, and success.

In my opinion, the above guidelines are a few of the most vital points you need to keep in mind. Focus on them 100 percent and implement them around the clock, 365 days a year if you are to gain the lion's share of the market and leapfrog your competition. And remember that this economy is truly on your side to help you gain your dream market share and make the most of it.

OLD-FASHIONED MARKETING HABITS CONTINUE

During my daily association with various CEOs and marketing executives, I find that many are committed to direct mail only or trade show only or e-mail only as the sole marketing vehicle for their companies. They act as if they have never heard of integrated marketing. Indeed, I have seen many companies that waste thousands of dollars on one or two media and ignore the rest. Obviously, these companies will never gain the full benefit of their marketing dollars.

I recently investigated such a company and discovered that in spite of the fact that thousands of dollars were spent on one or two media, the company did not commit to integrated marketing and that company's name did not appear in the appropriate categories in any of the major search engines. The bottom line is, the successful marketers of today are those that use integrated marketing and anything less will not do. In previous editorials, I have frequently mentioned that marketing is not a part-time job and there is no shortcut in marketing. And yet, many marketers are ignoring the above facts and their companies are losing millions of dollars in new business.

One of the most prevalent problems I have recently found with many marketers is that they are ignoring print, trade-show, telephone, and channel marketing. In my opinion, there is no greater disaster that can result from ignoring the above vital components of "integrated marketing." And yet, the mediocrity continues and many companies are completely oblivious to these facts and foundations of modern marketing.

Advertising blunders also continue. Indeed, many advertisements that I find in a variety of publications are guilty of the following problems. First, they are not communicating the benefits of the products or doing business with that company. Second, they are not differentiating themselves from the competition. Third, they have not positioned themselves effectively. Fourth, they are too busy or they do not say anything. Fifth, they are poorly designed and are using colors that turn off readers. Sixth, last but not least, many of them do not even have a powerful benefit-driven headline. To make matters worse, 70 percent of the sales leads generated from advertising are not followed up!

If the above is the case, one has to wonder, what is the purpose of advertising if you do not give the customer a reason to do business with you? And again, Corporate America seems to be oblivious. The lousy ads appear in many publications and newspapers without having any effect whatsoever! How do you solve the problem? The client must do a much better job of informing the ad agency about the benefits of the product and, most importantly, what differentiates that product from the competition.

As stupid and ill-advised as this may sound, believe it or not, a few marketing/PR people go out of their way to destroy relationships with the most powerful media companies in their industries! To me, this is like someone developing a new Bible for Catholics and, as the first order of business, he or she decides to break all relationships with the Pope! I know this sounds stupid, but it is also sad and it is happening! Unfortunately, this is also a true story. Who is to blame? Of course, top management for hiring and keeping such idiots on the payroll!

In any business, every now and then, one encounters an entrepreneur who has no experience in marketing who likes to take on the role of a marketing manager, or one meets a marketing director who simply speaks at the direction of the entrepreneur who has no experience in marketing. Unfortunately, often in these cases, if they market and do not sell something for a short period, they cancel all of their marketing without investigating why they did not sell anything. Such people should know that only properly prepared marketing messages that speak to the audience in a benefit-driven manner, which are properly placed in a magazine (or other media) that targets their audience, are the ones that will generate sales leads. In addition, unlike the common belief that all leads will turn into sales, sales leads, no matter how qualified, are worthless if you place them in the hands of unproven salespeople. In other words, a response-driven campaign that is properly developed, speaks to the audience with something to offer, and is placed in an appropriate, targeted publication will generate leads and only sales leads, but no sales by itself. Consequently, sales leads should first be qualified and then must be placed in the hands of a good salesperson with appropriate closing techniques to sell the product/service and convert the sales leads into customers.

THE BIGGEST MISTAKES OF ALL

In my judgment, two of the biggest blunders made by businesses are as follows:

1. The greatest mistake made by downsizing is laying off the core people who are the foundation of your business success. Let it be known that categorically I truly hate to lay off anyone solely because of economic conditions.

2. Many ill-advised senior managers also authorize drastic cuts in advertising, marketing, and trade-show participation. As far as I am concerned, these people are making the greatest possible mistake and thereby inflicting the greatest possible damage to their corporations. Here is why: in a slow economy such as the one we are now experiencing, every corporation loses anywhere between 50 to 70 percent of its current customers. We also know that all sales begin with a sales lead. Furthermore, the sole purpose of marketing, advertising, and trade-show participation is to generate qualified sales leads which, when handled properly by the sales department, will become new customers. However, when you cut all marketing, advertising, and trade-show budgets, and you lose 50 to 70 percent of your customers, how then can you replace the lost customers and still remain in business? To me, this is a very simple principle of business and yet in every recession, the majority of corporate leaders still make the mistake of eliminating their marketing, advertising, and trade-show budgets. In my judgment, this explains why so many companies go under at such times! It is like cutting off your nose to spite your face.

WHY SOME COMPANIES FAIL

Based on my years of experience watching businesses develop, grow, and then decline, I offer the following lessons or examples of the most common failures.

Lesson #1: Ignorance Is the Entrepreneur's Best Friend

I am a firm believer that ignorance is truly the entrepreneur's best friend. I once read a study made by a reliable research organization that stated that 90 percent of entrepreneurs are between the ages of 30 and 38, because that is a period in life when people do not know an excessive amount about business, but they do know some things for real. Consequently, entrepreneurs in that age bracket are more likely to take a plunge, and once they are in the water, they know that they have to sink or swim. That element alone leads the entrepreneurs to become successful.

Lesson #2: Why Do Some Companies with Poor Products Succeed and Others with Very Good Products Fail?

Believe it or not, this was precisely the case for a pair of companies, one with a great product and the other with a mediocre product. Ironically, the former (the company with a great product) nearly went bankrupt, while the company with the mediocre product maintained better than 80-percent market share! If you asked me to explain why this was so in one word, I would say, "marketing." If you allowed me three words, I would say "lack of marketing," and if I could use two more words, I would say "lousy marketing." Believe it or not, this is a true story, and I admired the company with the highest market share simply because the CEO of that company was a master marketer, while the CEO of the failing company considered marketing to be a necessary evil, and he gave it only lip service. The ironic thing, in this case, is that the above scenario occurred with not only many high-technology companies, but also with several teleservices companies.

Lesson #3: The Case for the Teleservices Companies

Company A and Company B ranked #48 and #49 in the Top 50 Teleservices Agencies ranking as selected by the editors of *Customer Inter@ction Solutions* magazine. The CEO of Company A was a master marketer and frequently consulted with Technology Marketing Corporation (TMC). He followed practically every suggestion that we gave him. He was also an excellent manager and had very talented and hard-working employees. As a result, the company rose from #48 to #2 in the Top 50 rankings (over a five-year period), and thanks to the tremendous business savvy of the CEO of Company A, the company went public in the mid 1990s at about $15 a share. Subsequently, the price rose to $80 per share. Later on, there was a two-for-one split, and the split stocks also rose to $80 per share. The bottom line is that the CEO and founder of Company A cashed in an estimated $600 million worth of stock, and through exceptional investing, he has now become a billionaire. Company B did nothing: no marketing, no promotions, no advertising and, therefore, the company went nowhere. Again, this is a true story.

Lesson #4: Having a Marketing Vice President with No Budget

Believe it or not, some companies are shortsighted enough to have a marketing vice president, but no budget. They try to rely completely on word-of-mouth marketing. Even if these companies have not gone out of business over the last 25 years, they have not made much progress, either. To me, it is incomprehensible for any company to have a director or vice president of marketing, but no budget for promotion or advertising.

Lesson #5: Rush to Market

Back in 1990, a leading company in our industry came up with a product that was supposed to be all things to all people. For political and personal reasons, this product was marketed long before it was ready. The powerful marketing and previously existing respect for this company in the industry led many innocent call-center executives to adopt that technology, only to find out that it was completely nonfunctional and, in fact, it was nothing more than a major headache. As a result, the company lost major market share and still has not recovered from that disaster.

Lesson #6: Suing Your Influential Customers

Another idiotic and totally incomprehensible action that a few CEOs have taken in the recent past was actually threatening to bring a lawsuit against their leading customers. The reason? The customer refused to renew its contract with Company A because of Company A's obsolete product and unreliable technical service. The shortsighted CEO of Company A was blinded by his ego and did not realize that the contact center industry, like many other industries, is an extremely well-connected group. In other words, when somebody screws up a great company by offering lousy service, yet does not allow customers to go elsewhere by virtue of threatening lawsuits, that CEO has no reason to exist, in my opinion. Fortunately, one such CEO was let go just before the company went under.

This was not the first time I had witnessed such an illogical and idiotic action of bringing a lawsuit against a prestigious customer. Back in my chemistry days, the CEO of a chemical adhesives company where I was employed submitted a completely defective product to the company's leading customer. When the customer refused to pay, the ill-advised CEO brought a lawsuit against the customer. That ill-advised action took the chemical company, which had heretofore been the number 1 supplier to the industry, to last place. Eventually, the company was sold for practically a song to a leading competitor. One wonders how the board of directors of any responsible company could put up with this kind of stupidity—instead of providing maximum care for their leading customers, they actually brought a lawsuit against them. Yes...it sounds utterly stupid, but it has happened and I have witnessed it.

Lesson #7: The Demise of Horizontal Trade Shows

Once upon a time, the granddaddy of all technology shows, COMDEX (Computer Dealer's Exhibition), featured exhibitors who offered soup to nuts in terms of products. Suddenly, there was a shift in the marketplace from exhibiting at horizontal shows in favor of exhibiting at small but highly focused and targeted trade shows. As a result, COMDEX no longer exists. What made matters worse in COMDEX's case were ill-advised managers who treated every exhibitor like dirt and dictated to those exhibitors that if they wanted a particular space the next year, exhibitors must increase their booth size by 20 to 50 percent. The rule was, "Take it or leave it." Eventually, exhibitors who were not getting much business out of COMDEX anyway declined to continue exhibiting, and COMDEX is now history.

Lesson #8: The CEOs Blinded by Ego

A CEO can be a double-edged sword. On the positive side, a CEO with the right frame of mind and the proper attitude can enhance the revenues of his or her company tremendously. The right CEO will actually build and reinforce relationships with all customers, or as many of his customers as possible and, in fact, will play the role of ambassador for the company. Alternatively, many CEOs would prefer to deal only with other CEOs. In such cases, the wrong CEO (who is rude and has a huge ego problem) would spell disaster. I know one CEO who inherited a company with about 80-percent market share. That market share was largely the result of an outstanding CEO who had run the company previously. The new CEO, a person with horrible interpersonal skills, came in and started to break most, if not all, of the company's relationships one by one! As a matter of fact, I became so disgusted with that particular company that I wrote an editorial about how lousy some companies are in treating both their customers and the leading media in their industry. One analysis that I used was that the company acted as if the world owes it everything and it owes nothing in return. Needless to say, that particular CEO was let go, and the rest of the company was extremely happy for that.

Lesson # 9: Build Great Products and Keep Them a Secret!

Another great lesson that we continuously learned from mistakes made by small to medium-sized companies is as follows: The tendency of technology companies has often been to build a better mousetrap only to find that the mouse died 15 years ago! Believe it or not, as funny as this may seem, this is still the case in 80 percent of technology companies. As mentioned, I once visited the CEO of a speech technology company who had an outstanding speech product. I was very taken by the natural speech that was incorporated into that company's solution. I said to the CEO, "You have a great product here. How are you going to market it?" He replied, "I have invested 35 years of my life and every penny I had in developing this product, and right now I have no money for marketing." Can you believe this idiotic comment? If you do not market, you do not exist. In fact, if you are not on the first page of Google and/or Yahoo! search results for your industry, you do not exist. Nevertheless, high-tech companies continue to ignore the rules of marketing, and they give only lip service to it. Ironically, the few companies that do market seem to have one or more of the following problems:

- The marketing pieces and advertising are not benefits driven,
- There is no differentiation statement,
- There is no positioning statement,
- There is a wrong message to the wrong audience, and
- There is no call to action!

With that many problems, it is no wonder that many who do a lousy job of marketing do not blame their lack of knowledge about effective marketing; they say marketing does not work or advertising does not work, whereas in reality, their poor marketing message has all of the above problems and, in most cases, their messages have no call to action. That should explain the reason for unusually high rates of failure within the technology companies—they typically spend 95 percent of their budgets on research and development of new products and next to nothing on marketing. Today...no company prospers without the implementation of well-strategized integrated marketing.

Lesson #10: Do Not Hang Your Hat on PR Alone

Many times, I have witnessed CEOs and vice presidents of many technology companies go on media tours with the public relations staff. The companies visit both the leading publications as well as the industry analysts. Often times, they feel that their visit will lead to press via public relations, and thereby they feel that their marketing job is done. Many CEOs, while visiting the leading media providers, rarely ask, "How do you think I should market my product?" And that is the source of the problem, because a leading publisher who really understands the industry can offer practical solutions and suggestions for effective marketing strategies at no charge. Yet, many companies are not receptive to it, and they feel that PR alone is going to do the job. In my humble opinion, that will never happen, and it is only wishful thinking.

Lesson #11: Merger and Acquisition Blunders

In the mid 1990s, when the contact center industry was flourishing and growing at literally 50 to 100 percent a year, Wall Street became extremely interested in the contact center industry, specifically in teleservices. Investment bankers started calling me and asking me what I thought about this company or that company. It looked as if there was a feeding frenzy or, more specifically, an acquisition frenzy going on. Every week or every month, I would hear of a new acquisition. I was concerned about this activity: not because I did not feel that consolidation would be good, but because many of the acquirers were financial buyers, which means they were strictly interested in making a profit and they were clueless about the many, many details that need to be considered in order to effectively run and manage a call center.

I recall talking to such a financial buyer who used to be a waiter in a restaurant; he then purchased the restaurant and subsequently went into the real-estate business and made a ton of money. At that time, he discovered the rapid growth of call centers. As a result, he borrowed millions and acquired half a dozen incompatible and subpar companies. Before too long, as expected, he ran into major problems. I recall receiving a call from that person asking me what he had done wrong. Unfortunately, it was too late. If he had called me prior to the acquisitions, I would have told him that his particular combination of incompatible companies would never have become a unified profit center. As a result, millions of dollars were wasted.

Lesson #12: The Unlikely and Unfortunate Story

A few years ago, a poorly funded company (Company X) claimed to have developed a new technology that raised the eyebrows of all technology-savvy people. The company made every claim known to mankind, and it made many, many promises. While no one was taking it seriously, Company X decided to manipulate an analyst to state that upon evaluation of all products in this category, the analyst found Company X's product to rank at number 1. Obviously, some monetary rewards must have changed hands; otherwise such nonsense never would have been presented. The industry was up in arms. All manufacturers were against this action, and they spent a considerable amount of time informing the rest of the industry to beware of Company X's questionable practices. To make a very long story short, eventually Company X went out of business.

I have always wondered what is in the minds of the people who continue to make mistake after mistake and misleading statement after misleading statement, getting involved in all of the problems that I have outlined above. I once explained some of these problems to a highly respected CEO of our industry who, in my judgment, was one of the most, if not the most, knowledgeable CEOs in our industry. I shared with him some of the errors that were being committed. I asked him what he thought about the issue. His answer was, "If this industry wasn't so good, many of those CEOs would be pumping gas!" The more I thought about it, the more I realized he was right. Obviously, the purpose of this chapter is not to embarrass anyone or bad-mouth any individual or any company; rather, the main objective of this chapter is to learn from some of the mistakes made in the last 25 years. If I can prevent anyone from making any of the above mistakes, I think I have accomplished what I set out to do!

MARKETING THROUGH EDUCATION—THE ONLY WAY TO GO

It has been proven that the only way to market high-technology products is through education. There is simply no other way. One of the best ways to address this is to come up with unique and innovative editorial/marketing strategies to get your message across convincingly. The key to successful marketing must include, at a minimum, the following:

- Think out of the box and think integrated marketing.
- Be innovative.
- Remember the top three rules of marketing and advertising, which are benefits, benefits, and benefits. If your marketing message does not have a powerful, benefit-driven message, do not expect any results.
- Positioning. Nothing is more important than all of the above, plus positioning.
- And . . . differentiation.
- Last, but not least, please note that, without question, an integrated print, online, and trade-show campaign is much more effective than focusing on only one or the other exclusively.
- The combination of positioning and differentiation is what gives your customers a reason to buy your product as opposed to your competitor's product.

To be successful, you need to follow the above guidelines to avoid wasteful spending and costly mistakes and, above all, do not put all of your eggs in the same basket. Online marketing can be extremely rewarding if you follow the above guidelines. That is, integrated marketing should be the foundation of your marketing program to include online, print, trade shows, and so forth to bring appropriate brand recognition and marketing through education in order to help you maximize your marketing return on investment.

THE 12 COMMANDMENTS OF CUTTING-EDGE MARKETING

While conducting my day-to-day CEO-to-CEO interviews for TMC's Boardroom Report, I ask, "What is your greatest challenge?" Over 90 percent of the CEOs say things such as, "We are not well known; most people don't know us; most people don't know our company or our products, etc." In plain English, most CEOs are admitting that they need to do a much better job of marketing! What hurts me the most is that nearly all of the companies I speak with offer truly unique products and services for our industry and literally only a few, if any, people know that they exist! I think that is a shame! I ask, if you do not plan to market it effectively, why do you build it? Following are 12 areas that successful b-to-b companies include in their marketing mix:

1. Out-of-the-Box Integrated Marketing—Given that prospects are bombarded with thousands of proposals, marketing messages, and advertisements, developing an out-of-the-box integrated marketing program is vital for success. The bottom line is that you need to differentiate yourself and the only way to do that is to stand above the crowd.

2. Marketing through Education—Over the last 25 years, I have learned that the only way to effectively market high-technology products and services is via marketing through education. There is no shortcut for this.

3. Targeted Online Marketing—Online marketing has gained tremendous momentum in the marketing discipline, to a point where no company can exist without conducting a major program online. Targeted messages, that is, selecting key words that clearly define your core competency, are vital to the success of online marketing.

4. SEO—Search engine optimization is truly vital to the success of modern marketing. We used to say, "If you don't market, you don't exist." Today, we are saying, "If you are not on the first page of the world's leading search engines under your selected key words, then you don't exist." Proper SEO can be achieved only through effective integrated marketing, which is the only way to have your company appear on the first page of the world's leading search engines.

5. Search engine marketing is a new concept, and not many people are doing a good job. But I am sure that in due course it will evolve to being one of the most, if not the most, effective components of modern marketing.

6. Print Advertising—The biggest mistake made by some marketers is to jump into online marketing and forget about all other components of integrated marketing. It is a known fact in marketing that no one buys anything from someone he or she has never heard of. Continuous print advertising solves this problem by creating awareness of your products and services. Print also creates a perception of your company's stability and commitment to CRM. After all, customers want to know that your company will be around when they need service. Continuous, effective, and targeted print advertising creates precisely the kind of perception you need as a viable supplier. And...we all know that perception is reality! There is no way a shortcut will give you the necessary results. In other words, if you do print only or online only, you will not get the optimum results.

7. Participation in Conferences and Exhibitions—The next commandment of cutting-edge marketing is participation in conferences: both speaking and exhibiting at related trade shows are a MUST. In this manner, you will communicate to your prospects that your company is a major player, and you can demonstrate your products and services in the exhibit hall.

8. Special Editorial Series—Thinking along the lines of out-of-the-box marketing, special editorial series are indeed a powerful vehicle by which you can not only conduct marketing through education, but also in an editorial environment, you can communicate the benefits of your products as they pertain to the editorial matter at hand. Examples of these special editorial sections are "advertorials," white papers, and case studies.

9. Webinars—Webinars are becoming another major component of online marketing. Not only are they cost-effective, but if proper preparation, positioning, and

differentiation are made by the Webinar sponsors, the audience will give the sponsor its undivided attention regarding the benefits of the technologies and services being presented at the Webinars. Indeed, the Webinars should also be a vital part of your integrated marketing and one of the most important "commandments."

10. ROS, Curl Down Page, Splash Page, and Other Forms of Online Marketing—Run of sight (ROS) by key words is an extremely powerful way to create awareness about your products and services. This powerful tool, which appears on highly popular industry Web sites (for example, TMCnet.com) draws the attention of hundreds of thousands of unique visitors and as such, you will have the most effective way to not only introduce your company, but also your products and services, to a tremendously large audience. Other forms of online marketing include curl down pages and splash pages, which draw the exclusive attention of visitors to the Web site, and its uniqueness is so powerful that visitors can hardly miss it.

11. The Principles of Effective Advertising—You need to follow the principles of effective advertising, that is, articulating benefits, positioning, and differentiation, to name a few.

12. Last, But Not Least—You must use effective business-to-business telemarketing/teleservices and direct mail as a vital part of your integrated marketing campaign.

Hopefully, by now, you will agree that the nature of marketing has undergone a revolution. Today, one can easily state that if you are not on the first page of the most powerful search engines, you do not exist, simply because 95 percent of visitors to search engines will not go beyond the first page. In other words, if you are not practicing the above commandments, chances are that you are not on the first page of the popular search engines under your chosen relevant term. And if you are not on the first page of these search engines (preferably number 1 on the first page), then YOU DO NOT EXIST!

Put simply, anyone who is interested in getting information about certain products to buy will usually refer to the industry's leading publications and/or the leading search engines first and then continue to get information prior to purchasing a product. Just following the above 12 commandments will give you satisfaction in knowing that you are doing a decent job of integrated marketing, but if you aspire to be number 1 on the leading search engines in your category, then you are doing only a decent job. That is not good enough. To me, there is no glory to be one among many. What you must aspire to do is dominate the above new paradigm of marketing in order to not only protect your market share, but also continue to expand it.

NOTES

1. Paul Fornier (Ed.), Reed Business Information, personal communication.

2. Ed Abram, personal communication.

3. Jack Trout, *The New Positioning: The Latest on the World's #1 Business Strategy,* with Steve Rivkin (New York: McGraw-Hill, 1996).

CHAPTER 8

BORDERLESS MARKETING SYSTEMS: THE EMERGING HYBRID MULTI-CHANNEL MARKET SYSTEM

Andria Evan and Dale M. Lewison

Successful marketing channel architectures of the future will require that "go-to-market" strategies be constructed as "borderless marketing systems" that deliver a consistent, high-quality exchange experience across all channel alternatives. No longer will you be able to conduct your exchange relationships within a single, independent channel or as a stand-alone business. Future channel systems will consist of several channel alternatives that have been integrated into a hybrid multi-channel structure capable of attracting and deepening relationships with high-value partners.

Dell Inc. has become the largest seller of PCs worldwide. Why? Today, Dell's online, telephone, catalog, and in-mall kiosks are completely integrated. Both Dell's front-end sales and back-end after-sales customer-service functions are performed by the most efficient and effective channel for a specific customer market. The highly focused nature of these hybrid channel architectures will permit Dell and you to create and sustain a superior "end-to-end" relationship experience with all parties to an exchange process within the channel system.

This end-to-end experience includes the best possible two-way communication and interaction encounters. From the initial contact through the completion of the transaction and subsequent follow-up, the total experience will be a win-win outcome for all parties within the hybrid channel. Any past concerns regarding shared information, coordinated scheduling, cooperative strategies, revenue sharing, territorial exclusivity, and a host of other control issues will require a considerable attitude adjustment. You will not be able to keep channels autonomous because you fear cannibalization of sales, comparison of prices, resolution of conflicts, and loss of control.

This chapter and subsequent chapters in this book will assist you in examining and assessing your needs relative to one of the most dynamic and important marketing trends for the next decade or two—that is, the emergence of the hybrid multi-channel marketing system and the creation of borderless marketing strategies between various channel alternatives.

CHANNEL SURFERS: "BORDERLESS" CONSUMERS

Channel surfing in search of the best value is rapidly becoming the norm for both final and business consumers. Channel surfers are shoppers who use different marketing channels to meet their needs at different stages in the buying process. One surfer might elect to search for information using one channel (Internet), place an order using a different channel (telephone), and pick up the order at a third channel (retail store). Each of these channels may or may not be part of the same marketing system: a fact that does not seem to trouble these advantage seekers. For example, the purchase of airline tickets has shifted from printed tickets and personal travel agents to paperless electronic ticketing on the Internet.

The multidimensional shopping experience is becoming commonplace as shoppers poach the best value from whatever channel regardless of the circumstances. The buying behavior termed value poaching is characterized by channel surfing shoppers routinely taking advantage of high-touch channels to shop and low-cost channels to buy. Channel loyalty suffered as buying behavior became more unfettered, unstructured, and unregulated. This lack of loyalty is simply a repeat of the decades-old complaint by small local retailers moaning the loss of business to large national chains. This detached and removed attitude of shoppers regarding channel patronage can be explained, in part, by the fact that buyers are better informed, have access to more channel alternatives, are more comfortable with new technologies, and are more experienced with the buying process. All is fair in the quest for better value and a more rewarding shopping experience. The trend toward channel surfing and multi-channel shopping is a marketing reality that will be with us for the foreseeable future.

CHANNEL ARCHITECTURES: MULTIPLE "TOUCH POINTS"

The critical issue that you will face in planning and designing marketing channels of the future will involve the structuring of channel architectures not in terms of *who shoppers are* but *how shoppers shop* and what type of channel flows (marketing functions) will be needed to accommodate these behaviors. This shift of emphasis toward buyer behavior and away from buyer traits has profound implications for the future of marketing segmentation and the development of target markets. For the channel designer, the ability to hone in on the specific buying behavior of high-value consumers will dictate a more comprehensive approach to the marketplace. Using the RFM (Recency, Frequency, Monetary) model, multi-channel marketers are better able to target those high-value customers who have made a purchase recently, who purchase on a more regular and frequent basis, and spend more money each time they buy.

To establish these additional and appropriate touch points, you will need more, better, and different market access strategies. Because individual shopping behaviors will dictate what type of channels will be required to meet and exceed the needs and expectations of shoppers at each stage of the buying process, you will need to ensure that you have the channel capability to deliver a consistent, high-quality shopping experience across multiple shopping venues. Generating and fulfilling consumer demand in a highly successful fashion can be achieved by matching how the consumer buys (five stages of the buying process) with the best vehicle (the five general types of marketing channels) for delivering key channel functions (five kinds of channel flows).

The Channel Design Model in Figure 8.1 presents a visualization of the major components structuring the channel flows that you will need for your portfolio of the multidimensional channels that you will need to deal with the multidimensional behaviors of your selected consumer markets. This basic tool allows you to lay out different variations and combinations of channel architectures based on various channel alternatives, stages of the buyer behavior process, and different kinds of marketing channel flows. Before we look at the dynamics of channel architecture, we briefly describe each of our three sets of design considerations that are used in structuring our go-to-market strategies.

BUYING PROCESSES: "MULTI-CHANNEL" BEHAVIORS

Multi-channel marketers continue to focus on selling "things" that comprise the offer proposition—product quality, style, selection, and price. While things are still important, you need to recognize that "how consumers buy" (experiences) is as important as "what consumers buy." For example, L. L. Bean, Inc. recognized that some of its customers need to have a live tangible sensory experience (smell, hear, taste, feel, or see) with the product before committing to ordering it from a catalog or over the Internet. Personal involvement with its products is one of the major forces driving the firm to open new stores and increase its market exposure in a effort to secure incremental growth.[1] As more and more product categories become commodities, shopping and buying experiences are becoming the things consumers' value most. The continuum of experiences that you might create can range from a maximum of efficiency to different and interesting socialization, entertainment, and recreational encounters. By recognizing this bipolar

Figure 8.1
The Channel Design Rubric

behavior, you position yourself to create strategies around either or both ends of the continuum.

Consumers make purchase decisions by passing through a five-stage sequential process consisting of recognition, consideration, evaluation, selection, and reaction. The duration and extent to which an individual gets involved in any one state of the buying process varies greatly depending on such factors as urgency of need, frequency of purchases, importance of purchase, availability of time and resources, the number of available channel alternatives, and a host of other considerations. We quickly review these five stages.

Recognition Behavior

A felt discrepancy between an ideal state of affairs and the actual state of affairs starts the buying process by creating an awareness and concern that a problem exists. Recognition is a feeling that things are not what they should be, and a process to create awareness of pending issues. For final consumers this state of tension might be triggered by internal physiological or external psychological stimuli—dissatisfaction with a current product or interest in a new product aroused by promotional efforts of competitors. Margery Myers, spokesperson for The Talbots, Inc. (upscale retailer of professional women's apparel), attests to the effects of physical stimuli noting that 70 percent of customers who receive a catalog subsequently visit a store. In this instance, it does not matter whether or not the client is a catalog shopper per se, the catalog's secondary function is to drive sales by reminding the recipient of the catalog of unmet needs and desires.[2] Organizational buyers might be facing a straight rebuy for a satisfactorily performing product from the same supplier, a modified rebuy for a product from the same or new supplier with new terms and conditions of sale, or a new task buy for a new product from a new supplier. The key outcome of recognition behavior is that the individual or organization is motivated to act in some fashion in order to reduce tension.

Consideration Behavior

Serious consideration of the problem identified in the first stage requires the consumer to gather new and additional information pertinent to the reasonable consideration of the identified problem. The extensiveness of the consideration will depend on the relative importance assigned to the problem. A low-level information search involves paying closer attention to advertisements, store displays, promotional literature, word-of-mouth comments, and other less intrusive forms of communication. For more serious consideration of identified problems, a high-level information search and deliberation can be achieved by talking to, reading from, and observation of more comprehensive and sophisticated sources of information. Surveillance (visiting different sources of supply), counterintelligence (talking with competitors), networking (interacting with trade sources), and researching (consulting reports, third-party experts, independent surveys, and government publications) are all means by which both final consumers and organizational buyers gather the intelligence needed for a complete reflection of possible solutions for an identified buying quandary.

Evaluation Behavior

This stage of the buying behavior process focuses on comparing the various alternative solutions using the information gathered from the previous stage. At this point of the buying process, final and business consumers are interested in discovering which alternative solution has the greatest likelihood of best achieving an acceptable problem resolution. Common evaluation criteria used by the ultimate consumer include functional and aesthetic features of the product, extra services that support the product, psychological benefits that characterize the product, product price points, degree of availability of the product, promotional claims, compatibility and appropriateness of the product to the consumer's need, and other factors such as the durability and quality of the item. In business-to-business channels, the evaluation process is more formal and rational. Typical evaluation criteria are terms and conditions of sale, level of vendor's delivery standards and special handling capabilities, suitability and availability of the product, the adaptability of product features to buyer's specifications, order cycle time, and error rate in filling orders.

Selection Behavior

Response decisions by final consumers center on the answers to two questions: "*if*" and "*when*" the prospect will make a purchase. The *buy decision* is a confirmation that at least one of the product/seller alternatives is capable of resolving an identified problem. On the other hand, the consumer might conclude that of the known alternatives evaluated, none meet minimum expectations for problem solution—*the no-buy decision*. The latter decision terminates the current cycle of the buying process, and the consumer can either dismiss the problem or start the buying process anew with hopes of gaining a different perspective on the problem. Each prospect is faced with the "when" decision, which involves deciding whether to make an immediate purchase (proceed) or wait (postpone) until some future date. One of your bigger challenges will be to develop offers that close the sale now; postponed decisions are very likely to result in lost sales. Organizational buyers generally face the same "if" and "when" decisions as final consumers. In addition, business buyers may elect to concentrate their purchases with one vendor (single sourcing) or spread orders over several suppliers (multiple sourcing) For both business-to-consumer and business-to-business channels, order placement and fulfillment must be convenient, easy, fast, reasonable, reliable, and secure. For both groups of customers, the ability to communicate and negotiate on a live, one-to-one basis is often crucial to future relationships.

Reaction Behavior

The final stage of the buying process deals with how final or business customers react to their concluded buying process—that is, a postpurchase evaluation of their buying experience. Most buyers have some doubt or concerns about both the purchase and the buying experience. They need reassurance that they made the right decision. A positive assessment of the experience results in postpurchase satisfaction and encourages the buyer to repeat the just-concluded buying process on a regular and routine basis. A negative response leads to postpurchase dissonance—dissatisfaction with the purchase and/or the process that led to it. Dissatisfaction leads to product returns or allowances, lost sales, bad word of mouth, and, most importantly, the lost opportunity to create a loyal and profitable customer.

MARKET PATHWAYS: GO-TO-MARKET CHANNELS

Today's marketing organization will face several different types of marketing channel alternatives as it prepares to design or modify the channel structures needed to reach selected consumer groups. The choices for accessing selected markets include personal, electronic, broadcast, print, and teleservices channels. Eddie Bauer uses the classic bricks, clicks, and pages combo of marketing channels; it offers its customers the opportunities to patronize its stores, shop online, or order from one of several catalogs. Each of these alternatives has individual strengths and weaknesses of communicating and interacting with the marketplace. Competition today is becoming a battle not between firms or products, but aggressive rivalry between channel systems that consist of a portfolio of two or more channel alternatives. It is the offering from one vertical and horizontal marketing system warring against another system. In the future, winners will be those organizations that have the best collection of channel alternatives and not the one that has the biggest promotional budget or product line. In order to develop a successful portfolio of channel alternatives, we first briefly profile the five pathways to the marketplace.

Personal Channels

The distinctive characteristic of personal (field) channels is the face-to-face nature of all communications and interactions between buyers and sellers. Direct-to-customer marketing features personal explanation and demonstration of the offer. The primary formats used in personal channels include the brick-and-mortar *store facilities* common to retailers and marketing intermediaries and *direct selling* in which the seller (manufacturer, wholesaler, or retailer) negotiates directly with the buyer (decider, influencer, user, or purchaser) without an intervening middleman. Personal contacts with the buyer in his or her home, place of work, or interceptor location (streets, trade fairs, or expos) are common examples of this channel approach. At the retail level, door-to-door solicitations, in-home party plans, and stationary and mobile kiosks are three examples of this direct one-on-one channel. Tangibility and socializing are two of the most important strengths of this channel alternative. The ability to physically interact (feel, smell, see, hear, and taste) with the product is still one of the most important competitive advantages of personal channels. Social interaction is the second advantage enjoyed by face-to-face marketers. Shopping is a socializing, recreation, entertainment, and buying experience. Personalization is a driving force for getting and keeping loyal and profitable customers.

Electronic Channels

Electronic channels encompass all of the pathways for buyer/seller communications and interactions over the Internet—the global superhighway of computer networks connected by landlines and satellites. A computer-based, electronic channel allows millions of people to communicate, perform research, find entertainment, and buy and sell products and services. The two most commonly used electronic channels are the World Wide Web and e-mail.

The Web is a collection of Web sites and pages that allows the user to access the Internet. Its nonlinear design enables users or "surfers" to jump from topic to topic and site to site. This easy-to-navigate channel uses text, pictures, sound, and video in interesting and informative layouts and designs to effectively do the following:

- Provide useful information,
- Communicate offers and responses, and
- Connect or link with other sites.

The Web's role within the marketer's channel strategy might include building a market presence, enhancing the firm's image, opening geographically dispersed markets, reaching different customer groups, providing product information, promoting new offerings, and acquiring customer feedback.

E-mail is a low-cost, one-on-one electric communication and interaction channel that allows you to offer greater exclusivity, customization, and convenience by providing links to information that is highly relevant to the buyer situation. E-mail channels allow personalization of the offer and can be effective in gaining the customer's permission (opt-in) to continue the relationship by providing additional information. Enhancing customer relationships, driving customers to a Web site, and directing customers to stores and other personal selling venues are the three most common commercial uses of e-mail. On-going electronic browsing by prospects is the equivalent of electronic window shopping that creates the awareness and interest that leads to trial and purchase. Chief reasons customers cite for shopping online include the ability to browse, buy at any time, save time and effort, greater product selection, and ease of price, feature, and benefit comparisons.

Broadcast Channels

Radio and television constitute the primary forms of broadcast channels. As a channel alternative, broadcast venues have traditionally been used for one-way communications and not for two-way interactions. While talk radio and various shopping channels represent notable exceptions, broadcast channels are poorly configured for direct customer response. Broadcast channels are generally outbound communications networks that use print, electronic, and teleservices for handling inbound responses and inquiries. Television offers the advantages of good communication effectiveness (both sight and sound), reasonably good audience selectivity through the use of programming material, extensive reach into almost every home, and considerable prestige due to its more glamorous and conspicuous presence. High costs, lack of flexibility, immediacy, and short life span are the limitations most relevant to television as a marketing channel. Radio has great immediacy in terms of lead times, good audience and geographic selectivity, good flexibility by providing words, music, and sound, and has a very favorable cost structure. Well-known personalities (radio show hosts like Paul Harvey) who have established programs and loyal listeners add creditability to the offer. Radio messages are short-lived, lack strong impact, and messages must be kept simple. Satellite radio has extended the effectiveness and usefulness of this type of communication vehicle.

Print Channels

The published word and visuals (pictures, tables, and graphics) are the means by which offers are extended and accepted with print channels. Direct-mail packages, magazines, and newspapers are the principal print media for generating customer response. Direct-mail packages typically consist of the outer envelope (creates awareness and interest), a letter (presents the selling proposition), a brochure (provides information for consideration and evaluation of the offer), and an order form or some other response vehicle (ask for the sale or response and provides a means for customers to communicate their decisions). Catalogs, syndication mailings, coupons, stuffers, and inserts are some of the choices for creating effective direct-mail programs.

The proliferation of special-interest magazines can be an excellent means of reaching a select group of customers who share a common pursuit. Modern printing technologies allow magazines to create printed collateral material of high quality at modest prices. Long life (customer often scans and reads several times) and frequent publication intervals are additional strengths of magazine channels. Newspaper channels are an extensively used medium for delivering direct marketing offers. Newspapers as a preferred channel can be justified on the basis of its excellent geographic and audience selectivity, good market coverage, shorter lead times, faster customer response rates, and a wide choice of formats (different sections, supplements, inserts, and editions). Lower-quality paper, basic newspaper print copy, and considerable advertising clutter are some of the less desirable features of this channel.

Teleservices Channels

The telephone is one of the most convenient and efficient communication technologies that you can use to meet your needs as a marketer and the service needs of customers. Teleservices operations assume one of two forms: inbound or outbound.

Inbound telemarketing is customer-initiated communications or interaction for the purposes of obtaining information on a wide variety of issues, ordering a good or service, requesting assistance or service, responding to a direct marketing offer, locating other marketing channels (store or service center), expediting or canceling an order, and a host of other service-based requests. This form of telemarketing usually involves a toll-free number (800, 888, 877, and 866) as a communication channel. Inbound calls are the common response mechanism used in conjunction with offers that have been extended through electronic, print, and broadcast channels

Outbound telemarketing is a proactive marketing channel in which the seller initiates contact. Because outbound calls are a fast and efficient means of communication that can be used to presell (initial call to create awareness and arouse interest), sell (second call to gain trail and confirm conviction), postsell (followup call to check on the customer's satisfaction), and upsell (attempt to sell additional complementary products and services or trade up to higher priced/quality products or greater quantities of the existing product). Lead generation and qualification are highly suited to outbound teleservices channels, while account management and postsales services are the primary uses for inbound telemarketing.

In general, teleservices marketing tends to be an immediate channel that facilities two-way communication, immediate feedback on an offer, higher customer contact productivity, a flexible and adaptable selling process, and acceptable cost structures. On the downside, teleservices marketing is an intrusive channel that relies on a single sense (hearing) that is incapable of providing the customer with tangible proof of the product's qualities. New voice technologies and voice-over-Internet protocols are having a positive impact on the growth of the teleservices industry.

MARKETING PIPELINES "FUNCTIONAL" FLOWS

How are you going to satisfy the different behaviors of different customers in different channels of distribution? The marketing channel is a distribution system that delivers the firm's entire marketing program to selected consumer markets. Channel flows are movements of several distinct, functional marketing capabilities that consist of several diverse yet integrated flows that travel over assorted routes (channels) in various directions (inbound and outbound or upstream and downstream) at different speeds. For BMW's Mini Adventures campaign this meant using online, direct mail, experiential, and promotional marketing coupled with additional media sources.[3] As a channel designer, you may eliminate one or more of the channels for delivering a particular functional flow, but you cannot eliminate that flow. Therefore, it is your responsibility to decide how you plan to accommodate the various buying behaviors and channel flows through your selection of marketing channels. There are two major categories of flows: (1) those that are primarily related to communications and (2) another set of flows that are concerned with interactions between members of the exchange parties. *Communication flows* consist primarily of information, promotions, and negotiations, while *interaction flows* take the form of transactions and relationships.

Information Flow

Meaningful communications among channel participants depend on transmission of useful and informative facts and data. The information flow is a two-way exchange of useful information between two parties within one or more channel settings. Outbound or downstream flows provide information on the seller's offer and business proposition. Inbound or upstream flows communicate the buyer's response in terms of inquires, rejections, decisions to buy, or feedback. Efficient flow of basic information is essential for informing, ordering, paying, delivering, tracking, and servicing within the marketing exchange process.

Promotional Flow

Marketing involves the art of influence. The promotional flow is a firm's presentation of persuasive communications directed at influencing the behaviors of customers (final consumer promotions) and other channel participants (trade promotions). The promotional flow consists of advertisement, personal selling, sale promotions and incentives, public relations, and publicity. Promotional flows are persuasive appeals that involve communicating the right message to the right audience through the right media. The right message is the right thing to say (message content) delivered in the right way (manner of message presentation). Message content is right when its emphasis is what the buyer is concerned with (product quality and selection, pricing points, service support, and warrantees) and explains how the seller's offer meets those concerns. Persuasive promotions tend to be formulated as logical arguments (factual presentation about the offer) or emotional appeals (messages that speak not to what buyers think but to how they feel).

Negotiations Flow

The interplay of sellers and buyers within the marketing exchange process encompasses the negotiation flow. Negotiation has been described as the "art of give and take" where discussions are directed at resolving differences and issues. Within the marketing channel context, negotiation is the act of reaching a resolution in response to an offer proposition. Deciding what features of the offer are open to conciliation and to what extent the parties are willing to agree to concessions and resolutions, the negotiations flow can be predatory or symbiotic in nature. If you decide that taking a hard line and an uncompromising position in negotiations with customers and other channel partners is in your best interest, your predatory style may lead to transactions (assuming that the other party is dependent on you), but it will fail to build long-term relationships and loyal patrons. If you believe win-win strategies are more productive, then you need to negotiate courses of action that are mutually beneficial. This symbiotic negotiation process is about sharing information and communicating freely in order to find concessions that foster successful transaction and fruitful relationships.

Transaction Flow

Order placement and fulfillment constitute the two key activities of the transaction flow. Favorable conclusions to the negotiation process are transactional closure—the convenient transmission of an order, and physical response—the timely delivery of the order. Inherent in the transaction flow are the transfer of the physical goods, the submission of required payment, and the transmission of title of ownership. Managing the transaction flow will require you to allocate to various channels such things as order processing, materials handling, warehousing, inventory planning and control, packaging, billing, and transporting.

Relational Flow

Channel structures need to support channel relationships. One of the more powerful movements during the last decade is the evolution of marketing into the relationship era. In short, the concept of relationship marketing stresses the viewpoint that all channel exchange activities need to be directed at creating value at every point and link in the marketing channel. Relationships are the glue that hold the channel together and ensure its cooperative advantage. You can decide to be a transaction marketer or a relationship marketer. The former is most concerned about making a sale and completing a transaction that is in his or her best interest. The latter strives to build a continuing relationship that results in mutual loyalty. Channels can be designed to support either one of these two flows. In practice, relational flows range on a continuum from discrete (independent, self-serving, short-term, and hit and run) exchanges to relational (interdependent, mutual, long-term, and win-win) exchanges. Successful channel design supports customized relationships that meet the other party's needs. Shared responsibility, mutual commitment, continuous interaction, effective coordination, horizontal alignment, and vertical integration are all traits of a well-conceived structural channel design.

CHANNEL MIGRATION "CHANGING ARCHITECTURES"

The architectural journey from single-channel structures to multiplicity of market pathways has picked up speed in the last several years. The catalyst for this dynamic has been the acceptance and expansion of the Internet as a vehicle for doing business and being an acceptable way to shop. The capabilities of various marketing channels and their usage by consumers have proliferated since the turn of the century. Buyers have unbundled the offering of various marketing channels and practice a form of "cherry picking"—selecting what they perceive to be the best channel alternative and flow for communicating their needs and interacting with their chosen exchange partners. As described earlier, consumers are becoming less and less mindful of channel boundaries. Given the speed at which consumers migrate from one channel to another, it will be necessary for channels to offer a "bill of fare" of features and functional flows. Prepackaged, standardized offerings will be less apropos to shopping behaviors of the future. Channel migration is an issue of customer preferences. People select the channel that best suits their purposes at any given point of time, and they often change their minds and preferences. Take consumer banking for example: customer preferences shifted from branch stores to automatic teller machines to online banking. Many banks closed branches or reduced on-site channels such as drive-through windows. Today, consumers expect banking services to be available through convenient and secure personal, Internet, and teleservice channels.

Channel migration can be viewed from the perspective of a continuum of channel architectures ranging from the traditional (single channel) marketing networks to the hybrid (multi-channel) marketing systems. Between these two ends of our channel architecture continuum is the transitional structure of the independent (multiple channels) option. Figure 8.2 summarizes the scope of options you have in constructing go-to-market strategies.

Traditional Single-Channel Marketing Networks

As illustrated in Figure 8.2, single-channel structures are largely vertical systems that provide only one option: to deliver your offer to the marketplace. As suggested by Figure 8.3, a single channel has the job of guiding the consumer through all five stages of the buying process, that is, by providing all of the various kinds of marketing functions and flows. The example in Figure 8.3 is a traditional retail store channel where each channel level (producers, distributors, manufacturers, wholesalers, and retailers) operates as a separate entity with a prescribed set of responsibilities assigned to that channel level. Customers and end users rely on the last or lowest member in the channel (for example, the retailer) for most or all of the channel flows and the fulfillment of their needs. For the most part, the single channel offers a "take-it or leave-it" bundle of channel flows and functions that move through a more or less standardized channel structure. Management of this traditional network is accomplished by a channel captain who typically is the most powerful member of the network. While manufacturers were historically the channel captain, power has shifted away from these upstream sources of supply to

Figure 8.2
Continuum of Channel Architectures

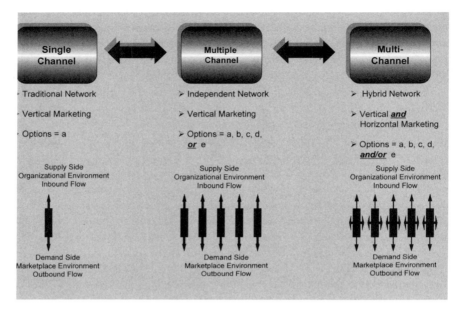

downstream sellers and retailers who control access to markets. By controlling vast market shares, Wal-Mart, Federated Department Stores, Inc., The Home Depot, Inc., Best Buy, and a host of other resellers have become the power source of the channel. This power affords them the opportunity to determine the structural dimensions of the channel's architecture and the managerial characteristics of the channel's operations.

Independent Multiple-Channel Marketing Network

Reaching various market segments via separate and independently operated marketing channels is the core concept behind the multiple-channel strategy. As portrayed in Figure 8.4, this option structures channel architectures as "either/ or" (either a, b, c, d, or e) vertical marketing choices that are designed to reach different target markets. Think of this option as choosing among one of the five types of marketing channel alternatives where each alternative is expected to deal with all aspects of the customer's buying behavior. All communication and transactional functions are carried out via a single channel for each selected consumer segment. This approach is the result of channel architects electing to add channels incrementally in the quest to achieve better market coverage and lower-cost structures. Figure 8.4 shows three different channels (retail outlet, Web site, and direct mail) as multiple yet independent approaches to the marketplace. This multiple-

Figure 8.3
The Channel Design Rubric for a Single-Channel Network

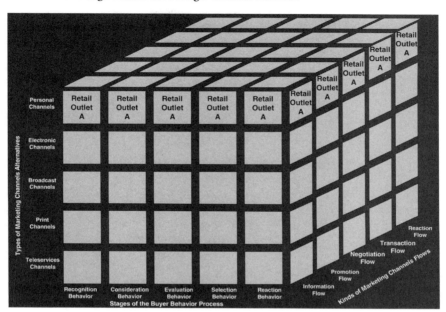

channel architecture has been the response of many firms to the increase in market fragmentation, product proliferation, and accelerated product life cycles. The "one-channel-fits-all" strategy is being replaced in some cases by "several different channels fit several different markets." The multiple channel architecture recognizes that different customers with different buying behaviors will seek out different channels for their different needs. If you employ this channel differentiation strategy, you are electing to demarcate your offerings by channel, thereby reducing or eliminating direct comparisons of offers. Even if multiple-channel structures are necessary to reflect market plurality, each channel within the portfolio of channels specializes in handling all stages of the buying behavior process for a specific group of consumers. The multiple-channel network appears to be best suited to dynamic marketplace conditions where rapidly evolving environments require faster reaction times.

Hybrid (Multi-Channel) Marketing Network

Hybrid channels are highly integrated vertical and horizontal marketing systems that seek to employ the channel best capable of meeting the behavioral buying needs of the customer by delivering the channel flow most suited to that stage in the buying process. Vertical and horizontal integration involve a high level of

Figure 8.4
The Channel Design Rubric for a Multiple-Channel Network

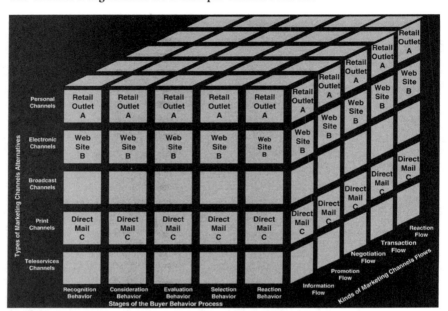

coordination and cooperation between different channel levels (for example, producers, distributors, manufacturers, wholesalers, and retailers) and different kinds of marketing channels (for example, personal, Internet, broadcast, print, and teleservices). Hybrid channels can be comprised of any combination of channel alternatives that supply any combination of channel flows to service the consumer at any stage of the buying process. Multi-channel structures are designed to build maximum customer value by optimizing the strengths of each type of channel. "A kiosk program creates a hybrid channel of sorts, as it leverages both the brick-and-mortar and direct marketing arms of a business (Internet, direct mail, catalogs, telemarketing). It relies on the direct marketing back end while providing the front-end retail location access to more SKSs [stock keeping units] and countless opportunities to offer information and customization."[4]

To implement a multi-channel strategy, channel flows have to be unbundled and sourced separating from one or more of the available channels. In the end, the channel design manager treats each possible channel option not as an independent, stand-alone, go-to-market effort, but rather as an integrated component of a larger marketing network that has been designed to build the best exchange scenario possible for both the seller and the buyer. As suggested in Figure 8.2, multi-channel strategies are and/or choices (a, b, c, d, and/or e) where any combination of channel alternatives and flows can be fashioned to maximize the most effective interactivity with the customer and to construct a superior multi-channel buying experience.

The Charles Schwab Corporation allows its traders to conduct transactions online, by phone, or in person. In addition to transactions, Schwab partners with its traders by providing actionable information, by sponsoring investment courses (face-to-face classes), providing portfolio consultations (inbound teleservice channel), and supplying links to useful sources of information (links to Web sites). A greater selection of channel options enhances the chances of the seller being more successful; a sharper focus on profitable buyers results in greater buyer loyalty and satisfaction. If you become a participant in a hybrid channel, you will be better able to share resources and competencies in novel ways. Hence, you will be in a better position to take advantage of profitable market opportunities and create strategic alliances that are more suited to exploiting those opportunities. In addition to better and greater market coverage, firms pursue hybrid channel structures in an attempt to share and lower cost structures. General trade data show costs for face-to-face selling time for sales representatives tend to average $300 per hour, teleservice solicitations average $17 per hour, while direct mail runs $1 per customer contact. Given the relative strengths and weaknesses of each of the above channels, design architects have a continuum of possibilities to select the most cost-effective channel alternative.

Figure 8.5 provides an example of a rather basic multi-channel marketing network. In this example, Kristopher's (our customer) awareness level of a felt need or desire for a new vehicle began while surfing the Internet and linking to a site with a story on the "hottest selling wheels." Of all the successes described in the article, what caught Kris's attention was the Toyota FJ Cruiser—a retro-looking off-road vehicle with distinctive styling and features. Having his interest peaked, Kristopher decides to Google the model to see what information was readily available. Finding a host of possible information sources ranging from official Toyota sites to auto-buying services to eBay traders, Kris starts gathering intelligence by visiting several sites. His search was fruitful in that he was able to secure a detailed description of the vehicle, its standard and optional features, together with several price quotes. Further investigation on the Web allows Kris to obtain a fairly good idea of the trade-in value of his current vehicle. By looking at several videos, viewing a gallery of photos, and reading numerous descriptions, an understanding and an appreciation of both the aesthetic and functional features were formulated. One major piece of information was not attainable from the Web. Being a rather tall and stout individual, Kris did not know if he would fit into the driver's seat comfortably. A personal visit and face-to-face encounter with the vehicle and the dealer now seemed appropriate.

An Internet search identified five Toyota dealers within a 38-mile radius of his home. Kris also checked the local newspaper in order to get a feel for each dealership and to see if they had the Cruiser in stock. No Cruisers were advertised.

Figure 8.5
The Channel Design Rubric for a Multi-Channel Network

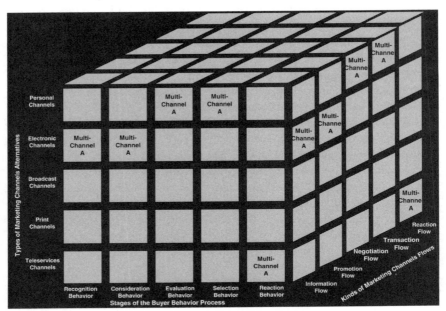

Short on time, Kris elected to call the three nearest dealerships to check on available units. Of the three, only one dealer had the FJ Cruiser on the lot. The selection was limited—one silver and one black. Conversations with the other two dealers revealed that these vehicles were often sold before they were delivered or they were sold within two days of delivery. This bit of knowledge put a damper on Kris's plan for being an aggressive negotiator and driving a hard bargain.

Using MapQuest, Kris was able to get precise directions to the dealership. Upon arriving at the retail outlet, Kris was quickly claimed by a professionally dressed sales representative. Physical contact with the vehicle answered concern number one—the driver's compartment was more then adequate for Kris's significant frame. Close examination of the Cruiser's sticker and various sales literature provided most of the information for an informed decision. The dealer's salesperson carefully reviewed all of the FJ Cruiser's finer attributes and benefits.

The demand factors surrounding this highly sought after vehicle dictated that the sticker price was indeed the actual selling price. Accepting this fact, Kris decided that the best negotiation strategy was to get the best price for his trade-in. Having checked several sources, Kris knew the trade-in value ranged from $8,500 to $13,000 depending on the condition. Using the sales pitch that he was willing to pay top sticker price for the Cruiser if he could get top value for his trade-in, Kris started the negotiations.

After numerous offers and counteroffers between Kris and the sales representative and the rep and the sales manager, the deal was concluded with Kris achieving his goal. The conclusion of the vehicle sale leads to the opening of a new set of negotiations regarding several "up-selling" efforts on the part of the dealer. Information and offers regarding financing arrangements, insurance coverage, extended warrantees, maintenance contracts, protective coatings, and roadside assistance plans were communicated to Kris through a finance and service representative using various forms of literature and face-to-face presentations. Both Internet and inbound teleservices channels were used to support the personal channel and finalize the transaction between Kris and the dealership. Additional after-sale communications and interactions were conducted via direct mail and teleservice channels. The whole point to this exchange scenario is to demonstrate that multi-channel approaches are both effective and efficient for all parties within an exchange relationship. For most consumers, they are or will be the channel structure of choice.

The favorables for hybrid multi-channel marketing systems are considerable. In sum, if you elect to compete through an integrated hybrid multi-channel marketing system, you should have the following comparative advantages. First, hybrid channels allow you to focus on high-value customers using the best combination of channel options. Second, multi-channel structures lend themselves to delivering a superior offering of "*ERs*"—bett*er* customer value, fast*er* customer service, new*er* product offerings, great*er* product selection, cheap*er* price points, bigg*er* promotional events, high*er* quality offerings, and fin*er* shopping experiences. Third, the more intensive market coverage commonly associated with horizontally and vertically integrated marketing systems is very supportive of customer acquisition and retention. Fourth, customer conversion rates (the success of turning prospects into buyers) are enhanced due to the ability to interact with customers within the environs of their preferred channel of exchange. Fifth, it forces the channel architect to focus on channel flows and functions and how they relate to buying behaviors as the primary design tool. Six, it encourages participants to willingly hand off customers to those channels best suited for meeting the needs and behaviors shared among customers; hence, it encourages fully customized offers that are more likely to exceed the expectations of the customer. Seven, it promotes a channel climate of sharing, cooperating, and partnering that ensures win-win relationships for all partners. Finally, clearly articulated multi-channel structures break down internal and external barriers and boundaries and subdue various channel conflicts while supporting cross-channel coordination of activities.

MULTIPLY AND BE PROFITABLE: SOME CONCLUSIONS

Today's and tomorrow's multi-channel communication and distribution networks are some of the great marketing frontiers open to you for both incremental growth and rapid expansion. Explicitly delineated hybrid channel architectures that carefully lay out each channel alternative's (in-person, online, on-the-air, in-print, and on-call) roles, responsibilities, formats, functionalities, and expected behaviors will permit you to exploit the ripe opportunity for capturing and holding high-value consumers. This is particularly significant given that 20 percent of your customers will account for 60 to 80 percent of your sales for any good or service. Major resellers of books and related product lines (for example, Borders Group Inc., Barnes & Noble Booksellers, and Amazon.com) have all developed frequency and loyalty programs to keep track of their customer purchases (for example, what they buy, when they buy, why they buy, and how they buy) and other behaviors (for example, product searches, returns, inquiries, and requests). The purpose behind these programs is to build a database of customers that will help in identifying, profiling, and selecting the most profitable, and potentially, the most loyal customers. To succeed in implementing an integrated multi-channel system, you will need to do the following:

- Articulate the strategic and tactical rationale for expanding into new channels and markets and its impact on the added value for both the firm and the customer.
- Gain support from all partners within the distribution system and mobilize the core competencies of all parties.
- Integrate channel flows across all new and existing channel alternatives while avoiding parallel operations of single independent channels.
- Synchronize operations, processes, policies, and procedures across all new and existing channels in order to ensure within and between channel consistencies.
- Coordinate all supply chain fulfillment activities in order to leverage inventory data across all new and existing channels.
- Boost intra- and interchannel responsiveness using channel architectures that promote flexible and configurable design principles.
- Avoid channel conflict between new and existing channels through relationship building, role definition, equitable treatment, benefit sharing, and superior communications on all issues.

NOTES

1. Louise Harbach, "L.L. Bean Retail Store Comes to Burlington County, J.J.," *Philadelphia Inquirer,* August 16, 2002.
2. Paul Miller, "Making Retail Buyers Mail Order Prospects," *Catalog Age,* August 1, 2003.
3. "Integrated Ideas Allow Brands to Transcend Media," *Precision Marketing,* September 3, 2004, p. 14.
4. Shayn Ferriolo, "The Key to Kiosks," *Catalog Age,* June 1, 2003.

CHAPTER 9

HEADS OR TAILS: IMPLICATIONS OF THE LONG TAIL FOR MULTI-CHANNEL MARKETERS

Mark Collins and Dale M. Lewison

What opportunities await you in the long tail of the demand curve? Will you recognize them? Will you be able to exploit them? Should you try to exploit them? The concept of the long-tail distribution and its impact on demand and marketing endeavors has recently been popularized by the publication of Chris Anderson's new book *The Long Tail*,[1] published by Hyperion in the summer of 2006. The long tail is the story about how new technologies are helping marketers challenge the tyranny of the mass-market culture of hits (the head of the demand curve) by creating the means for tapping the well spring of latent demand that lies within the niche and other submarkets of the long tail or the demand curve. In this chapter we explore some of the key concepts espoused by Anderson and attempt to examine those concepts within the context of the traditional marketing process and the emergence of multi-channel marketing networks. Figure 9.1 is a visual representation of the marketing process and its key components. It will serve as the benchmark for our discussion.

As described in earlier chapters, our marketing process starts with the marketplace. Analytic marketing involves the gathering, processing, analyzing, and interpreting of market intelligence. Mining the marketplace environment in order to discover market opportunities in both the head and tail of the demand curve constitutes the first phase of the marketing process. Customer, environmental, and competitor analyses are the three most common intelligence-gathering activities.

Figure 9.1
The Marketing Process

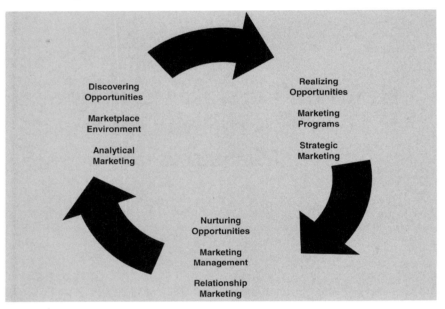

Discovering
Opportunities

Marketplace
Environment

Analytical
Marketing

Realizing
Opportunities

Marketing
Programs

Strategic
Marketing

Nurturing
Opportunities

Marketing
Management

Relationship
Marketing

Customers, cultures, and competitors can be significantly different between the "head of hits" and the "tail of non-hits." Planning and implementing strategic initiatives via well-conceived multi-channel marketing programs is the marketing focus for the second phase of this process. Selecting the right marketing strategy, developing the right market offer, and choosing the best channel alternative are the key decisions needed to realize those targeted opportunities that populate the heads and tails of demand.

Finally, the ongoing nurturing of realized opportunities is the stuff that marketing management is made of. In this final phase, the focus is on building and maintaining mutually beneficial relationships with customers, partners, stakeholders, and shareholders. Strategic marketing relationships typically take the form of alliances, coalitions, collaborations, or associations between strategic partners whose cooperation is essential to the proper care and feeding of market relationships. The aggressive winner-takes-all relationships that characterize mainstream markets are in sharp contrast to the more collaborative efforts found among the occupants of the tail. Using our simplified marketing process model, we examine the implications of long-tail distribution and some of its impact on multi-channel marketing.

HEADS OR TAILS: EXPLORING THE OUTER LIMITS OF THE DEMAND CURVE

Demand curves typically portray market structures characterized by a power-law distribution continuum where a relatively limited number of popular or best-selling products form a "big head" and many other progressively unfamiliar and less popular products comprise the "long tail." This standard demand curve could be applied to most goods and service industries as well as the less tangible world of concepts and ideas. In this type of distribution, a high-frequency population is followed by a low-frequency population that gradually "tails off." As seen in Figure 9.2, the vertical axis is popularity (for example, sales or profits) and the horizontal axis is product type (hits, misses, unknowns, and also-rans). The head of the curve (shaded area) reflects mainstream, best-selling hit products or ideas that have dominated traditional marketing for the last half century. "Hits" are the things that mass markets are made of; creating and building "hit" products for the masses represent the strategic focus of the "go-to-market" strategies for most consumer products companies. The long tail is that part of the demand curve characterized by a low-frequency population that gradually tails off. Anderson suggests that product demand in the tail can cumulatively outnumber or outperform the head of the curve.[2] This new and different look at this established concept poses numerous questions regarding the future structure of the

Figure 9.2
The Long Tail—The New Marketplace

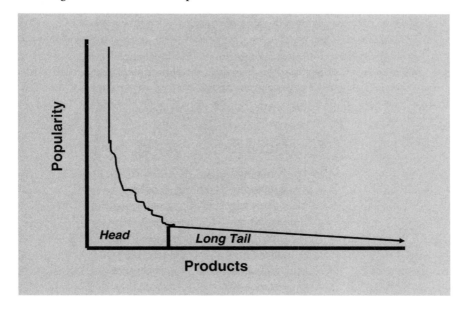

marketplace and the modifications that your marketing programs might need in order to take advantage of these new ignored opportunities and to avoid possible new threats to existing practices.

CURVES AND FORCES: EXPLOITING THE OUTER LIMITS OF THE DEMAND CURVE

The theory of the *long tail* can be summarized as follows: Demand is slowly shifting from mass-market hits and embracing long-tail marketplace opportunities. In the new era of the information/knowledge/experience/service economy, Anderson[3] suggests that narrowly targeted goods and services found along the tail of the demand curve can be as economically attractive as mainstream offerings (hits). As hypothesized by Anderson, the emergence of long-tail economics is a function of five forces. An appreciation and an understanding of these forces are essential to your ability to exploit the latent demand and new market opportunities that populate the outer reaches of the tail. As suggested by Anderson, long-tail efficiencies and capabilities are based on the following five premises:

- *Population:* The total number of tail goods (marginal sellers) markets significantly exceeds the number of head goods (best sellers) markets. This discrepancy is growing exponentially.
- *Affordability:* The cost of reaching long-tail markets is falling dramatically relative to mainstream hit markets as the cost of technologies fall dramatically.
- *Reachable:* The use of filters (rankings, evaluations, and recommendations) assist consumers in finding and assessing tail markets.
- *Selection:* The large number and extensive variety of tail product markets result in a collective (accumulative) market that rivals the hit market.
- *Modification:* The old demand curve becomes modified in such a fashion as to reflect the naturally flattened shape of the new demand without old operational distortions.[4]

Which of the above themes is the key factor in shape demand curves? The answer is affordability. The Internet and related technologies have created new economies *of scale* for production, distribution, and marketing. The result is that new and latent market demand in the long tail can be accessed with acceptable cost structures that result in acceptable operating margins. All marketing takes place within the context of the changing marketplace. The long tail is a marketplace phenomenon. The emergence of long-tail marketing is a reasonable response to some of the environmental dynamics being faced by firms as they explore and navigate uncharted waters of the marketplace. Consumers behave differently, competitor relationships vary from collaborative to aggressive, social and cultural norms are shifting, the economic environment is becoming less tangible, the global legal environment is much more complex, demographic profiles are undergoing major alternations, and the political landscape has been transformed by the global movement. With all these forces for change, it is hardly surprising that demand curves are undergoing transformation.

SHIFT AND DRIFT: DEMASSIFYING CULTURES AND MARKETS

Mass culture is diminishing, subculture is ascending. From a marketing perspective, it is informative to view this movement from the perspective of market segmentation—the fragmentation of the heterogeneous mass market into more homogeneous submarkets. Anderson suggests that we have traditionally been a gregarious society that is highly influenced by what others do and think.[5] Communications and entertainment technologies (telephone and television) have been the great American unifier over the last several decades. As in the past, the introduction of newer communication and entertainment offerings has prompted a new culture shift and drift from *following the crowd* to *going it alone*. While evolutionary changes in our mass culture have been the subject of books, the shift from a mass-directed culture to an individual-based culture is seen by Anderson to be something a whole lot more than a passing fad. He sees this shift in our cultural focus as a new economic era in which there is a significant shift of power from the masses to specific groups or individuals.

The demassifying of society is not a new concept. In his book *The Third Wave*, Alvin Toffler argues that the Second Wave Society of mass production, mass distribution, mass consumption, mass education, mass market, mass media, and mass recreation and entertainment leads to standardization, centralization, concentration, and synchronization of society and its organizations and activities.[6] Toffler's new Third Wave Society is the postindustrial culture where customization, personalization, diversity, extensive choice, and entrepreneurship will be the norm. Kevin Kelly, another futurist, in his book *New Rules for the New Economy,* describes the shifting sands of culture. "The new economy has three distinguishing characteristics. It is global. It favors intangible things—ideas, information, and relationships. And it is intensely interlinked. These three attributes produce a new type of marketplace and society, one that is rooted in ubiquitous networks."[7] The world of "soft" (for example, the intangibles) will command the world of "hard" (for example, the tangibles).

SCARCITY OR ABUNDANCE: NEW ECONOMIES AND MORE CHANNELS

The needed scales of economies for producing, promoting, and distributing mainstream high-demand product hits as part of a mass-marketing channel effort results in a self-selecting process where only a few products go to market and remain in the market. High absolute (initial) production, distribution, and marketing costs associated with mass marketing acts like a funnel in which lower profit potential goods and services are filtered out either by the product development process or little or no support for the product launch and subsequent marketing effort. Lower-demand products become scarce because of physical limitation imposed by a finite amount of shelf space in brick-and-mortar outlets and the limited geographic drawing power (primary and secondary trading areas). Figure 9.3 illustrates this restrictive nature of mass marketing on the economies that support it. Best-selling, high-margin products that offer fast turnaround, brand recognition, and known attributes dominate the vertical and horizontal display shelves of the big box retailers and the trading areas that constrain it. Store trade area economies and the marketing effort that supports them create the backdrop for the heads over tails approach to demand curves. Boundaries on store drawing power, restrictions on time and place availability, as well as limitations on product variety and selection all act in concert to confine traditional marketing efforts to the head of the demand curve.

According to Anderson, the dawning of a new day for tail-end products is coming;[8] the genesis of this new era is the result of such emerging trends as peer

Figure 9.3
The Restrictive Nature of the "Hit-Product"-Making Process

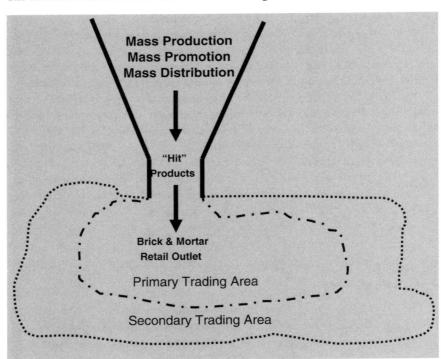

production and database marketing. In the knowledge/information/experience/ service economy anyone can have product to sell or give away. While a lot of it is crap, much of it has some value to someone. The trick is to create the right marketing, promotion, and distribution system for matching up these obscure producers (peers and otherwise) with equally obscure suspects, prospects, and customers. Database marketing involves the use of real-time computerized database systems (a list of customers and prospects containing useful and meaningful information) that is capable of predicting the likelihood of response and the type of reaction. These *one-to-one* direct marketing systems are ideally suited to mining the sales nuggets of the tail. While the focus of Anderson's inquiry into the means for successfully tapping into the world of abundance represented by the tail is largely concerned with outbound and inbound one-line distribution channels, any of the direct one-to-one multi-channel marketing systems (for example, certain types of print, broadcast, and other electronic, teleservices, and direct personal sales channels) offers considerable opportunity for capturing some part of this endless demand curve. The key to success is the careful construction of databases that allows the multi-channel marketer to use pinpoint marketing to target a specific and limited target market and to access that market using one or more of his or her direct marketing channel networks.

SLICE AND DICE: MASS MARKETS AND INDIVIDUAL TARGETS

Anderson expresses a dichotomous view of the marketplace—markets tend to be seen as either a mass (hits and knowns) market or a niche (misses and unknowns) market.[9] In reality segmenting the marketplace is a more gradual process of dissecting markets into more consistent and uniform market delineations that support better marketing efforts. There is a continuum of markets that range from mass markets to markets of one. Figure 9.4 identifies five market categories —mass markets, market segments, market niches, micro markets, and individual markets. As illustrated, mass markets are comprised of big, mainstream product hits at the head (left side) of the demand curve. Traditional economies of scale in the production, distribution, and marketing of hit products have made them the most desirable target markets. While their hit status offers considerable opportunity, it also attracts significant competition. To improve your marketing effort, you can elect to disaggregate mass markets into market segments of consumers that tend to respond to a marketing effort in a similar fashion. Niche and micro markets are simply smaller and smaller market segments that offer you less and less total sales potential, but make it easier to develop a successful marketing effort by presenting you with more uniform expectations. Individual markets are markets of one and represent the epitome of personalization of the marketing effort.

Figure 9.4
The Continuum of Markets

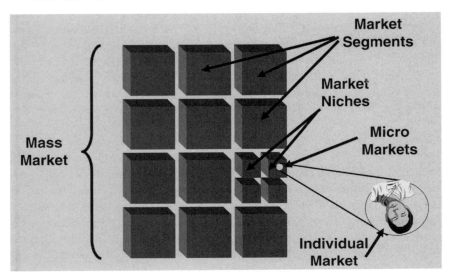

The long-tail distribution is a very visual illustration and justification of why you need a well-designed and executed market segmentation process. If you are capable of identifying and targeting each market level (mass market, market segment, niche market, micro market, and individual market) in the head of the distribution curve by employing various multi-channel marketing networks, you will have similar capabilities to tap the demand in the tail markets (niches, micro groups, and individuals). Strong core competencies in market segmentation and multi-channel marketing will allow you to go after demand wherever you find it in the long-tail distribution.

COMMODITY NEEDS AND SPECIFIC DESIRES: FRAGMENTING CONSUMER INTERESTS

Mainstream mass media tended to focus on the general or generic needs and interests of mass-market consumers because that is where production, distribution, and marketing economies of scale were satisfied. Catering to the communalities of consumer needs became the battle cry for the widely heralded "marketing concept," which trumpeted the notion of "customer satisfaction at a profit." The "at a profit" side of the marketing concept equation usually involved finding a broad homogeneous need that could serve as the anchor or hook for the marketing effort. With time and advancement in the lowering of marketing costs, mass markets were able to be segmented into market segments of somewhat more focused needs and interests. As one moves down the long tail, larger group needs become more sharply focused on specific desires of small groups and individuals. Until recently, a typical consumer did not have access to multi-channel marketing networks. The traditional marketing norm was mass advertising on mass media for mass products distributed through mass retailers to mass markets. Anderson argues that more and more consumers are discovering their specific desires and the means for satisfying these fragmented interests that have always been just under the surface of an evoked set of needs.[10] Today, satisfying consumer needs is no longer an "either/or" decision between one mainstream hit or another; rather it is rapidly becoming a "this/and/that" choice of both top selling hits that exist at the head of the curve and bottom dwelling specialties that populate the curve's long tail. The advantages of having multi-channel marketing networks capable of reaching the entire demand from generic/commodity head to the specific/specialty tail are substantial and achievable.

The aforementioned market opportunities are realized by developing and implementing marketing strategies and creatives that are tailored to the particular needs and preferences of the market that is being targeted. The key word in the previous statement is *tailored*. The better tailored the strategies and creatives, the greater the likelihood of successfully tapping the market demand wherever you find it on the curve. Products, prices, promotions, and places that are well suited to the buying behavior particulars of chosen consumers have greater success in garnishing the loyalty of those consumers.

VARIETY AND SELECTION: PARADOX OF CHOICE

What would happen if your customers had unlimited choice? The consuming public has come to expect an extensive variety and selection of products from which to choose. Creating the traditional product mix offering always involved the careful selection of the best-selling product lines (for example, men's, women's, and children's apparel) and product items (for example, brands, styles, sizes, models, colors, and so forth). The history of retailing formats from the general store to merchandise catalogs, department stores, discount stores, and big box retailers was focused to a large extent on finding the right choice of product lines and items. In the hits-based economy choice was restricted largely to those select few items that could support the production, distribution, and marketing economies associated with the mass market. Limited selection associated with the head of the demand curve simplified the consumer buying process; the complexities of generating product awareness and interest, promoting product trial and evaluation, and making purchase commitments and decisions were reduced mostly to a choice of hits. In contrast, the number and type of choices associated with the long tail are greatly expanded.

In the online age almost everything can be available. Anderson[11] believes that there could be an infinite number of choices found within the long tail; if that is true, is there a choice overload? While consumers want choice, too much choice can be problematic for the time-stressed consumer who needs help in finding the right choice. Unlimited choice can be confusing and debilitating. As a multi-channel marketer, a tenet of your marketing effort should be an abundant meaningful choice offering supported by easy product searches and convenient access channels. As postulated by Anderson, the secret to creating a thriving long-tail business is wrapped up in two imperatives:

1. Make everything available, and
2. Help customers find it.

BENCHMARKS AND GUIDELINES: CHASING THE LONG TAIL

So, how are you going to take advantage of the opportunities that can be found in the long tail? There is still a great deal to learn about the structure and nature of long-tail demand curves and how best to harvest their bounty. Anderson suggests several rules for chasing long-tail demand; his suggestions are consistent with emerging marketing practices for targeting micro and individual markets. The following guidelines are a composite of some of Anderson's rules and emerging one-to-one marketing practices for reaching tail-end consumers.[12]

Do Not Hoard It, Share It

Nothing is more important in the information economy than information. Connecting the nontraditional producers, distributors, and consumers that comprise the long tail is absolutely essential to successful marketing endeavors with respect to the tail. The more information possessed by each party of the exchange process, the greater the likelihood of a successful transaction and lasting relationship. The introduction of new communication technologies has eliminated many of the technical problems with real-time communications. The remaining hurdle is an issue of trust—the willingness of parties to share information. Transparency, the availability of reliable and useful information, is a powerful tool in the trust- and confidence-building efforts of marketers. Equally important is the ease by which each party has access to the information and how the information is structured and presented. As Anderson describes it, "deep information about products, from reviews to specifications, can answer questions that would have otherwise halted a purchase."[13]

Do Not Predict It, Measure It

One of the chief advantages of using multiple direct response marketing channels is that each marketing effort can be pretested and postassessed. Direct multichannel marketing goes well beyond making estimates of the sales potential of a market or making guessimates of the likely market shares any one competitor might capture. The highly targeted nature of direct marketing efforts relative to tail opportunities allows the seller to gain highly reliable measurements of the responses to each marketing campaign. Response categories can range from purchases to inquiries to consumer rankings and rates to no response at all to the offer. Regardless of the type of response, you will have hard data on how targeted consumers accepted your offer. What is more, you will have the makings of a sophisticated database the will assist you in pretesting and measuring your next effort at reaching your chosen markets along the long tail.

Do Not Advertise It, Mouth It

The declining trust and faith in traditional mass advertising campaigns and the rising confidence and reliance on personal one-to-one communications further supports Anderson's convictions that the long tail is within reach of emerging online marketing strategies of viral marketing and the off-line strategies of buzz marketing. Bottom-up promotions are consistent with long-tail marketing, and they create the pipelines for those consumers who reside at the end of the tail. Peer-to-peer promotions are becoming a pillar of multi-channel efforts to reach each market niche and individual consumers.

Viral marketing and advertising entails various marketing techniques that attempt to use preexisting social groups and networks to pass on marketing messages to its membership and to others outside of the unit. "Viral marketing sometimes refers to Internet-based stealth marketing campaigns, including the use of blogs, seemingly amateur web sites, and other forms of astroturfing, designed to create word of mouth for a product or service. . . to the idea that people will pass on and share interesting and entertaining content (funny video clips, interactive Flash cards, images, and text material)."[14] Some of the more common viral marketing campaign strategies that you might consider are as follows:

1. Pass-along messages that ask the receiver to send your message on to others,

2. Incentive messages that provide rewards for passing your message along or for supplying an address to someone else,

3. Undercover or mystery messages that make an appeal (cool or unusual activity or news) in which it is not immediately apparent that anything is being marketed. Activities that surround solving the mystery generate the word-of-mouth needed to build consumer awareness and interest.

Your viral marketing effort can be transmitted in the form of Word-of-Web (forwarding an article from the Web), word-of-e-mail (forwarding an e-mail), word-of-instant-messaging (forwarding hyperlinks), and blog publicity (spreading messages from one blog to another).

Buzz marketing is a highly intense and interactive form of word-of-mouth marketing in which the multi-channel marketer attempts to generate personal recommendations and referrals for a product or brand within a select group of individuals. One of the most common forms of buzz marketing is to identify trendsetters and tastemakers for a particular peer group, convince them to use the brand or product, and recommend that the sellers offer them to their friends and followers. "By orchestrating a tsunami of chatter, marketers are hoping to replicate the pattern set by such overnight sensations as independent film The Blair Witch Project, the Harry Potter book series, and Razor kick scooters."[15] The slightly subversive nature of buzz marketing with its underground tactics is suited for several direct marketing delivery channels. Because it is an individualized promotional tool, buzz word of mouth works best with a narrowly defined selection of products that consumers care deeply about—ideal characteristic for tail products and consumers.

Do Not Store It, Move It

The goal of distribution is movement. The design of your merchandise logistical systems needs to manage the integrated flows of goods and other materials from the original source through each appropriate channel level to the ultimate consumer. For most multi-channel marketers, physical storage is not an option for any length of time. Steady and continuous product turnover rates are essential. Costs for ordering, carrying, handling, and delivering goods need to be kept at a minimum; storing adds to these costs, while moving helps to reduce them.

Contemporary multi-channel distribution systems are gaining efficiencies by developing and implementing virtual and, where appropriate, digital inventory systems in additional to their normal physical stock practices. Virtual inventory networks consist of a virtual warehouse that makes inventory of all vendor partners available to partnering resellers. These national "back-end" operations feature lower costs, secure transactions, standardized operating practices, automated service, and fast turnaround. Such firms as Staples, Inc. and Amazon.com are able to greatly expand the variety and selection of their product offerings without expanding the physical size of their facilities. Selling function is handled by multi-channel alternatives (for example, electronic kiosks, print catalogs, and telephone kiosks). A typical Staples brick-and-mortar outlet stocks 7,500 product stock keeping units (SKUs); by using virtual kiosks, an additional 45,000 virtual SKUs are added to the product offering of the store.[16]

In the information/entertainment/education economy where a significant share of new age products can be produced, stored, and distributed as binary numbers and non-numeric symbols, the efficiencies of digital inventory will continue to open up the opportunities of the long tail. Anderson puts it this way: "Digital inventory—think iTunes—is the cheapest of all. We've already seen the effect the switch from shipping plastic discs to streaming megabits has had on the music industry; soon the same will come to movies, video games, and TV shows. News has left the paper age, podcasting is challenging radio."[17] On-demand production and distribution of digital products via electronic channels of distribution will allow tail-end marketers to capture micro markets of a size that was hitherto unreachable and unprofitable. The ability to produce and distribute digital products after they have been purchased creates the possibility of successfully pursuing a market of one.

Do Not Do It, Source It

Creating mass-market hits usually required a tightly controlled, centralized mass production process. A "do-it-yourself" production mentality (self-sourcing) was the normal for "hit makers." As competition heated up, the actual production of hit-based products was often outsourced to a select few partners, many of them offshore. Outsourcing involves the delegation of selected production and other operating functions to external entities that specialize in them. This sourcing activity helped mass marketers to lower their costs, focus on their core competencies, and secure intellectual capital. The big hesitation about pursuing an outsourcing strategy was that the practice involved transferring a considerable amount of decision-making power and control to an outsider. This issue of trust was a significant barrier that had to be overcome. Trust can still be an issue, limiting the complete vertical and horizontal integration of multi-channel marketing networks.

Production economies of scale for sourcing hit products found in the head of the demand curve are not transferable to locations along its tail. New alternative sourcing opportunities are needed to exploit the tail demand. Two such alternatives are open sourcing and crowdsourcing.

Open sourcing involves free access to a source code that can be read and modified for production and development purposes; outsiders can improve it, adapt it, and fix it. Open sources are communities of individuals who have a common interest in a particular industry, product, or problem. Using open sources, people are free to modify the products of others and to communicate those modifications to others. Often, open-source products have a public goods aspect to them. The marginal cost of improving products is substantially lower because improvements may be added at zero costs. The power of open-source collaboration is illustrated by the development of a cola recipe (OpenCola) that is comparable to the secret cola formulas guarded by The Coca-Cola Company and PepsiCo.[18] Educational training, government services, political commentary, journalistic news gathering and fact checking, shared scientific research, film and video presentations, software development, and a host of other product innovations are being developed in an open-source venue. Bogs and message boards are two common platforms for open-source sourcing.

Crowdsourcing is a production model that relies upon unpaid or low-paid amateurs, and "want-to-be" entrepreneurs, who are willing to invest the time, money, and effort needed to create content, solve problems, conduct research and development inquiries, test product concepts, build product prototypes, plan product launches, and generally provide the effort needed for the new product development process. Who makes up these crowds? Sources of crowdsourcing include garage scientists, amateur videographers, freelancers, basement musicians, photo enthusiasts, data companies, writers, smart mobs, and those who crowd the Internet electronic business channels. Procter & Gamble employs more than 9,000 scientists and researchers in corporate research and development (R&D) and still has many problems they cannot solve. These unsolved problems are posted on a Web site called InfoCentive, which offers large cash rewards to the more than 90,000 "solvers" who make up this network of backyard scientists. iStockphoto is a Web site with over 22,000 amateur photographers who upload and distribute stock photographs.[19] The emergence of "peer-to-peer" paradigms is shifting the way things are designed and used. This phenomenon is beginning to be taken seriously by small independent venture businesses to huge R&D departments at major corporations.[20]

Do Not Sell It, Give It

Free is a hard price to beat. When one starts with a zero price point, enhancing the value of an offer is a whole lot easier. The endless variety of products found along the tail of the demand curve is bound to pose a problem of buyer trust: unknown sellers, unknown brands, and lack of previous buying experience. The cost advantages of tail products created by peer producers and marketers encourage cost-effective use of free samples, free trials, free premiums, and other risk-reduction incentives. Consulting firms frequently provide insight into their offerings by providing white papers, newsletters, state of the industry reports, and complementary assessment models. These product quality samples are risk-reduction incentives that are provided free of charge in hopes of alleviating buyer concerns.

Do Not Standardize It, Customize It

The creation of hit products requires the production and distribution of standardized products that cater to a market large enough to support hits. In a product marketing context, standardization involves the development and promotion of products that have common product attributes, features, and benefits that meet an acceptable level of functionality and quality. One of the reasons why "hit products" are able to achieve the desired status of hits is that standardization promotes compatibility, interchangeability, and commonality in producing, promoting, distributing, and selling these uniform product packages. In the world of hits marketing, standardization of product offerings is required.

However, in the demassification of the marketplace along the long tail, firms must find acceptable alternatives to the growing heterogeneity of demand. Whether one presumes that the product is available from stock on hand, on a build-to-order basis, or will be made only after it is sold, customizing product is a necessity for marketing to the individual taste along the long tail. Mass customization is the personalization of goods and services for the individual taste of the customer at prices that rival that resulting from mass production. Dell Inc.'s "build-to-order" model was a major contributor to the firm's dominance of the personal computer industry. Customization and low price are no longer mutually exclusive.

Collaborative customization involves the firm talking directly with customers to determine their precise requirements and expectations. New interactive technologies allow buyers to interact with sellers and help design a good or service that is then manufactured and marketed by automated systems. Donal Reddington, editor of the MadeForOne blog makes the following comments: "Anderson rightly states that if digital manufacturing can be developed to output more complex products, then almost every market will become a digital market. In the same way that online music can be downloaded someday the design for pretty much everything else might be downloaded someday and manufactured at home. Then every market will be a long-tail market, and the cost of carrying infinite variety of stock will be zero for everything."[21]

Is the "head of hits" becoming a commoditized offering of goods and services? The more generalized appeals of mass-market hits are starting to look more and more like commodity offerings. With their greater personalizations, products that populate the tail have the potential for being better value-added offerings. In their book *The Experience Economy*, B. Joseph Pine II and James H. Gilmore argue that businesses must orchestrate memorable events for their customers and that memory itself becomes the product—the "experience."[22] In the book, products are classified along a continuum from undifferentiated to differentiated offerings. The evolution of products can be described as follows:

- *Commodity business*—charge for undifferentiated stuff,
- *Goods business*—charge for distinctive tangible things,
- *Service business*—charge for activities you perform,

- *Experience business*—charge for the feeling customers have because they engaged you, and

- *Transformation business*—charge for the benefit customers receive as a result of spending time with you.

In the world of experiences it is more than "just do it," it is all about how and why you do it and the mental states resulting from the experience.

CONCLUSION

The opportunities presented by the long tail are both real and challenging. The forces behind the long tail are largely technological: cheap hardware and software that lessen production costs, ubiquitous broadband that lowers distribution, and elaborate filters (search engines, blogs, and online reviews) that support a more effective marketing effort by better matching supply and demand. "Think of each of these three forces as representing a new set of opportunities in the emerging Long Tail marketplace."[23] While the long tail of demand does not threaten the world of blockbuster hits, it does present new, different, and significant market opportunities for a wide range of business enterprises.

NOTES

1. Chris Anderson, *The Long Tail* (New York: Hyperion, 2006).
2. Ibid.
3. Ibid.
4. Ibid., 53.
5. Ibid.
6. Alvin Toffler, *The Third Wave* (New York, Bantam Books, 1980).
7. Kevin Kelly, *New Rules for the New Economy* (New York: Penguin Books, 1999).
8. Anderson, *The Long Tail.*
9. Ibid.
10. Ibid.
11. Ibid.
12. Ibid.
13. Ibid., 222.
14. http://en.wikipedia.org/wiki/Viral_Marketing.
15. Gerry Khermouch and Jeff Green, "Buzz Marketing, Suddenly This Stealth Strategy Is Hot—But It's Still Fraught with Risk," *Business Week,* July 30, 2001, 98.
16. Jennifer Libbin, "Staples Taps into Virtual Inventory," *DSN Retailing Today,* February 19, 2001, 1.
17. Anderson, *The Long Tail,* 218–19.
18. http://en.wikipedia.org/wiki/opens_source, p. 3.
19. http://en.wikipedia.org/wiki/Crowdsourcing, p. 1.

20. http://www.smartmobs.com/archive/2006/0531crowdedsourcing.html (accessed Summer 2006).

21. Frank Piller, "Mass Customization and *The Long Tail*—A Review of Chris Anderson's Book," *Mass Customization & Open Innovation News,* http://masscustomization.blogs.com/mas_customization_open i/2006/07/mass-cusomi (accessed Summer 2006).

22. B. Joseph Pine II and James H. Gilmore, *The Experience Economy* (Boston: Harvard Business School Press, 1999).

23. John Cassidy, "Going Long—In the New 'Long Tail' Marketplace, Has the Blockbuster Met Its Match?" *New Yorker,* July 10, 2006.

Part II

FOCUS IS THE KEY

CHAPTER 10

A FRAMEWORK FOR ELECTRONIC CLIENT RELATIONSHIP MANAGEMENT IN SMALL BUSINESSES

Jeffrey C. Dilts and Paramjit S. Kahai

In the past few years, small businesses have increasingly migrated toward the Internet. In addition to providing online informational catalogs about the products they sell, these businesses are also facilitating completion of purchase transactions online (Dilts and Kahai, 2004). As a consequence, customer retention and building solid client relationships are receiving considerable attention today. For a small business, in particular, developing long-term client relationships is the lifeblood of the business, and a primary reason why the business exists and is successful.

This focus on customer relationships represents a fundamental shift from the more traditional customer acquisition and transaction mentality that was the reigning paradigm only a few years ago. During the late 1990s, the focus of many Internet-based marketing programs was to present products and attract new customers. Not only did this strategy not achieve its desired goals, it proved to be both time and cost ineffective for many companies, especially resource-constrained small businesses. Today, while attracting and converting new customers is essential, the key to business profitability is the retention and long-term, lifetime value of existing customers. With the current technological advances of the Internet, it has become feasible for small businesses to develop timely and inexpensive programs to solidify and grow these relationships.

For years, sophisticated client relationship management (CRM) tools have been considered the purview of large corporations due to their multi-million-dollar cost, and the resources needed to develop and implement them. Large client databases and sophisticated data mining are not part of reality for most small businesses. However, at a fundamental level, what is required is the ability to identify meaningful customer segments, tailor offerings to their needs, and deliver these in a reliable manner that meets or exceeds customer expectations and encourages them to keep coming back. Using today's Internet technology, it is very feasible to create an electronic client relationship management (eCRM) program that will not deplete a small business of its resources, but will provide the company with the tools needed to improve business profitability and give them a compelling advantage over their competitors.

The focus of this chapter is to examine ways in which small businesses can develop and implement their own unique and workable CRM programs using the Internet. We also propose a framework for the use of eCRM in small businesses. The chapter is organized as follows. First, it outlines the foundations of relationship management; therein, it examines the costs of customer acquisition, especially via the Internet, and discusses the process of managing relationships with customers. Next, the chapter identifies the role of eCRM and each of its component parts in the relationship. Here, the discussion focuses on the applicability of eCRM for small businesses. Finally, it offers a number of practical suggestions the small business owner can use to create a workable and profitable eCRM program.

RELATIONSHIP MANAGEMENT AND ITS FOUNDATIONS

The notion of "build it and they will come," once prevalent before the dot-com meltdown, does not apply anymore. Given that a high proportion of online traffic goes to a small proportion of Web sites (Lake, 2000), a firm will need to consider how it will drive traffic to its site. One way of getting out the message about the firm's Web site is to promote it both online and off-line. Tables 10.1 and 10.2 provide the online and off-line promotional methods most frequently used by businesses in the United States. The key driver of profitability, however, is the conversion of visitors to customers and their retention (Reichheld and Schefter, 2000). This is especially important online since the customer's search cost is lowered and alternatives are but a click away. Online firms will not break even on a one-time shopper, and it will take a number of transactions before a profit is realized for that customer (Reichheld and Schefter, 2000). In fact, only one in 14 visitors becomes a customer, and only one in 75 customers returns to buy again (Agrawal, Arjona, and Lemmens, 2001).

Customer acquisition represents a major cost, and only those firms that are able to control these costs will have a better chance of survival today (Hoffman and Novak, 2000). Customer acquisition costs refer to the overall expenses of converting a prospect into a buyer and include all online and off-line marketing

Table 10.1
Online Web Site Promotional Methods Ranked by Use

1. Search engine and directory positioning
2. Online public relations and press releases
3. Buttons and links
4. Reciprocal ads and links
5. Affiliate programs
6. Paid banner ads

Source: Active Media Research (2001).

and advertising, and general brand awareness efforts. While costs vary by industry, they are estimated to be 20 to 40 percent higher among pure "click" than "click-and-mortar" firms (Hamblen, 2000).

In recent years, acquisition costs have been cut in half, as online firms have shifted away from the expensive, broad mass-marketing campaigns, including television and nationwide radio, to more direct marketing programs involving targeted e-mail and online advertising (Kelsey, 2000). As a result, average acquisition costs for online retailers dropped from a high of $71 in 1999 to $12 in 2001 (Juptner, 2002; Pastore, 2000).

MANAGING RELATIONSHIPS WITH CUSTOMERS

Customer loyalty, as reflected in a customer's repeat purchase behavior, is fundamental to the profitability of a firm (Heim and Sinha, 2001). By strengthening the firm's relationship with its most valuable customers, a firm can increase retention and enhance its profitability. According to a study conducted by Bain & Company, a 5-percent increase in customer retention rate can increase profits by 25 to 95 percent (Reichheld and Schefter, 2000).

Table 10.2
Off-Line Site Promotional Methods Ranked by Use

1. Paid print and display ads in newspapers and magazines and billboards
2. Trade shows, conferences, and seminars
3. Brochures and other collateral materials
4. Direct mail and catalogs
5. Paid TV and radio commercials
6. Sweepstakes and contests

Source: Active Media Research (2001).

The role of customer retention and loyalty in the online world today is only as important as, if not more important than, it is in the physical world (Reichheld and Schefter, 2000). Given the high customer acquisition costs, one may surmise that it is more expensive to recruit new customers than to keep existing customers happy. Furthermore, loyal online customers tend to purchase more frequently and in greater amounts, and frequently refer new customers to a supplier, thereby cutting acquisition costs and enhancing profits (Reichheld and Schefter, 2000). Since it costs over five times more to acquire a new customer than it does to retain and keep existing customers satisfied (Reichheld and Schefter, 2000), it would be more cost-effective if firms shifted their emphasis more to customer retention than acquisition (Strauss, El-Ansary, and Frost, 2003). As indicated in Table 10.3, such an emphasis would serve to maximize the number of total customers, particularly the number of retained customers that tend to spend more than newly acquired customers.

The key to retention is to encourage a continuation of online visits and interactions by strengthening the customer relationship. Typical of such efforts is Hewlett-Packard's (HP) "e-relationship" e-mail marketing program. The e-mail campaign generated a 42-percent loyalty rating among subscribers and served to increase sales annually by $300 million (Soltoff, 2002). E-mail marketing programs, such as this, can serve to strengthen the customer relationship by providing value-added information as well as offering additional opportunities for cross-selling and cost reductions. Hyperlinks embedded in the newsletter can guide customers back to the Web site for additional information, including offers for other products that might be of interest to the customer. By including a *forward to a friend* button, the firm may be able to generate favorable word-of-mouth advertising and generate new valuable customers, thereby reducing acquisition costs. Links to frequently asked questions (FAQ) Web pages can help customers get answers to questions more quickly and reduce the need for, and the cost of, live service representatives.

Table 10.3
Retention versus Acquisition Emphasis: Maximizing Number of Clients

Retention Emphasis	Cost	Acquisition Emphasis	Cost
Gain 4 New Clients ($500 each)	$2,000	Gain 8 New Clients ($500 each)	$4,000
Retain 25 Current Clients ($100 each)	$2,500	Retain 5 Current Clients ($100 each)	$ 500
Number of Clients = 29 Total Cost	$4,500	Number of Clients = 13 Total Cost	$4,500

Source: Adapted from Strauss, El-Ansary, and Frost (2003).

Retaining customers is less about technology and more about the delivery of a consistent superior customer experience, where online service quality meets or exceeds customer expectations. Based on an analysis of repurchasing patterns at highly successful online sites, researchers have observed that the primary determinants of customer loyalty are "quality customer support, on-time delivery, compelling product presentations, convenient and reasonably priced shipping and handling, and clear and trustworthy privacy policies" (Reichheld and Schefter, 2000, p. 112).

According to a recent study conducted by McKinsey & Company, best practices include reliability in basic operational execution (that is, the online fulfillment process) and personalization of communications based on customer profiles and buying histories (Agrawal, Arjona, and Lemmens, 2001). Although personalization is emerging as a driver of retention, the sophisticated CRM and data mining tools needed to support effective personalization may be too costly for many small firms and, while nice to have, are not mandatory. What is required is the ability to identify meaningful customer segments to tailor offerings to their needs and to deliver them in a reliable manner that meets or exceeds their expectations (Agrawal, Arjona, and Lemmens, 2001), a topic to which we now turn.

WHAT IS ELECTRONIC CUSTOMER RELATIONSHIP MANAGEMENT?

In a nutshell, electronic customer relationship management (eCRM) can be defined as using the Internet to grow deep and enduring relationships with the most profitable customers. In breaking down this definition into its component parts, one quickly sees that eCRM is a strategic vision and plan and not simply a set of processes or programs. At the heart of this definition is the customer (individual or business). The customer is the center of attention, and everything done centers around meeting and exceeding the customer's needs and expectations.

During the 1990s, retailer and manufacturer off-line CRM programs focused on delighting the customer. In today's technologically sophisticated environment, the use of the Internet to interact with customers, and their increasing acceptance of it, has both accelerated and enhanced relationship management. By going past a product/service mentality and offering customers unique solutions that meet their needs and solve their problems, companies that emphasize CRM offer customers more than what is expected and, consequently, delight them. A delighted customer is a satisfied customer and is eight times more likely to repurchase and provide benefits to the firm that he or she is delighted with (Reichheld and Schefter, 2000). A satisfied customer is more likely to acquire additional products/services and, therefore, become a more profitable customer. A satisfied customer is also more likely to maintain and grow his or her relationship over an extended period of time. Most importantly, the customer will become a loyal supporter and advocate, thereby referring other customers to the business.

The key term in the above definition is deep relationships. This means going past the list of products/services currently owned by the customers and understanding their aspirations, preferences, lifestyles, and life-cycle stages. It also means understanding their current needs, anticipating their future needs, and then communicating solutions to them in a nonthreatening, trusted advisor manner. This entails offering customers the products/services that they will personally find most useful via the channels they prefer to use.

By definition, deep customer relationships should be long-term growth relationships. As customers experience continued delight with good solutions, they will continue to increase their level of comfort that the company is providing them with the best solutions. The cumulative effect of these positive experiences will further solidify the relationship and, more importantly, allow it to grow. It is extremely important to remember here that good relationships are a reciprocal process. As one provides customers with profitable solutions that meet and exceed their expectations, they become more comfortable with the idea that the company is looking out for their best interests. As this comfort level builds, customers will be more likely to allow and expect the company to provide them with expert advice. The unique blending and cross-selling of products, programs, and services becomes the logical outcome of this process. As with any type of relationship, the continuous meeting of expectations and the growth of trust will continue to deepen and strengthen the relationship. In the end, these delighted customers are (or become) the most profitable customers.

COMPONENTS OF AN ECRM PROGRAM

Although they are called by different names, most eCRM programs are based on four major interrelated components. These are (1) using the Internet to understand the customer, (2) targeting the right products to the right customers, (3) selling to the customer online or off-line, and, most importantly, (4) providing the customer with the service he or she needs. Based on the four above-mentioned components, we present, in Figure 10.1, a proposed framework of eCRM for small businesses. In and of themselves, these components do not look or sound much different than the way business is normally performed. It is the Internet-based, customer-centric, integrated approach that makes eCRM different.

The first component is *understanding the customer*. This means collecting and analyzing not only product/service data, but also data on aspirations, preferences, lifestyles, and life cycle. By integrating all of this information into a profile of the customer, one is able to identify current needs and anticipate future needs. One is also able to look for tendencies that will enable the company to provide

Figure 10.1
A Framework for eCRM

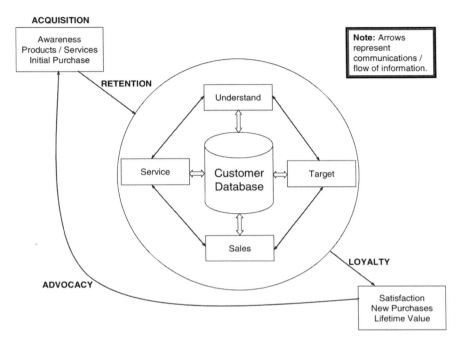

appropriate product/service solutions to the customer. This could mean products or services synchronized to life events or needs; it could also mean knowing the customers' delivery preference for the products/services and then optimizing their usage of that channel. Collecting and manipulating the data constitute only one aspect of this component. Thoroughly analyzing and interpreting the data constitute the other more important aspect and the key to success.

The second component, *targeting the right products to the right customers,* is a logical extension of knowing the customer. Because electronic customer knowledge bases have been created, customers with similar tendencies can be grouped together. This is where the notion of mass customization comes into play. No company has the resources to perform actual one-to-one marketing and sales. But by linking those customers with similar characteristics into focused target groups, one can provide personal solutions to a larger group with similar needs. Targeting the right information to the right customer is not only cost-effective from an acquisition sense, it also increases the customer's level of comfort that the company he or she is dealing with truly does know his or her unique needs.

The third component is *selling to the customer*. Understanding what the customer needs is not selling him or her just any product, but products that are personally right for him or her. The knowledge about the customer provides the appropriate information for selling a given product or set of products. It moves the company away from a "Chinese menu" approach to one where the customer views advice and recommendations as helpful and relevant. Not only does this enable customers to feel that their wants and needs are known, it increases their level of comfort that they are receiving sound, timely advice and the company has their best interests in mind.

The fourth component, *service,* is the glue that holds the entire relationship together. The majority of interactions or touch points that customers have with companies are in the area of service. Delighted customers are ones that receive timely, appropriate solutions. One interaction, as inane as the problem or question may seem to the representative, can easily and quickly make or break the relationship. If, at first, customers build the confidence that the company really does know them and has their best interests in mind, but later perceive that they are being treated as just another face or voice, they quickly begin to wonder how important they really are to the company. World-class customer service is providing actionable solutions in a timely, friendly manner that once again gives the customer the impression that the company cares and really does want his or her business.

Creating a successful eCRM program is not an easy task. Changing the modus operandi of an organization is both difficult and time-consuming. While there are numerous Internet tools available to make the data gathering, targeting, and selling easier (see, for example, Microsoft's small business Web site at http://www.microsoft.com/smallbusiness/bc/default.mspx), it is still the personal touch that will drive the relationship with the customer. This is why the service component is so important in a customer relationship management program. Perceptions become reality. No matter how much one knows about a customer, if he or she perceives that the company views him or her as just another face in the crowd, the less likely she or he will be to want to enter into a deep and enduring relationship with that company. Customer relationships are like fine crystal. If not handled with care, they are easy to break. However, if treated properly, they last for many, many years.

There are a few software tools available that allow small businesses to manage relationships with customers. These tools, however, may tend to be expensive and possibly be out of reach for the smallest of businesses. Microsoft offers a CRM product (see http://www.microsoft.com/smallbusiness/products/mbs/crm/detail.mspx) that requires companies to purchase server hardware and software, and the CRM software. The disadvantage of such a solution is the costs associated with purchasing the required tools, and hosting and maintaining them. However, companies like NetSuite Inc. (http://www.netsuite.com) and Entellium (http://www.entellium.com) offer solutions that do not require the purchase of additional hardware or software. These tools are hosted on the servers of the respective companies and accessed over the Web. The tools are also modular; that is, companies pay a nominal fee (usually less than $100 per month) only for modules they use. This solution is a more palatable one, especially financially, for many small firms.

We now turn to outlining the components of an eCRM program in greater detail.

UNDERSTANDING AND TARGETING CUSTOMERS

Every individual or business is a unique customer. However, it is both financially and physically impossible to treat each customer as such. For these reasons, marketers attempt to group or cluster customers according to certain characteristics they are likely to share. In doing so, it is assumed that each group of customers will have common demographic attributes, needs, interests, and attitudes. These clusters, or customer segments, enable marketers to design products and services emphasizing these unique collectivities and their shared social milieu.

Historically, the problem with most segmentation schemes is that they have tended to be monadic and static, while customers are multifaceted and dynamic. The most rudimentary schemes are based on purchase behavior and product ownership. In many cases, the scheme is as simple as either owning or not owning a given product. The assumption (albeit erroneous in most cases) is that if the customer does not own the respective product, he or she is a likely target for the next campaign. Another common approach is based on customer demographics. In this case, customers are partitioned around structural characteristics such as age, income, gender, and education for consumers and type, size, and sales for businesses. The problem with this type of scheme is the assumption that individuals or businesses with the same demographic characteristics will have the same wants and needs.

Recently, a third approach has surfaced and is receiving significant attention. This scheme attempts to ascertain the customer's attitudes and aspirations at both a macroscopic and a microscopic level. For example, these attitudes can range from the customer fearing an economic downtown (macroscopic) to being risk aversive (microscopic). This framework can be used both with individual customers and businesses. The only problem with attitudinal/aspirational data is that this information is unique to a given customer and, therefore, both difficult and costly to gather. Also, as social and economic events influence changes in customers' lives (life-cycle and business trends), their attitudes and aspirations will change, too. Thus, monitoring customer attitudes requires regular, ongoing communication with the customer to make sure that the attitudinal information is current. Even with the use of the Internet, this tends to be cost and time prohibitive for most businesses.

Where traditional demographic segmentation schemes may give a sketchy and sometimes false picture of consumer behavior, and attitudinal schemes are hard to collect and maintain, a multiattribute segmentation framework can be more insightful (Cassedy, 2002). For example, conventional demographic profiles using family status (for example, married with children, households with multiple sources of income, and level of income) have been used to highlight consumers as promising technology/online buyers. However, product failures (for example, WebTV) have convinced many firms (for example, Sony Corporation and Royal Philips Electronics) that conventional demographic segmentation frameworks are not precise enough in predicting behavior. Instead, what is needed is a multiattribute model that goes beyond the simplistic use of demographics and is capable of examining behavior along multiple, relevant dimensions (Judge, 1998).

An example of a multiattribute framework is Technographics, a proprietary segmentation scheme developed for the Internet era by Forrester Research. The framework is useful in identifying and understanding online buying behavior, thereby enabling marketers to better target the right audience with the right product and services, and using the right messages and channels to reach the audience. Potential customers are categorized into ten unique categories using three dimensions (Rubin and Bluestein, 1999): (1) attitudes toward technology (optimists or pessimists), (2) their motivation to use technology (career, family, or entertainment), and (3) their ability to afford technology (high or low income). For a more complete description and understanding of Technographics, the reader is referred to the Forrester report, "Applying Technographics," which may be found at http://www.forrester.com/ER/Marketing/0,1503,84,00.html.

Such a framework might have benefited WebTV, had Sony and Philips focused on the segmentation category "Mouse Potatoes" with the proper marketing message that emphasized entertainment over education (Judge, 1998). This category consists of relatively young, high-income households (mostly singles and families without children) that enjoy entertainment and view technology as a means by which to improve upon their lives and make them more enjoyable. In short, a multiattribute framework that focuses on a richer source of data, which are intelligently analyzed, can lead to more meaningful and profitable insights.

Therefore, the best segmentation schemes are a combination of a number of dimensions. Segmentation schemes based on a single dimension or factor are not only limiting, they also stand a good chance of being incorrect. For example, a broadly defined segment such as mass market is so large and encompassing that it begs the question of whether it is a unique and mutually exclusive segment at all. Similarly, creating a segment that consists of individuals between the ages of 24 and 49 includes so many life-cycle and lifestyle differences that one finds it difficult to identify and focus on any one of the many groups within that segment. Also, placing all small businesses into one segment would be inaccurate given that small businesses range from small single-person entities with little revenue to a moderate number of employees with revenues in the millions. Likewise, past customer purchase behavior, by itself, is not the best indicator of future behavior, especially in industries where the products (for example, financial and informational) are not created to be disposable. Therefore, this chapter proposes the use of a triangulated, balanced segmentation scheme that encompasses and integrates demographic, behavioral, and attitudinal dimensions into one comprehensive view.

It is very important to realize that segmentation is a tool used to group individuals in a manner similar to the use of stratified random sampling in consumer research. In its most effective form, segmentation allows researchers to better understand the unique clusters and then provide the right products at the right time to this "right" group of customers. At its worst, improperly defined and used segments can easily create chaos out of confusion, somewhat akin to following a road map down a dead-end road just because you had the road map!

Segmentation schemes are meant to be dynamic processes. They will continuously change as the composition of the customer base changes. Since customers are living, changing beings, the process must have enough fluidity to move in concert with these changes. Good segmentation schemes identify where a customer is at a given point in time. Excellent schemes capture and predict future customer trends and then evolve in anticipation of these changes. When this happens, businesses understand their customers and are able to provide them with a sense of comfort that they will offer them the most profitable solutions. When companies do this, they create delighted, loyal customers.

Finally, segmentation schemes are not meant to be turnkey or automatic. Identifying and placing an individual customer into a segment does not mean an automatic product purchase. If done correctly, it does create a greater likelihood that customers perceive the company as understanding their needs and providing them with the best possible solutions. It is for this reason that segmentation schemes require ongoing analysis and the flexibility to change to meet the changing environments.

SELLING TO THE CUSTOMER

Having attracted the right customers to the site, the challenge now turns to engaging and converting the customers into purchasers. There are several best practices that may be employed to enhance online performance and purchase conversion, including (1) simplifying the purchase process, (2) making payments easy, safe, and reliable, and (3) personalizing offerings, even for first-time visitors (Agrawal, Arjona, and Lemmens, 2001).

First, the simpler the purchase process, the higher the chance of converting visitors to buyers. This means that the site should download quickly, within approximately eight seconds, and enable visitors to easily navigate the information and find what they are looking for within approximately three clicks. In addition, real-time assistance, such as *call me now* buttons and live online customer assistance, will help facilitate the process (Agrawal, Arjona, and Lemmens, 2001). Since privacy is a major issue, disclosure of the firm's privacy policy regarding use of personal information collected should be clearly stated. In addition to the above, business-to-business Web sites should focus on site functionality that enables users to quickly find desired information, real-time information regarding inventory and shipping status, and comprehensive product information, all of which would enable users to evaluate and compare product features and determine appropriateness to their needs (Hansen, 2002).

One of the main reasons why visitors abandon shopping carts and do not complete a transaction that they started is "data greed," according to consulting firm A. T. Kearney (2001). Many sites request extensive information on visitors' preferences and behavior, resulting in an invasion of privacy and an intrusion on time. Information required should be limited to payment and shipment details. One or two targeted questions may be requested at other significant interaction points in exchange for offering other site functions such as registering for product updates or newsletters (Agrawal, Arjona, and Lemmens, 2001).

Second, best practice online firms offer multiple payment options for transactions that are easy, safe, and reliable, and obtain certification from TRUSTe and VeriSign. In addition, information regarding response-time guarantees and return policies are prominently displayed or are easy to find (Agrawal, Arjona, and Lemmens, 2001).

Third, successful sites personalize their offerings, even for first-time buyers (Agrawal, Arjona, and Lemmens, 2001). A nationally know paint manufacturer asks Web site visitors to identify themselves as members of one of three categories: do-it-yourselfers (DIY'er), contractors, or decorators. The site is then tailored based on users' responses. For example, if a user responds as a DIY'er, a paint estimator is provided that allows the visitor to determine the amount of paint needed to complete a project. This serves not only to help the user but also reinforces the brand relationship, thereby enhancing the possibility of conversion.

CLIENT VALUE AND SATISFACTION: GIVING CUSTOMERS REASONS TO RETURN

Given the availability of numerous alternative Web sites, consumers must be given a compelling reason for visiting and returning to a given site. Understanding the consumers, and their needs and wants, is paramount! The key point to remember is that the Internet is really not just about technology. Instead, it is also about understanding the customer and taking that understanding of the intended target market and translating it into effective Web strategies and actions.

This means that the firm, if it is to succeed and stand apart from its competition, must create a focused value proposition—a cogent reason why consumers should visit the firm's site and buy from the firm, either online or off. For example, Amazon.com offers consumers four compelling reasons to visit and shop on its site: (1) selection—a database of 1.2 million titles from which to choose, (2) convenience—24/7 availability and a simplified "1-click" express-purchasing capability, (3) cost—discounts on best sellers, and (4) service—e-mail and phone customer support, automated ordering conformation, and tracking and shipping capability (Laudon and Traver, 2001).

The Internet-enabled marketplace has diminished, if not eliminated, the search cost for purchasing goods and services, thereby empowering the customer. By analyzing the online visitor's "footprint" (for example, cookies, log files, and site registration), site information and communications can be personalized to the needs of the individual, thereby enhancing the value of the site to the customer (Albert and Sanders, 2003). This, along with quality customer service, should serve to enhance the customer relationship, leading to a higher probability of customer retention and site profitability.

IMPLICATIONS OF ECRM FOR SMALL BUSINESSES

Given the limited human and financial resources, most small businesses may view the creation of an eCRM philosophy and a segmentation scheme as an onerous task. However, the sophistication of the Internet has made these processes quite feasible and cost-efficient. At the core, businesses must collect timely and accurate data on their customers. While this information should not be too intrusive, it should include data on customer purchases, demographics, and attitudes (if possible). Responses to online advertisements, e-mails, and actual purchases generate a substantial amount of customer information. Additional information can be quickly gathered from short online customer surveys. As importantly, online and off-line client satisfaction queries provide important information on client attitudes and comfort with the relationship with the company. These data then need to be integrated into a customer database that is easy to understand and use. The database can be as simple or complex as needed, but should be planned out in advance of its creation. By planning in advance, each of the data touch points can be integrated and used most effectively to generate information and minimize on redundancy. Depending on the size of the database, everything from simple spreadsheets to advanced database marketing software can be used to store, analyze, and use the information.

Once the database is constructed, a number of data elements should be selected to create a customer segmentation model. Again, planning is required here to make sure that the model philosophically fits both the business and the collectivities of customers. Wherever possible, a number of different elements should be used in order to provide a more comprehensive, triangulated profile of customer groups. Next, the segments should be prioritized and e-marketing campaigns created to deal directly with the selected segment or segments. It is important to remember that because the focus is on characteristics demonstrated by the customer and the campaign is customized around these factors, the customers will feel that they are understood and that their needs can be met. Also, each subsequent interaction with the customer will provide information that when added to the database will update and enhance the segmentation.

However, segmentation, in and of itself, is not eCRM. Once interaction has been initiated with the customer via the Internet, it is important that an ongoing dialog be developed and maintained. The best one-to-one personalized Internet interactions with the customer are those that quickly and seamlessly respond to customer query and concerns. This creates an expectation of trust and loyalty on the customers' part and gives you their permission to continue the relationship with them. With this permission, trust and loyalty via an ongoing interactive dialog, eCRM, can be achieved.

CONCLUSIONS

Customer relationship management is not a new concept. It has a long and varied history in the retailing and manufacturing industries. However, only recently have companies grasped its importance and begun to view it as a strategic vision. The advent of the Internet and eCRM strategies has made it more feasible and economical for businesses to create one-to-one relationships with their customers. Small businesses, traditionally lacking resources for larger formal CRM programs, can effectively create their own program over the Internet. Customers will feel that they are receiving special treatment, while the company maximizes resources in the manufacturing, marketing, and sales of its products and services.

Whether called customer lifetime value, one-to-one e-marketing, permission marketing, or mass customization, eCRM has one underlying theme: the customer rules. Actually eCRM is much more than a theme: it is a philosophy or way of thinking that must permeate through all levels of the corporate culture and processes. If not followed thoroughly and comprehensively across all aspects of an organization, it stands a very good chance for failure and, even worse, can be very unprofitable for a company.

Realizing that eCRM is a strategic vision and not just a set of tools or processes requires a dramatic philosophical shift from how companies traditionally think about and do their business. For example, many interpret eCRM to simply be the cross-selling of products and services. This is only a small part, or actually the outcome, of a successful eCRM philosophy. That is, in the course of knowing, understanding, and servicing customers, companies should be able to provide them additional products/services or unique combinations of the two that are right for them and profitable for the business. This profit is immediate in the sense of incremental products and services sold; more importantly, it is long-term in the additional loyalty and business a company will receive from the customer over a sustained period of time.

REFERENCES

Active Media Research (2001). Real Numbers Behind Successful Web Site Promotion 2000. *Entrepreneur,* June. Retrieved March 24, 2004, from http://www.Entrepreneur.com/article/0,4621,289554,00.html.

Agrawal, V., Arjona, L.D., and Lemmens, R. (2001). E-Performance: The Path to Rational Exuberance. *The McKinsey Quarterly.* Retrieved March 24, 2004, from http://www.mckinseyquarterly.com/article_print.asp?ar=975&L2=24&L3=45&srid=13&gp=1.

Albert, T.C., and Sanders, W.B. (2003). *E-Business Marketing.* Upper Saddle River, NJ: Prentice Hall.

A.T. Kearney (2001). Abandoned Shopping Carts Online: Top Reasons Why. *Client Help Desk,* March 30. Retrieved November 25, 2003, from http://www.clienthelpdesk.com/statistics_research/abandoned_shopping_carts.html.

Cassedy, K. (2002). Know Your Online Customer: Forrester Research Creates Technographics. *HSMAI Marketing Review,* January 25. Retrieved March 24, 2004, from http://www.hospitalitynet.org/news/Association_Update/AHLA/4010740.html.

Dilts, J., and Kahai, P.S. (2004). Taking A Small Business Online: A Systematic Approach. *Journal of Business and Entrepreneurship,* Spring 16(1), 29–45.

Hamblen, M. (2000). Customer Acquisition Costs. *ComputerWorld,* August 21. Retrieved March 24, 2004, from http://www.computerworld.com/industrytopics/retail/story/0,10801,48712,00.html.

Hansen, E. (2002). Must-Have Features for B-To-B Websites. *Catalog Age,* March 15, 19 (4), 37.

Heim, G.R., and Sinha, K.K. (2001). Operational Drivers of Customer Loyalty in Electronic Retailing: An Empirical Analysis of Electronic Food Retailers. *Manufacturing & Service Operations Management,* Summer, 3(3), 264–271.

Hoffman, D.L., and Novak, T.P. (2000). How to Acquire Customers on the Web. *Harvard Business Review,* 78(3), 178–188.

Judge, P.C. (1998). Are Tech Buyers Different? *Business Week,* January 26. Retrieved March 24, 2004, from http://www.businessweek.com/1998/04/b3562090.htm.

Juptner, O. (2002). Online Customer Acquisition Costs Down. *e-gateway,* January 10. Retrieved March 24, 2004, from http://www.e-gateway.net/infoarea/news/news.cfm?nid=2116.

Kelsey, D. (2000). Online Retailers Buying Fewer Offline Ads. *ComputerUser,* November 29. Retrieved March 24, 2004, from http://www.computeruser.com/news/00/11/29/news18.html.

Lake, D. (2000). The Web: Growing Two Million Pages A Day. *The Industry Standard,* February 28. Retrieved March 24, 2004, from http://www.thestandard.com/article/0,1902,12329,00.html.

Laudon, K.C., and Traver, C.G. (2001). *E-Commerce: Business, Technology, Society.* Boston, MA: Addison-Wesley.

Pastore, M. (2000). Internet Retailers Look Toward Profitability. *CyberAtlas,* August 30. Retrieved March 24, 2004, from http://cyberatlas.internet.com/markets/retailing/article/0,1323,6061_449371,00.html.

Reichheld, F.F., and Schefter, P. (2000). E-Loyalty. *Harvard Business Review,* 78(4), 105–113.

Rubin, R., and Bluestein, W.M. (1999). Applying Technographics. *Forrester Research, Inc.,* April. Retrieved March 24, 2004, from http://www.forrester.com/ER/Marketing/0,1503,84,FF.html.

Soltoff, P. (2002). HP Gets It Right. *Clicz.com,* July 29. Retrieved March 24, 2004, from http://www.clickz.com/em_mkt/em_mkt/article.php/1433721.

Strauss, J., El-Ansary, A., and Frost, R. (2003). *E-Marketing,* (3rd Ed.). Upper Saddle River, NJ: Prentice Hall.

CHAPTER 11

The Creative Process in the 21st Century

Joel Sobelson

What makes the 21st century so special to the creative process? On the face of it, one could argue that the creative process is the creative process. Who cares if it is the mid-20th century or the new 21st century? Left brain and right brain are still doing battle. The theory of flow still prevails. New ideas are still defined as two unrelated thoughts that you combine to make a new thought or idea. But, as you will see, the 21st century does raise some interesting issues to consider when creating marketing communications for today's consumers. We begin by exploring the "creative process." And the best way to do that is by understanding what creatives are asked to do.

THE METHOD TO THE MADNESS

As much as creative folks like to think they are freewheeling, free-spirited, irreverent, iconoclastic, and occasionally even endowed with supernatural powers that enable them to simply conjure up creative solutions from some mysterious inspirational force, that simply is not the case. Whether they are aware of it or not, they go through some kind of "process" to arrive at a creative solution. There is a method to the madness. I have always relied on what I believed was my intuition to create a solution, not realizing (or maybe denying) that there was a lot more of a rational and logical process going on in my subconscious. But once I understood what was going on and what kind of input I needed to get better output, that blank sheet of paper staring back at me was less intimidating. My solutions were more strategy focused, relevant, less complicated, and more creative.

What is it creatives are being asked to do? They are being asked to create fresh ideas to sell products and services. Ideas are the fuel that makes creative engines run. Ideas are the inspiration. Few things are as satisfying as coming up with a killer idea that everyone loves and sells the crap out of the product, for which you win a bunch of awards. But before we go pack our bags and run off to Cannes for the yearly Advertising and Direct Marketing Awards Festival, let us look at what an idea is all about.

WHAT IS AN IDEA?

This is a big question, so let us find a point of reference. Think about an idea you recently had. Dissect it. Realize that it represents nothing more than taking facts you already know and putting them together into a new combination in order to discover a relationship between them of which you were not previously aware. In other words, it is nothing more than making a new combination of known elements in a new and unexpected way.

But in our business it is not enough just to have an idea. We must have an idea that demonstrates a proposition *so differently* that it can break through all the clutter, get someone's attention, and engage the consumer in a fresh new manner.

THINK DIFFERENTLY

So we are after "different" ideas. What is that about? Let me give you a few examples. A while back, one of my clients was a car rental company that had just revamped the way it did business. It looked at its customers' behavior and found out that their first stop after leaving the rental lot was at a convenience store. So my client installed a small convenience store right inside the rental centers. This allowed the customers the convenience of shopping in the rental center so they did not have to begin their vacation looking for a convenience store. This was pretty revolutionary thinking in the industry at the time, because no one else had done anything like this. As far as the advertising campaign, the normal route would have been to show grandiose photos of the new rental centers, which essentially would have been the client patting itself on the back for coming up with the idea. But in thinking about the problem differently, we changed the perspective 180 degrees, looking at the opportunity from the consumer point of view. We decided to show a steaming mug of hot coffee with the client's logo on it accompanied with a copy line that read, "This is not just a cup of coffee. It is an entirely new way of renting a car." This simple twist on the expected highlighted the single major point of difference between my client and its competition. We ended up with an ad that was far more attention-getting and provocative than what was expected.

Another example of thinking differently happened at a presentation I recently gave to a conference of creative directors at a beach resort. I asked a few of the creative directors to describe, in words, the scene outside the window. Most began their description talking about the blue sky or the blue water or the white hotels, the expected responses. I urged them to look at the scene differently, not from the picture postcard point of view. I suggested starting their descriptions with a single grain of sand and then artfully working their way out to a description of the full scene. Once again it was a 180-degree shift in thinking from the expected to the unexpected. Their descriptions became much more vivid, entertaining, and creative.

Creatives are supposed to think differently. To do that they need to train themselves to look for and consider alternative points of view. Question everything. Keep the doors open to all possibilities. They need to be sponges and continue to take in information, advice, opinions, and input from all sources. This is a collaborative business. They cannot be selfish. They are not doing art for their own sakes.

One of the most effective techniques for coming up with creative ideas is through the technique of brainstorming sessions. Just get a few people in a room, and select someone as the moderator. The moderator then poses the problem to the group and writes down anything that anyone says. There are no bad ideas here, so naysayers and cynics need to understand that or leave the room. Collect all the ideas at the end of the session, edit out the ones that do not work, and then merge the thoughts that do work together to create new ideas. But the key is to stay open, stay open, stay open, and see what comes. As Linus Pauling said, "You need to have a lot of ideas in order to have a good one."[1]

Another place to start to understand what it is like to think differently is with a simple exercise. Go home a different way tonight. Take your time, look around you, and feel how different it is from your normal route. Bring new conclusions to what you experience. And smile; it cannot hurt.

GET SMART

So now that we understand what an idea is and how to think differently, what do creatives do next? Remember that an idea is simply putting together stuff you already know in new ways. So does it not seem logical to increase the stuff you already know? This will give you more possibilities, which will give you a better chance to come up with something new and fresh. This is where the phrase "garbage in, garbage out" comes to mind. Or in other words, the better the input, the better chances for great output.

First, creatives need to get smart about consumers so they can create ideas that are relevant to them. They should become an advocate for the consumer. Consumers are really our clients, when you think about it. They are the ones who choose whether an ad works or not by opting in to the offer or ignoring it. Get into their minds; walk in their shoes. When evaluating an idea, view it through their eyes as criteria for effectiveness. To learn more about the consumer, you should consult with research or data folks. They have vast stores of knowledge about consumers. Creatives need to be detectives looking for clues that will lead to unusual, unique, and rare insights. Then they need to turn that information on its ear to form new conclusions on how to address the consumers' wants and needs.

Next creatives need to research the client. They need to try to understand the client's "big picture." They should understand that clients are not really asking for a mail package or TV spot, even though that may be what the brief says. Clients are asking you to help them market their products and services, expand the value of their brand, and create a long-term transactional relationship with their customers. To succeed, creatives should know as much as possible about the client, its marketing philosophy, its corporate philosophy, even its management philosophy, to gain insights into what and how it thinks. Creatives cannot be shy here. Ask clients what they think good marketing and good advertising is. Ask for examples. Conversely, ask what they hate and why. Ask how they view their consumers as well as their competition's customers. Their answers will give creatives the opportunity to not only get to know clients better, but it will give some insight into how they judge good work, as well as what criteria they will be using to buy ideas.

Finally, creatives need to research the competition. If you are going into a game, it is always good to have a bit of a scouting report on the opposing team, knowing its strengths and weaknesses. It is also a good idea in marketing. Scouting may uncover differentiating insights that may work in your client's favor and help it create a great idea. You should visit the competition's Web site and look at its current work in every channel. Buy the competition's product and give it a try; evaluate it against your client's product. Then use the findings as a basis for some of the ideas.

LET IT FLOW

This is where the fun comes in. If you have been asked to come up with an idea for a piece of marketing communications, and you followed my suggestions about filling your head full of information about your client, the product, and the consumer, now is the time to put down your knife and fork and step away from the table. Forget about the problem at hand. Go get inspired. Go out for a walk, go to the movies, have a beer, play with your dog, take a nap. Basically get away from it all and just let all that information percolate a bit. If you find yourself beginning to think about it, force yourself not to. It is not cooked yet. If you have ever heard of the "Theory of Flow,"[2] this may be a good time to experience it.

Take a shower. In the warmth and quiet you can relax and make your mind a blank sheet ready to be filled up with ideas. Ideas will come to you as you begin to relax. There seems to be a psychological reaction to the flowing of the water around you and through you. Some type of release happens. I find I usually emerge from the shower with a bunch of ideas.

If a shower or bath does not do it for you, find something that does. Go for it. Subconsciously you are making connections, putting things together. And when the time comes to start to work on the problem, you will find that you have begun to formulate some strategic and creative thoughts. Ideas will begin to come to you almost effortlessly.

IT IS ALL IN THE EXECUTION

Now that you have a great idea, it is time to put pencil to paper. This is where the "art" of the craft comes in. Execution is everything. It all comes down to not only *what* you say, but more importantly, *how* you say it. The tone of voice needs to be one that is appealing to your target, *not* your own artistic whims.

The other element you must consider is the brand's voice. Hopefully it is one that speaks in a straightforward, honest style so that the brand and its values come across that way. If not, you have your work cut out for you. Know that people do not want to be reminded that they are dealing with a large corporation. So any chance to prove the corporation's human side should be taken. But most importantly, speak to the target consumers as if you were speaking to them on a one-to-one basis. Short declarative sentences in a conversational tone work best.

Consider using graphics, photography, and iconography that can speak volumes. Consider both its content and style carefully. Continue to ask yourself if the target will get this or relate to this. Here you have to rely on your knowledge, judgment, and research of the target to make that determination. And finally, I have a personal thing where I never make anything too perfect. Call it superstition, but I do not trust anything that is perfect. Would you?

The bottom line is that the solution you create comes from your creative ability to rethink insights about the consumer based on your knowledge of the marketplace. When all is said and done, success is really based on 50 percent knowledge and 50 percent intuition. It has to feel right; trust your gut. Think about the creative process and how we fashion a marketing message this way. There are four steps creative folks need to know to create great work. These steps will make the work relevant to consumers in order to get them to pay attention to your message and consider buying its offer or product.

1. *Understand what creatives do.* They take what clients want to say and turn it into what consumers want to hear. For example, a financial client who is looking to market its online banking product may want its marketing message to talk about how it allows consumers to transfer funds between accounts, how it enables them to pay bills

automatically, and how it delivers a statement of the transactions to them automatically each month. That is all well and good, but is that what a consumer wants to hear?

2. *Understand what the consumer wants to hear.* Consumers want to hear about issues relevant to their lives. To some it is about gardening; to others it is about motorcycles. But the key is to know the target consumers and what interests them and then fashion a relevant message directly to them. In the case of the client's online banking product, consumers want to know what is in it for them and how the product features add up to something that will make their lives easier, more fun, and simpler. Not having to get in the car, drive down to the bank, drive around the block a few times to find a parking space, then stand in line waiting for a teller, and so forth, will all add up to saving a load of time for the consumer—time better spent with family and friends or even napping or enjoying a good bottle of wine. That is what consumers want to hear. And what will give consumers that leisure time? The online banking product.

3. *Understand how creatives create what consumers want to hear.* They ask themselves, "If I buy this product, what will it give me that others like it will not? What is in it for me?" That is called the product proposition, or the product promise. Once they understand what the proposition is, they can then go on to the final purchasing step.

4. *Understand how creatives bring the proposition to life.* Creatives "dramatize" the product's proposition. We think of some relevant yet unexpected way to bring that product promise to life so that it is relevant to our consumer.

AND NOW FOR THE 21ST CENTURY

Now that we have defined the creative process, you might wonder how these principles are applied to what is going on with consumers and media in the 21st century. Today there are new communication challenges facing us that are vastly different from the ones that faced us five to ten years ago—challenges that we need to understand and consider before we begin creating marketing communications for today's consumers. For instance, with more brands trying to get your attention, shouting at you about more products and services than ever before, there is a palpable din out there. Did I say din? I meant cacophony! And it is not just the same old media channels of radio, TV, and print making all that noise. Now there is more of everything: more TV channels and radio channels, more magazines and newspapers, more out-of-home messaging, more product placement efforts, not to mention the overwhelming "moreness" of the entire online effort.

The ways a marketer can communicate with consumers is staggering and at times overwhelming. This alone justifies the thought that an individual consumer may receive over 2,500 marketing messages a day! Maybe "receive" is not the right word, because I am sure none of them are aware of that many messages. In fact, I would be surprised if they actually pay attention to ten of those messages. And if they do pay attention, that does not necessarily mean they remember them or care about them. And that is just the point. Would you pay attention to something that you do not care about? So why do marketers continue to "carpet bomb" us with their messaging? John Wanamaker's claim of knowing he wasted half of his advertising dollars, he just did not know which half,[3] must be revised; today I am sure that marketers are wasting well over 50 percent of those precious dollars.

SO WHAT IS A MARKETER TO DO?

First of all, as the guide in *The Hitchhiker's Guide to the Galaxy* reminds us, "Don't panic."[4] No matter how many channels of media exist, the relevancy of the message and the way it is delivered are still the keys to breaking through and engaging the consumer. Therefore the new marketing challenge is to understand how all this media bombardment affects the consumer and then to use this understanding to create engaging messages that will break through the clutter.

Let us look closely at some of the issues creatives have to consider in order to create relevant marketing messaging. In some ways, today's consumer is dumber than ever—and I say that noting I am a consumer. Today's consumers have the attention span of a flea. We know a little bit about a lot of stuff. The "sound-bite and key visual communications" we are exposed to daily are enough for many of us to think we actually know something about a particular subject, which fools us into believing we are making informed purchasing decisions. But we are not.

Another issue to consider is that more and more surveys and polls indicate that consumers are spending less time reading. I have even heard it said that many of us are functioning illiterates. Look around your environment. There are more and more signs that give us information with pictographs on them rather than signs with words on them. We are not a nation of readers any longer, thanks to how we have been trained by the marketing community.

While I am sure there are other issues, these two factors alone create a major challenge for any marketers. Now is the time for them to reconsider the outdated marketing strategy that believes frequency of message really can be a beneficial selling tool. They need to begin to be more open-minded about using new ways to engage consumers. Simple messaging (a fancy headline and visual on an ad) is no longer enough. Now they have to begin to practice marketing, which is a lot more of an *engagement strategy* that uses *new tactics* in order to get the consumer to sit up and pay attention.

BUT THERE IS SOME ENCOURAGING NEWS

All is not lost. Marketers have some new insights and tools with which to reach today's consumers. First, realize that in some ways, consumers are smarter than ever—and I say that noting I am a consumer. They have developed a set of defenses that actually work in their favor in regard to today's marketing hype. They have honed a fine-tuned and rather accurate "B.S. meter" that tells them when they are being sold a line of crap. They can see right through those flashy adjectives, overpromises, and "copy weasels" that have worked so successfully in the past to hype a product. (A copy weasel is a line of copy that distracts a consumer about the true essence of a product. My favorite weasel was written by a friend working on an ad for a cheese product that was totally fabricated in the lab. His weasel was "Made with dairy cows in mind.")

In addition, consumers' values and attitudes toward their lives and the society they live in have changed radically over the years. What was once love, peace, and happiness evolved into excessive greed, which has further evolved into a more balanced approach to life. Today, families, home, and good health are the barometers of happiness. This means that today consumers are more value conscious than ever before. And I am not just talking price here. What a brand stands for is just as important as what the brand's products deliver.

Somehow consumers have learned how to deal with this onslaught of media; we multitask as never before. I come home and see my kids, the next generation, sitting in the TV room with the TV blasting, while they chat on their laptops, and manage to speak on the phone, all somewhat simultaneously, not missing a beat. But the key to making messaging work effectively is to understand consumers are willing to give up their attention to advertisers who give them something in return, namely, information that the consumer cares about.

IT IS NOT ONLY HOW YOU SAY IT, BUT WHERE

Coming up with the right thing to say to the target is only half of the battle. The home run is to tailor this message to the different media channels consumers use to access their messages. The old model of "carpet bombing" the consumer in the familiar media channels (print, TV, and radio) with iterative messages—a bunch of little soldiers all dressed in the same uniform, marching to the same beat—is not as powerful as it once was. Today consumers relate to each media channel in a different way and expect different things from each one. Messaging now must be created with each individual media channel in mind so that it can create more of an engaging "brand experience" with the consumer. To do this creatives need to understand the essence of each individual channel. Knowing these simple principles will help to ensure crafting the right message to the right channel for a better chance of connecting with today's consumer.

Now that you have the creative process down pat, let us venture into the world of the 21st century creative director. Fasten your seatbelts; it is a fast and furious world. But at the heart of it all, it is fun, it is exciting, and it is my life.

MESSAGING VERSUS MARKETING

Five years ago, I could have easily defined integrated marketing as a marketer finding a good messaging headline and visual and then duplicating it on TV, radio, in the mail, and perhaps online (if a marketer was so bold to be there then). Marketers simply did not fully understand the qualitative core value of each individual medium; they were just looking to have their message read in one or perhaps two media channels, hoping frequency of sightings would get the consumer to sit up and take notice. Since then, consumer media viewing has evolved. What I am finding is that people expect something different from each channel. Marketers need to understand this or else their marketing dollars will be wasted.

TV is a "lean-back" medium that is best used for creating an emotional bond with the brand. Print is a bit more involving and can deliver more about product specifics; it therefore can do some of the heavy lifting for the brand. Online is a "lean-forward" medium, a high-engagement vehicle where the brand can really come to life with dialogues beyond just a simple product offering. With this in mind, you can understand how the same repetitive, iterative message used time and again across all media channels may not work in all media channels. It needs to be tailored for each channel's specific capabilities.

The new definition of integrated marketing is moving from simple messaging, that is, a snazzy headline and visual, to true marketing. Here, the agency creates one big brand idea that can be tailored for effectiveness for each media channel. Messaging is created with each media channel in mind so that it works collaboratively. When done successfully, the brand then can begin to move from the world of transactions to the world of relationships.

I have just completed some work for a sick brand that was losing share rapidly. We were asked to create a print ad and a TV spot to stem the leak of customers from the franchise. But we knew that was not the solution. Instead we recommended unbranded tease direct mail, radio, high-impact print, regular print, e-mail blasts, big public relations events, and outdoor billboards, all slicing and dicing the brand idea in a bunch of different ways in order to drive the consumers to a branded site. Once they arrived at the site, offers for coupons, sweepstakes, information, and community were available for them to get involved. Early results look very promising, validating that the time to try a new form of marketing is here.

These new media opportunities create a greater stickiness than ever before.[5] This stickiness results in adding value to the marketing experience for consumers, making them more willing to engage with the brand. They are willing to give their attention to advertisers who give them something in return. And we are not talking refrigerator magnates or sippy cups with client's logos on them. I am talking about a simple value exchange where consumers say, "Entertain me; teach me; tell me something I want to know. Make me laugh; support events that interest me. I'll watch the screen, open the mail package, click through the banner, and pay attention, if you tell me something I really care about." Sharing information is a powerful thing for a brand to do, so why not make it the currency of the value exchange with the consumer?

EXCESSES, INDULGENCES, AND OVERAGES

Let us talk about TV commercials and their production. I have been involved with TV shoots for a single 30-second spot where production costs are equal to the gross national income of a small country. And I think that is okay if the result turns a company's fortunes around and makes it the "Microsoft" of its category. But it rarely ever does. On the other hand, I have produced short commercial films with terrific production values—about a third of the cost of a 30-second spot—that resulted in tremendous sales for my client.

The difference is working with people who are ardent about what they do and are willing to get the job done without the excesses, indulgences, and production cost overages. That means for crew, cast, client, and agency personnel, there are no private Winnebagos, no special golf course tee times, no hotel suites, and no luxurious car rentals. No private cabanas at the hotel pool. No over-the-top banquet dining with imported wines by the case. No one-of-a-kind expensive wardrobes earmarked for eventual ownership by special crewmembers and their "assistants." And, most importantly, there are no unbelievable day rates for talent, whether that talent is in front of or behind the camera.

But even today, overindulgence on commercial shoots is still going on. Get real. We are *not* producing feature films nor are we part of the Hollywood film scene, no matter how hard we try to delude ourselves that we are. A while back I was shooting a spot for orange juice, and I requested that a bowl of oranges be placed in the shot. I did not think it was an outrageous request—a bowl of oranges in an orange juice commercial. Well, by the way the director reacted, you would have thought I had asked for the *Queen Mary* to be flown in and parked on the set. I let him vent and dress me down in front of everyone. My rebuttal, just as loud and in front of his crew was, "Why should we put a bowl of oranges in the shot? In case you've forgotten, we're making a *commercial* about *orange juice,* and yes, this is what your career has sunk to, so wake up and just do it." The oranges ended up looking great.

But some commercial producers still believe they are filming full-length features. A while ago my agency was producing a spot in which one of the scenes took place between two actors in a baseball dugout. Where did we shoot this simple shot, one that could have been shot in any little league dugout in any American town? We shot at Shea Stadium in New York. What was the director thinking when he made this decision? Bragging rights to simply say he did it?

And what about excesses on the set? I recently came from a set where the newbie account person wanted to know who all the people with different rolls of tape hanging off of their belts were, who seemed to be doing nothing. I explained that while they appear to be standing around waiting for the lunch call, they really all do some very important stuff. A *reasonable* number of crew is essential to a shoot going off without too many snags. But that is not always the case. I have been involved in productions where there was an army of production assistants on call to individually cater to the whims of each client and agency person. And it is just not the client and agency who are indulged. Too many times I have seen certain crew members have a first assistant who has a second assistant who has a third assistant. Talk about excessive. Did they ever consider that maybe someone on the crew is actually capable of lifting two boxes at a time instead of having enough production assistants on the set to go on a 40-day safari through the Congo? Clients and agency personnel can surely find their own chairs to sit in or get their own bottle of water from the ice cooler.

There are three things you need to make cost-effective and marketing effective TV commercials or sales films.

1. *A good idea.* No amount of overproduced film or overscale payments to talent will mask mediocrity.

2. *A passionate director* who has the proper perspective on what the client and agency are trying to accomplish with the production. He or she needs to be willing and anxious to work *collaboratively* with both the agency and the client. And he or she needs to give it his or her best shot for a reasonable rate. In these situations, my motto is, "Remember, we're making a *commercial* here."

3. *A smart and creative agency producer* who will spend client money as if it is coming out of his or her own pocket and has the courage to say no to agency, client, and production company excess.

Anyone can produce a commercial for half a million bucks. The real talent comes when you have only $150,000 to produce the same idea. It is being done every day by talented, smart, and passionate folks who work in our industry. If you want to end up producing great work and protecting your client from wasting a whole lot of money, let me know. I know where the folks who can do it live; just ask.

UH OH, DIRECT MAIL IS DEAD!

I recently heard that financial direct mail marketing has resulted in poorer results than ever before. It is no surprise; I can understand it. I see my own personal mail. It has gotten to the point where it has very little to do with me anymore, but rather it is just blanket mailings with irrelevant offers. The overmailed and abused mail recipient really has no other choice than to just toss this clutter if only to clear some counter space to make dinner for the family. But again, "Do not panic."

The big thing is to realize that this does not mean the mail channel is dead. It just means there is an evolution going on that smart agencies will take advantage of—an evolution that creates new opportunities for their clients to reach their prospects. Smart Direct Marketing agencies now are beginning to understand that data used to drive the marketing effort, but now media needs to take the lead. And what is really cool about these new media channels is that they can be used in support of each other while actively engaging the consumer like never before. Unlike the lean-back medium of TV and print, these new channels create a lean-forward phenomenon, enabling a dialogue between consumers and a brand that not only enhances the brand's value with the consumer, but sells its products and offers as well.

Make information the currency of the value exchange between business and consumer. With the explosion of new media channels, a smart Direct Marketing agency can offer its clients a range of options to help them lead to new learning, which will enable their next marketing opportunity to be even smarter, more responsive, and more impactful. Did this ever happen to you? You get home after a long day, start in on the pizza you picked up on the way home, open a beer, and plop down in front of the TV, hoping it will all just go away. But all of a sudden this crazy hip-hop Volkswagen (VW) "scientist" Hans and his hot assistant Greta are jumping off the screen at you as he outdopes the brothers from the hood with the new campaign for the VW GTi. These are hilarious, entertaining, informative commercials that break through all the TV clutter; they are just what good mass-market advertising is supposed to do. (Check them out at http://paultan.org/archives/2006/02/23/volkswagen-golf-gti-un-pimp-your-ride/).

But the execution is only part of the genius of these three spots. The other part is the smart way this campaign has tapped into an insight about drivers that makes these spots appeal not only to the GTi target—young drivers under the age of 25 —but goes beyond it. I spoke with drivers under 25 as well as drivers over 35 and found that both groups not only loved the commercials, but both groups expressed an interest in checking out the car as well. Even my 16-year-old saw the spots and said this was the car he was thinking about getting once he gets his license.

This new campaign proves that VW continues to have an internal marketing culture that seems fearless. It continues to push the envelope just as it has since it redefined advertising with "Think Small." VW's marketers understand their brand, they understand their product, and they understand how to speak to their target like few others in the field. These spots add up to another memorable campaign from VW, establishing it as one of the premier marketers today.

INTERNET: WHO IS DOING IT RIGHT?

With the Internet being an $18.1 billion a year business, maybe it is time we take a look at who is doing it right. So many sites come off as simply online catalogs of their company's goods, and that is okay if a company is not looking to use the interactive channel to help build its brand. But some companies realize that this media channel can take their brands from being simply transactional to relational. They realize that this channel can be more than merely a company's online catalog of goods and services, but a destination for a consumer looking for dialogues, entertainment, and information.

I do not think anybody does it better than Amazon.com. For me it began a few years ago as simply a place to track down the books of a new author I had discovered. Amazon was able to expeditiously fill my order for his books *and* at a discount. Soon after placing several orders, a sentence appeared on my personal Amazon.com page suggesting that if I liked this author so much, maybe I would also like "so and so," a similar writer. I bit, and Amazon was right; I enjoyed its recommendations.

I expanded my purchases from books and CDs to videos and electronic gaming gear, all the while trusting Amazon's suggestions. When I wanted to purchase a digital camera, Amazon took the confusion out of the shopping experience with suggestions based on my needs and budget. Recently I took a chance and typed in a seersucker suit in the "find" bar. You guessed it; Amazon had it. I bought it.

Over time Amazon earned my ear, my trust, and a share of my wallet. Through good data gathering, it was able to market to me in a truly personal and relevant way, responding to and satisfying my needs. Amazon simply got it, making me feel comfortable spending my money with it. This past holiday season, not only did I find myself purchasing 90 percent of my gifts from it, but I also found myself spending a lot of time at Amazon.com because of the video and music presentations it had streaming on the site, the reviews from purchasers, and the money-saving opportunities it offered me.

Amazon allows consumers autonomy, freedom, and control, making them feel comfortable with the buying experience. This marketing strategy breaks through all the clutter and makes meaningful connections to develop loyal consumers.

Amazon has proven that the Internet can go from being a sales adjunct channel to one that can actually help develop a brand. And in a world of parity products, that is really an insightful use of a channel that we are only beginning to understand. A smart marketer recognizes the online experience as an opportunity to market to *individuals,* speaking to them on a one-to-one basis.

PROMISES, PROMISES: BEWARE WHEN AN AGENCY PROMISES *INTEGRATED SOLUTIONS*

So many agencies are talking about integrated solutions these days. How integrated are their solutions in actuality? Here are a few things to consider when it comes to an agency offering integrated solutions.

1. Before reviewing any work (it is easy to be misled by very snazzy executions), be sure to see a comprehensive marketing strategy that justifies integrated solutions. Then look to see if the strategy demonstrates how these tactics collaborate with each other while enhancing the consumer experience with the brand.

2. If you are introduced to an account person whose role is "integration," make sure he or she is supported by the appropriate personnel, such as a strategist, a creative, a media person, a data person, and a creative services person.

   - A *strategist* must understand that integrated marketing is not a bunch of divergent tactics held together with a common logo, but rather a strategy that uses multi-channel tactics that are collaborative and complimentary in delivering a brand's marketing message seamlessly across all media channels.

   - A *creative* must understand the brand and have multi-discipline experience (general, direct, and online) so he or she can execute the variety of tactics properly. He or she should also fully understand the core values of each individual media channel (that is, which one establishes the emotional connection best, which one can do the heavy lifting best, which one can take a brand from transactional to relational best, and so forth) so that the right message is in the right channel.

   - A *media person* must be able to suggest a plan that includes a combination of various innovative and unexpected media opportunities that collaborate and compliment each other to create seamless integrated messaging.

   - Someone from *data* needs to analyze the results. No back end to analyze all that new data could mean you lose a valuable opportunity.

   - An experienced *creative services person* with specific experience in the tactics you are considering is essential as well. If not, you will pay through the nose to produce, mail, or post things that could be produced for far less.

3. For digital work, get a site audit of your present work first so you know what is working and what needs to be improved. Creative solutions that look cool may not be furthering the brand experience, nor will they lead to the sale or the data gathering you want.

4. If an agency does not staff the necessary personnel with capabilities to strategize, create, execute, and analyze, ask the agency to demonstrate that it can collaborate with other marketing groups that do have those capabilities as their core competencies. The last thing you want to do is to manage the process, so make sure your shop can drop its ego to be able to work seamlessly with others.

   There are agencies that are actually capable of creating integrated solutions, but it is not the agencies you would expect. It is a new breed of smaller, more innovative shops. The point of difference with these shops is that they have a mélange of *experienced talent* from *all* aspects of the industry, not just a single marketing discipline. It is rather like having a tool box with only a bunch of hammers versus a tool box with a hammer, a screw driver, a drill, some sandpaper, and so forth. They see integrated marketing as a strategy with collaborative tactics from the start, not as an afterthought. And they have the talent sitting there right around the table to do it seamlessly and more efficiently.

NINE THINGS YOU NEED TO KNOW ABOUT CREATIVES

Based on my years of experience, following are nine helpful hints to better understand this unique creature called a "creative."

1. A *good* account person does not interrupt during the creative presentation. But a *great* account person does not shut up after the presentation, championing the work to the client in the room, on the ride home via the phone, and back in the office via e-mail until it is sold.

2. "Process" is perceived as suicide for creatives. They just do not choose to recognize its existence. However, as previously discussed, there is a method to their madness.

3. Art and commerce are two separate concepts. Sometimes the two shall meet, and that is okay as long as it does not ruin the concept.

4. Moving an element on a page or site or screen ¼ inch to the right or ⅛ inch down is critical to those designers and art directors who do it. God is in the details, and that ⅛ inch move is piety in action.

5. Good copy does not just flow like the swollen rivers after a rainstorm. It is constructed word by word with an ear to the rhythm and cadence of their read. So when someone starts to mess with it, he or she needs to understand the damage and indignation he or she is creating.

6. They see the answer to half of 13 not only as 6.5, but 6½, thir & teen, 1 and 3, and so forth.

7. They recognize we are all just consumers at heart. Answering "What's in it for me?" and then creatively dramatizing it is their creative muse.

8. They have an innate sixth sense. This allows them to suspend logic when making a creative decision with no apparent justification other than "It just doesn't feel right." Trust them.

9. When you are explaining the marketing problem to creatives, and they seem to go off into outer space and sit in front of you with a blank stare, they are not being rude. They are simply watching their inner movie screen play the creative to solve your client's marketing problem.

WHAT DO YOU BRING TO THE TABLE?

Not too long ago I was sitting across the table from one of my client's new junior brand managers: shaved head, black-rimmed glasses, slight British accent, not to mention a shirt and tie pattern combination that came straight from Clarabell's closet. You know the type—someone way too full of himself. My creative team had prepared work to show for his approval. Even though we all thought the work was terrific, I could tell he was not a "happy-chappy." The first thing he asked was why "his" offer was not in the headline. He took a deep breath and sighed, "My in-house group could have done better." (Good thing he was not too rude.) Then my favorite part of the meeting came when he proceeded to ask, "What actually is it that your group brings to the table?" He did not realize that he was putting his brand's positioning in jeopardy over a simple "offer" ad, not to mention his agency relationship.

I calmly smiled. I knew here was someone who grew up in a transactional world, never understanding nor paying any attention to the value his brand brought to the marketing message. His wore his ignorance of what makes a good ad and a smart advertising agency on his ill-fitting suit's sleeve. After all, if all he wanted was his parity offer in the headline, he was right, his in-house group could have done better. But I do not believe that is what we were asked to do, nor do I believe that strategy would have made for an effective ad.

Then came the hardest part of my job: not pissing off the client, that is, walking the line between not giving him what he wanted and convincing him of what he needed. I began by explaining that clients have an awful lot of information about their customers, but what they lack is enough insights into them. It is these insights that make the connection to the consumer, not an offer in bright red across the top of an ad. Good ads are not about the offer, just as good advertising is not about the brand. Good marketing is *all* about the consumer.

I quoted Lester Wunderman's insight about effective marketing: "The consumer, not the product, must be the hero. You must meet a customer's specific need and bring value to that customer in order for him to purchase your product and remain loyal to your brand."[6]

People are not sitting around waiting for the latest offer from a brand. But they are willing to pay attention if they are told something about what they really care about—the proverbial "What's in it for me?" So I looked across the conference room table and said, "The key to what we bring to the table is that *we take what a client wants to say and turn it into what a consumer wants to hear.*"

SOMETHING IMPORTANT TO REMEMBER

The creative process, what with all these tools to make us smarter about the consumer, is still not a refined science from brief to solution. There is no science to doing great creative work, no processes or rules to come up with great creative solutions. As the rest of the communications business gets more and more quantitative and process driven, creatives need to remain outside all of that. How creatives get from one of the most intimidating things they will ever have to face—a blank sheet of paper—and fill it with exciting, entertaining, creative solutions will always be a mystery. And that is good; that is how it should be. Give them that space. They just need a healthy understanding of whom they are talking to so the dialogues they create can truly resonate, creating brand affinity. A brand now has more places to grow than ever before, and in the right hands, its chances of connecting are greater than ever before.

NOTES

1. The quotation by Linus Pauling was found at http:/www.quoteland.com/author.asp?author_20=453 (accessed September 15, 2005).

2. Csikszentmihalyi, Mihaly (1990). *Flow: The Psychology of Optimal Experience,* New York: HarperCollins Publishers.

3. Ershkowitz, Herbert (1998). *John Wanamaker: Philadelphia Merchant,* New York: Da Capo Press.

4. Adams, Douglas (1980). *The Hitchhiker's Guide to the Galaxy,* New York: Del Rey Books.

5. Gladwell, Malcolm (2002), *The Tipping Point: How Little Things Can Make a Big Difference,* Boston: Back Bay Books.

6. Wunderman, Lester, Chairman Emeritus and Founder of Wunderman Advertising (personal communication).

CHAPTER 12

DATA STRATEGIES TO SUPPORT MARKETING: ACTIONABLE BUSINESS INTELLIGENCE OR DATA OVERLOAD?

AnneMarie Scarisbrick-Hauser

These days, it is hard not to laugh as you listen to energetic and passionate business experts or gurus explain the business benefits associated with taking time and making the effort to "know your customer," especially by focusing on a "one-to-one" marketing message (Peppers and Rogers, 2005). At the same time, architects of customer relationship management programs explain how these approaches are designed to create what they considered (until now) a seemingly unattainable relationship dynamic that provides a measurable return on investment for the client by leveraging that well-worn cliché of a database that provides a "360-degree view of the customer." Given the challenges associated with corralling the contents of customer data from hundreds of databases into some kind of manageable analytical structure, it appears that "knowing our customers" or strengthening the relationship with them is but one among many of our problems. Today, finding, consolidating, analyzing, interpreting, leveraging, and retaining their information in one location poses an even greater challenge. Think about the excellent job your frontline personnel do with the quality of the customer information you provide them as they establish and maintain customer relationships. Now think about how much better the entire client relationship might be if the right information was provided at the right time to your employees.

Sometimes it seems like the customers know more about our ability to serve them than we do. For years, businesses depended upon information gained from their frontline client facing relationships and anecdotal episodes before large corporations decided that it was more profitable to consolidate and migrate customer data into large databases to enable analysis of their business strategies, including marketing efforts. However, in many cases, these large databases were created using a basic database programming code, mostly COBOL, without any means of analyzing or leveraging those data using reporting or statistical software. As the understanding of data mining grew and statistical analysis (SAS and SPSS) and business intelligence tools (Brio, Actuate, Microstrategy, and Cognos) became commonplace, programmers began to extract customer data and publish customer demographic and performance information to the business leaders.

As awareness increased around the potential for leveraging information from customer data to acquire new customers, analytical efforts turned toward identifying patterns of purchasing behavior or characteristics that would guide future prospect marketing campaigns. In the marketplace today we discuss the quantitative aspect of the benefits of the science of marketing in terms of customer data profiling, client segmentation, campaign response modeling, and lifetime value estimations and then couple this with the qualitative aspect as a means of enhancing the art of marketing to the customer providing value to the customer and the company (Pettit, 2005; Wasserman, 2000).

While there is no doubt that making a connection with the customer will be greatly enhanced by knowing something about the purchase history, demographics, economic conditions, life-cycle stage, and other pertinent information; let us not forget that the nature of the customer relationship is driven by the overarching business strategy and initiatives selected by the business development team. Therefore, it is essential that one start with an understanding of the business purpose for the analysis. Irrespective of the type of business (that is, business to business, commercial, or retail), customer data need to be prepared and available for extraction into meaningful and actionable reporting databases. Information (facts and figures) gleaned from customer databases is only as useful as its contribution to the objectives of the selected business initiatives. The information needs to be actionable; that is, it must be relevant and meaningful and must have the ability to be readily integrated into the business decision-making process. Over time, using and building upon that information provides additional intelligence leading to knowledge that can be leveraged for future decision making. *Actionable intelligence* is generated through the use of the information used not only to drive the decisions used to drive the business initiative, but also in the analysis and interpretation of the results of marketing campaigns.

As the marketplace changes from an orientation centered on product sales to one centered on the customer, direct marketing efforts to target profitable customers across the multiple channels, especially the Internet, have resulted in reams of data waiting to be analyzed and converted into knowledge for use in enhancing future marketing efforts. It is important here to remember that any company, irrespective of size, can collect data on every customer transaction. These data are then stored in some format in a database for some future use, such as financial tracking or inventory management purposes. The larger companies have amassed hundreds of such databases over time and have hired hundreds of technology programmers and developers to maintain these bastions of customer data. However, while some companies have mastered this better than others, the major challenge today is enabling internal databases to surrender their data in a suitable format for data analysis and interpretation. Over the past ten years, especially as commerce transitioned to doing business via the Web, it has become clear that many internal databases were designed to collect data as a record of a interaction (that is, recording customer information, customer transactions, orders, and shipping information) and not for actionable intelligence designed to enable customized targeted marketing. Sadly, in many cases, historical data have regularly been purged from the systems to save money and make room for future transactions. These data would have helped the companies perform different types of trend analysis and predictive modeling which, in turn, would have increased business efficiencies perhaps more than compensating for the money allegedly saved by purging the data.

During the past decade, some of the more forward-thinking companies have spent millions of dollars extracting and consolidating customer information across numerous internal databases to create an overall view of their customers. These databases are often referred to as customer warehouses or data marts and are designed to provide a comprehensive portrait of the customer and to enable data analysis that will generate critical information on that customer. In today's fast-moving marketplace, successful businesses, especially those in direct marketing and Web-based commerce, are likely to be the ones that have established centralized customer databases designed to quickly convert data into actionable information using business intelligence tools to identify timely business opportunities of value to customer and business and deploy marketing campaigns with competitive advantage (Dyche and Levy, 2006).

The way that the information is converted to actionable knowledge is through the use of marketing analytics that is designed to extract intelligence about characteristics such as customers' demographics, interests, motivations, purchase behaviors, next likely product purchase, likelihood of attrition, or estimated long-term value as a customer, to name just a few. This intelligence provides a context for many aspects of the direct marketing campaign. In particular, it is the foundation for segmenting and targeting the appropriate groups of customers and then designing the creative messages to achieve the best results, increase revenue, and enhance long-term customer relationships.

Given all of the positives of data mining and analytics, confidence in the marketing information is usually threatened by challenges to the quality of the data and whether the results represent an alignment with the business goals and objectives. For example, how confident are we that we are targeting the right customer or business through the best channel with the most effective offer? Issues with the quality of business databases affect not only the ability to retain and generate business, but increasingly also a business's legal obligations to maintain an accurate database. This ever-growing interrelationship of legal and business requirements for quality data has increased adoption and use of quality-assurance processes such as Six Sigma or Lean, which originally were deployed solely in the manufacturing world. Fortunately, these same processes can be adopted for use in monitoring performance of current direct marketing campaigns and marketing new ideas.

This chapter gives a brief overview of the processes used today to translate data into actionable intelligence within a customer-centric business process strategy. It also identifies and discusses challenges associated with constructing analytical databases, recruiting staff, and providing general guidelines on how to establish an end-to-end analytical process.

DATA AND DATA QUALITY

Data: Where, How, and When Will They Be Ready?

Early in the 21st century, it appears that many companies have more data in their databases than they know what to do with. They are more likely to find too much data on too many systems using too many tools and, thereby, providing too little usable information. The loudest cry heard in the marketplace these days is the call for a "single source of truth" where the required critical business data are stored in one place accessible by the people who have a business need to use it. Until recently this problem was resolved by the creation of an enterprise data warehouse. However, many of these warehouses were built to support the product-driven marketing framework and are not as nimble as is required for a customer-centric view. Efforts are now turning toward integrating critical customer data in a nimble structure or a service-oriented architecture permitting operational, service, and analytical data to coexist in the same environment (Dyche, 2005).

One of the major challenges in data management is the inability to link diverse customer databases, thereby obstructing the ability to consolidate a customer's entire relationship history in one place. These unlinked databases serve different purposes, some of which are operational or constantly changing, and others that are analytical designed to investigate current as well as historical data. Another challenge is duplicative customer information where a customer has multiple customer account records with dissimilar information in each record that cannot be readily corrected due to an inability to link together. This lack of data linkage is referred to as "siloed" data and is at odds with the optimal view of a customer's relationship, which is referred to as the "360-degree view" or "single source of truth." Proponents of the latter view are pushing for a change in the way data are collected, recommending the use of a Common Data Integration or CDI approach (Dyche, 2005; Dyche and Levy, 2006). Because developing analytical systems is a vastly different undertaking than building operational ones, understanding their proper creation and uses can mean the difference between successful business intelligence and a scrapped project (Dyche, 2005).

What Is Data Quality?

The seeming inability of linking diverse data sources coupled with the lack of ability to verify the correct customer information reduces the credibility of the data used in analysis and reporting and evokes strong calls for data quality solutions. Cleaning data and maintaining data quality is an expensive proposition, and the costs for such work are not always supported or viewed essential by management. Because of the large quantity of data, it is cost prohibitive and does not make good business sense to try to clean all the "dirty" data. Therefore, it makes more sense to isolate and prioritize critical business data points that require special data cleansing and maintenance support. Moreover, this has become even more necessary with the increase in privacy and customer data protection regulations, which has led to a tighter focus on a specific number of critical data points addressing business and compliance needs as a valuable business activity.

It seems more useful to consider data quality as a value proposition where quality data are valuable data. The value of the data is derived based on prioritized business needs where critical data elements are classified in terms of the value they contribute, including a consideration of their value from a compliance perspective, to the business (English, 1999). What constitutes a critical data element? For example, any information considered critical for the legal identification of a customer, particularly those mandated by law: birth date, full name, address, and social security number. Other examples include data used in business calculations critical to the business, risk ratings, credit scores, loyalty calculations, summary revenue, or potential future client value. It is important to remember that everyone in the company is responsible for the quality of the data used to run and support the business. Data quality is not only the natural outcome of a strong strategic data management program, but is also a core component of a client service program such as a call center, branch office, or relationship management interaction with a customer. Good data quality combined with systemic linkages between databases will increase the likelihood of establishing a consolidated view of the complete customer relationship.

Six Sigma for Direct Marketing

Establishing strong data management programs does not happen overnight, but there are plenty of successful programs out there that can be used to support direct marketing efforts (Fairfield, 2004). According to Fairfield, companies that have implemented Six Sigma initiatives have reaped benefits that include the enhanced awareness of customer needs and the integration of those needs into core processes, as well as ingraining a corporate culture of continuous improvement (Fairfield, 2004). The Six Sigma process focuses on a systematic approach to data quality, and the steps outlined to design or create a quality process have many direct applications to direct marketing (Pyzdek, 2003, p. 240). For example, the Six Sigma process focuses on the creation of an error-free business performance and has established a standard of 3.4 problems per million opportunities (Pyzdek, 2003, p. 240).

Adopting the principles of Six Sigma for Direct Marketing is primarily implemented through a commitment to delivering the best customer service and analysis to measure the outcome of those efforts. The Six Sigma approach incorporates a number of methodologies for managing and driving quality and process improvements, including one that would appear to have beneficial application to marketing analytics, namely, the Design for Six Sigma or DFSS. Designing and enhancing new processes or DMADV (define, measure, analyze, design, and verify) is probably the most applicable component of the DFSS methodology. Some of the documented benefits of this approach on direct marketing efforts include increasing marketing campaign response rates, reducing duplicate mailing addresses, and increasing the number of fully integrated campaign response records suitable for response analysis (Fairfield, 2004). Table 12.1 briefly summarizes the similarities between the Six Sigma DMADV approach and the data analytics process implemented in direct marketing (Scarisbrick-Hauser, 2006).

Data Latency

Answering the question of how many data are needed for analysis prompts concerns related to latency and costs of data. We define "real-time" data as data generated in large operational databases with the expectation of providing immediate turnaround in information. "Right-time" data are data available when the business management and customers expect them. Clickstream data are designed to enable measurement of the number and site of clicks on a Web site using cookies. Session data consists of providing a record of behavior across a Web site usually measured, analyzed and sold by third-party data brokers. Finally, historic data are vintage data that permit analysts and decision makers to view business performance over time.

Today, business decisions using data-driven intelligence are made in seconds, minutes, hours, weeks, months, quarters, and years. There is a cost-to-benefit ratio to be considered for each of these time-driven events. The shorter the time available to make decisions, the costlier the technology and data analysis required to enable those decisions. However, if the benefit of the transaction is dependent upon a timely turnaround in providing business service or in generating expected

Table 12.1
Six Sigma for Direct Marketing

Six Sigma DMADV	Data Analytics for Direct Marketing
Define • Goals of the design activity • Identify what is being designed • Why? • Test that goals are consistent with demands and enterprise strategy	Define • Objectives driving direct marketing team • Research questions of interest • Prioritization of research questions
Measure • Determine Critical to Stakeholder metrics • Translate customer requirements into project goals	Data • Establish sources of data for analysis • Collect data into centralized data set • Evaluate data quality and compliance with privacy
Analyze • Options available for meeting goals • Determine performance of similar best-in-class designs	Analysis • Analysis of data • Descriptive statistics • Hypothesis testing • Results interpretation • Deliver results to direct marketing teams
Design • New product, service, or process • Use predictive models, simulations, prototypes, pilot runs, and so forth to validate the design concept's effectiveness in meeting goals	Implement and test • Direct marketing campaign launched • Test and learn activities monitored • Output/Performance data collected for analysis
Validate/Verify • Design effectiveness in the real world	Confirm • Measure performance against expectations • Estimate Return on Equity (ROE) • Celebrate and measure successes • Confirm and address weaknesses

revenue, then the costs of the data are justified. The amount of data generated daily, particularly from Web commercial traffic, is more likely to be measured in millions of rows of data and, due to increasing regulatory and data-mining needs, requires storage in a database that is designed to service day-to-day operational needs and complex data-mining processes.

Finally, the business need to be competitive may require access to and the use of data that are not available in internal databases. Prospect lists, competitive intelligence data, data from business affiliates, or data brokers are purchased at regular intervals and merged with internal data to conduct customer profiling or identify acquisition opportunities suitable for inclusion in marketing campaigns or business initiative planning (Coremetrics, 2004; Syracuse, 2006b).

While it might not seem, from a marketing professional's perspective, that spending time identifying the appropriate data required to support data analysis is time well spent, rest assured that time spent on this activity will save countless hours looking for errors in the published results later on.

Now that we have agreed about the importance of identifying data requirements, we need to consider how to build an analytic database as opposed to one that just collects operational data. However, there is one more important piece of information needed to get started. Knowing what your objectives are and what is expected of the data in a customer database are critical information and are pivotal in guiding the establishment of an appropriate source of data for business analysis. Business and marketing professionals are responsible for the identification of the expected business outcomes and associated analytical needs. The nature and design of a database must be aligned with the overall business strategy and objectives.

The first step is actually to ask the business managers to identify their business process and analytical needs and how they intend to use the results. How do you do that? Start by identifying at least three important business concerns that remain unanswered today due to a lack of useful information. Then use these concerns as a starting point for the identification and location of data necessary to answer these important questions. First, what data do the business managers feel are currently available to answer those questions? Second, once this data source is located, the next step is to identify whether you will use all or some of the data points for analysis and reporting. Third, once you look at the data you need to evaluate the "noise" or quality of the data, particularly if you plan on merging data from different databases into one analytical database. Data may be missing, corrupted, nonexistent, or duplicated. Fourth, you then need to confirm whether you have the expertise available internally to assemble the database, conduct the analysis, and interpret the results. Finally, it is also important to ascertain whether your company has the appropriate data analysis tools, such as mainframe SAS, Microsoft Office Excel (with advanced analytics), and business intelligence tools such as Actuate, Cognos, or Business Objects to name a few. If this is your first data analysis adventure and you lack experienced resources and tools, you may find that you need to contract with a consulting company experienced in the creation of an analytical database.

Mining Data: Profiling, Analytics, and Prediction

The customer-centric approach uses analytics to identify specific customer information including the estimated lifetime value of the customer, preferences, and areas of differentiation for service management. Understanding a customer's channel preference, scoring customers according to certain criteria, or segmenting the customer base permits the company to differentiate the customer experience according to a customer's value or potential to the company. For example, some companies have used analytics to rate their customers in terms of profitability, preferred status, or as an opportunity for cross-selling activities. When customers contact the company and enter their account numbers, they are likely to be routed to a specialized staff person who will already have knowledge of their scores and associated marketing treatment, a fee waiver, a special discount, free shipping, and so on (Wasserman, 2000).

Analytics is the term commonly used in the business world to describe a variety of data analysis, reporting, and business intelligence activities. Analytics can be characterized by activities such as data mining, automated algorithms, decision analysis, statistical analysis, scorecards, and dashboards. Following is a brief definition of the terms used to describe data analysis today.

Data mining for direct marketing is an automated or systemized process of database inquiry used to explore, discover, understand, and predict quantifiable patterns of consumer behavior (Linoff and Berry, 2001). Data-mining processes data in large databases (millions of rows of customer data) containing records of customer transactional or purchase behavior and campaign performance analysis searching for patterns of behavior. These types of analysis are usually conducted using an especially designed programming code, such as SAS Enterprise Miner. The results enable direct marketers to develop marketing programs and strategies, test customized creative ideas, modify and implement campaigns across multiple channels, measure response results, and then refine future marketing programs. Today, one of the most common applications of data mining is credit scoring, that is, assigning every customer a credit-risk rating. This use of data mining has taken on a much higher public profile in the past two years as federal laws have mandated free access to one's FICO (Fair Isaac) score so that he or she can review the data for errors and therefore have the information corrected (Wasserman, 2000).

Large databases enable customer data to be processed into segments or clusters of customers who display similar attributes or characteristics. Using more sophisticated methodologies, for example, customer data, contained in large databases, can be processed and segmented using predefined automated business algorithms to identify likely candidates for targeted offers, up-sell, cross-sell, and specific treatment opportunities including waived fees or discounted rates (Pettit, 2005). Increasingly, data from commercial Web site activity has been analyzed using data-mining approaches with some success (Linoff and Berry, 2001; Martin, 2006).

Some of the challenges associated with the data-mining process include the length of time necessary to produce the analysis and lack of linkages with other data not necessarily available in the company or available in coded formats. Data-mining programs conducted on IBM DB2 databases sometimes result in long hours of processing linkages (known as "joins") across hundreds of data tables, on a monthly basis, to produce data extracts suitable for populating report spreadsheets using Microsoft Excel and are expensive to produce. Internal customer databases often have missing data through lack of data entry at the time of initial customer registration, a lack of historical data, or some other reason. In many cases, externally generated customer data (called third-party data) are purchased from data brokers and appended to the internal customer data to populate missing data and add data that enhances an understanding to the customer's characteristics. Third-party demographic data for retail customers are available from companies such as Acxiom Corporation, Experian, and Equifax, Inc. to name a few, while firmagraphic data for commercial customers are available from companies such as The Dun & Bradstreet Corporation, Experian, and Equifax on a daily basis. Companies like Acxiom, Ascential Software, and Meta Integration Technology, Inc. work with clients to convert data to a common platform that can be accessed by various business applications and programs (Krol, 2006a). However, quality is also an issue for third-party providers. For example, there may be less confidence in the quality or currency of the data contained in the third-party databases if they are updated quarterly while your private database is usually updated monthly (Syracuse, 2006b).

Appending third-party data to your internal database can be an expensive activity that needs to be balanced against the business initiative's expected return on investment. Companies interested in targeting prospects usually rent lists from public cooperative databases, but more and more they are moving toward customized private prospecting databases to serve their special population needs at a more costly fee. The companies that are more likely to use private databases are business-to-business (b-to-b) firms with a large retail presence or those in financial services and insurance (Syracuse, 2006a). According to Krol, marketers are under pressure to not only rent the standard integrated postal, e-mail, and phone lists, but are also increasingly requesting e-mail appending, the creation of customized databases and other services to save time and maintain business with one vendor. In response to these increasing demands, b-to-b list companies are creating integrated cross-channel lists tying them together for their clients. One of the companies, ALC, analyzes and tracks commercial e-mail identifying trends in the frequency of messaging, level of personalization, and kinds of promotions offered by a company. The information is summarized and sold as a monthly report for clients (Krol, 2006b).

Finally, data mining as a systematic activity parsing data from large databases lacks sensitivity to detect the value of creative ideas in a marketing campaign. Until recently, data analysis, such as data mining, focused on "hard" behavioral data related to product performance and purchase behavior. Little or no focus was spent on the characteristics of the customer. Data-mining activities do not easily lend themselves to an analysis of the more emotional or "soft" data associated with the customer's preferences, financial aspirations, perception of quality, or measures of customer satisfaction (Martin, 2006, Wasserman, 2000). However, as these factors become more and more important in targeting and segmenting customers, the need for blended (that is, hard and soft data) databases is becoming imperative.

Decision analysis, is an automated process that uses a variety of business rules, generated by predictive models programmed as part of a database structure or "decision engine" to customize the search for specific patterns of customer behavior. This results in a series of recommended marketing or business process activities, such as discounted offers, lower fees, or bundled product costs. These are then electronically transmitted to customer sales and service personnel during their interactions with a customer. The results of these recommended activities are also recorded and stored for future analysis of customer behavior. The difference between decision analysis and data mining is that decision analysis is conducted using knowledge already gleaned from data mining, which is combined with other information about expected customer behavior using statistical analysis and expected customer patterns of behavior. Decision analysis can be automatically triggered by a customer event such as a large savings withdrawal or deposit, a request for information, or a predetermined set of conditions programmed for a business offer using business rules that have been programmed in the decision-analysis engine. Decision analysis can be used with real-time, right-time, or static customer data, but its ultimate design is to provide timely data to enable positive customer experiences generating value for both the customer and the company (Morris, 2004).

The principles of mining large databases to identify patterns of recurring or consistent performance have been adopted to create business intelligence from commercial online transactions, Web transactions, and content analysis of customer-service call conversations. These same principles can also be applied to qualitative analysis of data, such as customer surveys in malls, analysis of frequent flyer mile usage, content of Web blogs, e-mails channel activity, club memberships, e-mail communications, and other channel information not captured electronically (Linoff & Berry, 2001).

Statistical analysis can be used for either large-scale data extractions from mainframe databases or statistical hypothesis testing using smaller samples of data. Available for use on mainframe or personal computer, statistical analysis works best using samples of large databases incorporating sampling methods, hypothesis testing, predictive modeling, and campaign response analysis. The statistical software is designed to not only work with small or large databases, but also has the power to consolidate and standardize data from various sources. For example, one of the challenges with consolidating data from different databases is the formats used to classify the data may be different; statistical software can reclassify these data including open-ended text data, behavioral data, or demographic data into one dataset suitable for analysis (Pettit, 2004).

Scorecards and dashboards are tools used to display results of performance over a given time period. A scorecard can also be considered as a summary high-level report card of how a given strategy, business initiative, or department performed with respect to expected outcomes or goals over a given period of time. While the data used in the scorecard are presented at the summary level, the mechanics involved to roll up the data to the summary level may involve months of database construction, analysis, and interpretation using the lowest level of raw data. The production of scorecard reports and the analysis of data necessary to populate these reports is best handled by any of the sophisticated business intelligence tools, such as MicroStrategy, Business Objects, or Cognos (Linoff & Berry, 2001; Eckerson, 2006).

A dashboard report, on the other hand, is a report that presents analysis related to the performance of specific indicators over a specific point in time. Results presented in dashboard reports are at a much more granular level of detail than those presented in scorecard reports. The data analysis required to create dashboard reports is best handled using sophisticated business intelligence tools such as MicroStrategy, Business Objects, or Cognos. One of the major advantages of utilizing scorecards or dashboards is the ease of presenting results in a standardized format as they relate to business goals over a certain period of time (Eckerson, 2006).

Analytics—Turning Numbers into Business Value

Over the past 20 years economies across the world have been evolving from the old marketing framework designed to support manufacturing industries to a new economy and marketing framework supporting information-driven industries. As a result of this evolution, marketing strategies focus less on standardization of the message, or the efficiency of the marketing campaign process, and more on aspects such as speed to market, personalization of the marketing message, customization of the marketing offer, and evidence of the return on investment of marketing dollars. The manufacturing-driven marketing model was driven by a product-oriented strategy, whereas the new approach focuses on a customer-centric, demand-driven marketing framework. The emphasis in the new marketing model is placed on achieving client value and creating a culture of client service. From a direct marketing perspective, continuous data analysis is now necessary to establish a variety of value propositions for use in marketing campaigns. Customer data are now analyzed and modeled to identify their respective positions within strategically chosen customer or business segments, their market segment value, or their individual predicted lifetime value over time. Using selected data points, analytics is conducted to identify opportunities to extend customer relationships or to differentiate service and for prospects, opportunities for acquiring profitable new customers. Cost-to-value calculations based on customer information are used to drive customized offers and treatments to targeted customers. Over time, as the richness of historical data matures in the analytical databases, there will be opportunities for life-cycle stage analysis designed to identify the optimal timing of offers to customers and households.

Perhaps the largest change brought about in direct marketing analysis has been the increase in Internet commerce. Doing business on the Internet requires customer-driven and, ultimately, one-to-one marketing. Once one can extract or access the data produced by the Internet, subsequent analysis can be conducted to identify likely target customers, ways to differentiate your customers by their likes, dislikes, needs, and potential value to you. Analysis may also provide you with insights as to how to customize your products, services, and messages (Peppers & Rogers, 2005). Last, but not least, companies today are more intent than ever in identifying and tracking marketing return on investment dollars, which is more of a journey than a series of isolated observations (Costello, 2006).

There are a number of tangible benefits that focused data analytics can bring to direct marketing. Let us consider three factors, intimacy, accuracy, and immediacy, and the role they play in successful direct marketing activities (Scarisbrick-Hauser, 2006).

Intimacy

An active and nurtured customer relationship is key to creating a customer-centric experience. Creating and maintaining this customer-intimate relationship require a consistent, accessible, and timely flow of data about this customer's preferences, behavior, perceived needs, beliefs, and attitudes that need to be located and maintained in an available, centralized location. The use of frequent shopper points leading to special awards, preferred member cards, private sales for preferred customers, special coupons or discounts generated due to someone's VIP shopper status, used by leading department stores such as Nordstrom or Macy's, are just some of the examples of marketing strategies designed to build a lasting valuable and intimate relationship with the customer. Customers are active participants in this intimate relationship throughout the year as they earn and choose to maintain the preferred status using the discounts and special services provided by the company. Relationship management like this surely increases the likelihood of your retention as a customer. And yet, the analytical demands of generating and maintaining timely data to support these customer intimacy activities increase exponentially.

Irrespective of size or annual sales, the company Web site represents the best opportunity for maintaining that emotional connection with the client. Delivering the salient marketing message containing relevant information to the customer in a timely manner depends upon the breadth and depth of actionable customer intelligence that a company can store and access in a timely manner. Analytical data, or the scientific side of marketing, is critical as a support to the context of the marketing message designed to maintain the emotional connection with the customer thereby enhancing customer intimacy. For example, Electronic Boutiques Inc., more commonly known as EB Games, holds about 2,000 retail outlets generating about $2 billion in annual sales. Marketing is expected to not only contribute to generating sales, but to focus on influencing the unaware consumers to increase their awareness of the brand. Customers who are aware visit the store and may complete a one-time purchase. The value of the customer begins, in EB Games' view, with the repeat purchase (Koulogeorge, 2006).

The use of automated marketing analyses conducted using business rule decision engines provides the structure and process to enable direct marketing teams to create, strengthen, and maintain our knowledge of and connection with our customers' consumer behaviors. Regular reinforcement of customer intimate marketing messages enables us to stay ahead or current with customers' changing purchase intentions or relationship changes. For example, Coremetrics, one of the leading Web analytics solution providers, has developed a Web technology analytics solution called LIVE (Lifetime Individual Visitor Experience) designed to evaluate and measure the marketing return on investment delivered by each visitor's activity on the Web site and other metrics designed to test, in real time, responses to page design, creatives, and promotions (Coremetrics, 2004).

Accuracy

The quality of customer information, meaning the timeliness, correctness, and completeness of the data, impacts our ability to deploy successful marketing campaigns. The state of quality means more than having the accurate name and addresses of customers; it involves adding additional customer information as it becomes available, continually monitoring the data for errors or missing data, and updating the information in every company location. A lack of linkage of the critical analytical customer data will impact confidence in the value of the data.

It is important to keep the issue of data quality in perspective as it is neither possible nor cost-justifiable to clean up all the company's data. Maintaining quality data entails regular checking and data correction. Efforts to maintain data quality should be part of a proactive strategic process in response to requests for data to support company activities including marketing analysis. For example, it is well known that direct marketing mailings are returned or lie somewhere undelivered due to errors in mailing lists. Do you take the time, or do you think it is too expensive, to assess and fix the errors associated in the data used in your direct marketing practices, fixing the source of the problem? Do you have a continuous monitoring program assessing your data quality before you use the data as a driver of direct marketing decisions? A company needs to review and decide its strategic direction regarding data quality. The value of your relationship with the customer increases when you establish a culture of quality around the collection, storage, modification, and maintenance of your customer information (Scarisbrick-Hauser, 2006).

Immediacy

"Right-time" availability of quality customer information means that the sales force is enabled to use or document the most accurate timely customer information, retail or commercial, based on an understanding of its clients' needs, preferences, and lifestyles, to create an attractive customer offer. In some cases, companies seek to create a sense of immediacy associated with their products to provide a customized customer experience and also to generate as much market share away from competitors as possible. I am sure that you have noticed the hundreds of e-mail sale notifications that wait for you in your mailbox. The only drawback is that these sales are online sales and have very short-term windows of opportunity. In addition, have you ever received multiple offers from a credit card company with varying interest rates offered inside with short time frames for accepting the offer? Careful planning and data mining go into the testing of various marketing activities, targeting programs and the timing of the sales using historical data from prior months, quarters, years, or sales events. In addition, test results from ongoing marketing programs provide timely information to proceed or change marketing programs to achieve goals (Krol, 2006b).

Thinking about your marketing goals and objectives, the results of the last campaign you deployed, how successful were you in placing timely offers into the marketplace? Are you well positioned with marketing intelligence to respond to customer requests for service? As has been mentioned previously, it takes time to find the relevant customer data, prepare the database for analysis, and analyze and prepare findings to distribute to the business managers. The faster you can get a well-planned direct marketing offer into the marketplace, the greater the likelihood of increasing revenue and customer base; a well-prepared customer information process will increase the likelihood of faster time to market.

However, achieving immediacy and maintaining a profitable bottom line is not as easy as it sounds. Netflix, Inc., a video rental mail service company, has successfully signed up millions of customers who, through their rental patterns, provide the company with marketing tracking and analysis data. Netflix uses a formula to identify the most likely rental patterns that will keep current customers satisfied and also generate new customers. Customers pay a flat fee of $17.99 per month, giving them unlimited access to as many videos as they want a month. Customers return the DVD in a postage-paid envelope to the company and then receive the next choice from their account's wish list. Each customer's rental usage patterns are analyzed and service to customers is differentiated accordingly. Some customers noticed that, as they began to order larger numbers of videos per month, their shipments started to experience longer shipping delays, longer than the one-day delivery promise in their membership contract. Netflix's market analysis identified a class of users, heavy renters, who would rent somewhere around 18–20 DVDs a month. From Netflix's perspective, more profit would be made from customers renting 4–5 DVDs per month. Customers renting more DVDs were diluting the estimated profit margin. A class action lawsuit was taken out by angry heavy renters against the company for use of a "throttling" or fairness algorithm. Four months after the announcement of the lawsuit, the company issued a statement indicating that priority shipping was given to those renters who ordered the least number of DVDs per month. Customers, specifically heavy renters, were warned that they would be likely to face shipping delays and would be unlikely to immediately receive their top DVD choices. Without Netflix acknowledging any wrongdoing, the case was settled out of court, appealed, and subsequently resettled with an award of $2 million to the plaintiffs (Associated Press, 2006).

DATA STRATEGIES—DATA ANALYSIS APPROACHES

Once the need for analytics has been identified, there are a series of standard steps for conducting analysis that are reviewed briefly here. These steps include identification of high-level business requirements, data requirements and validation, data management or database construction, data analysis, results publishing, reporting and presentation, analytics debriefing, and creating performance metrics or dashboards. [Further detailed descriptions of how to conduct data analysis are available in the Berry and Linoff text *Data Mining Techniques: For Marketing, Sales, and Customer Support* (2004), and a recommended text for Web analytics is *Mining the Web: Transforming Customer Data into Customer Value* (Linoff and Berry, 2001).]

Translating Business Requirements into Data

First, we need a sound understanding of the overall objective of the business initiative. What are the business questions that need to be answered through data analysis? There needs to be clarity regarding the expected outcomes and uses of the results. Understanding the business strategy will enable a better focus on the analytic activities, increasing the likelihood of using the correct data points to conduct the analysis. These types of analyses go beyond the creation of the usual customer demographic profiles produced daily in companies focusing more on answering identifying patterns of customer behavior, assessing their attitudes, and identifying their demographics with a view to identifying segments of customers with similar characteristics, purchasing power, value, and opportunity or niches of customers requiring customized attention. Here are some examples of questions ranging from simple basic questions to complicated questions requiring years of analysis. Sometimes we find that we have not spent the time to ask and answer the most basic questions about our marketing performance or the customers targeted by marketing campaigns:

- What are the demographics of the customers reached by your last campaign?
- Have any of your customers received more than five campaigns in the past year?
- How many customers have you lost in six months? two years? five years?
- How many customers have purchased more than one product from you?
- Which channel do your customers use?
- What were the campaign results in dollars earned on your last campaign?
- How long have your customers owned their businesses?

Once you have identified your objectives, prioritized the list of objectives, or aligned objectives with overall company goals, you are ready to proceed with database construction and analysis (Pettit, 2004; Scarisbrick-Hauser, 2005).

Data Management—An Analytical Database

Today, it is not a question of finding data to construct a database (many would say there is too much data in our systems), it is finding the right data. One of the main problems is that the data may not be accessible in a format ready to use for analysis and decision making by direct marketing teams. In the past ten years, there have been major improvements in the consolidation of data into single locations through the development of data warehouses designed to store large amounts of customer data and the increasing demand, by legal entities, to store historical data for future review. Prior to the advent of the Internet, a macro level analysis of large internal company customer databases, parsing and searching for general patterns of customer behavior related to product purchases, sustained large company direct marketing activities for years. Usually the searches produced large lists of customers' names and addresses listed by the products currently held and potential new products to be used in outbound telemarketing or mail campaigns. With the relative low cost of Internet advertising, today's data mining focuses on a more micro level analysis, designed to provide customized information about targeted specific groups or segments with identifiable needs that may or may not fit the target market profile.

The main objective in data analytics is to organize, analyze, and publish the most valuable data about your customers or prospects that seem to share the same characteristics as your most profitable customers. Whether looking at retail or commercial customer data, you are interested in learning more about your clients, their needs, past purchase behaviors, demographics, attitudes, preferences, and beliefs with a view to better understanding your target market audience (Parr-Rudd, 2001; Pettit, 2005; Scarisbrick-Hauser, 2006).

Smaller to mid-sized companies do not need large data warehouses and can conduct their data-mining activities using small servers or databases populated with a smaller collection of data to meet their needs. Some smaller companies are setting up "data co-ops" to load their data, paying a fee for shared access to purchased data such as demographic customer data or informatics, business demographic data. Smaller companies can purchase Web site traffic information from Web advertisers and create lead lists from various opt-in programs offered by Web site browsers today (Syracuse, 2006a).

Is there a readily available data set or database for your use today to start analysis? If yes, all you will need to do is verify the sources of data to conduct your analysis and add the other data necessary to meet the needs of the analysis. There is a tendency to use data input fields or variables representing customer behavior, attitudes, and demographics for analysis and not to remember the additional data fields necessary to create reports of business performance, known as output data fields, variables, or performance data fields. Examples of input data fields you might be interested in adding to your database are sales volume, SIC (standard industrial classification) code, gender, occupation, number of employees, number of transactions, volume of spending on products, product suites, subscriptions, memberships, social activities, age group, social profile, and transaction dates. Examples of output data fields are purchase data, contact history information, application date, and other data indicating performance measures (Scarisbrick-Hauser, 2006). It is also important to remember and plan to include soft data in your database. For example, attitudinal, preference, and perceptual data cannot easily be gathered by technology; data are usually produced using marketing research techniques such as survey research using random samples of customers (Pettit, 2005). If you find that you need to build a database, create a centralized inventory of required data from internal and external sources. Design the database to accept future new data fields for information, as it develops, in this centralized area.

Again, as mentioned previously, one important component to consider when building a database is the quality of the "noise level" of the data. Data quality is a high-profile topic today, particularly when associated with customer information. Data quality is usually assessed by a series of measures such as percentage of populated data, percentage of valid data, and percentage of consistency by data field of interest. Privacy regulations such as the GLBA, or Graham Leech Bliley Act, have a zero tolerance for data quality errors in specific data fields associated with name, address, and Social Security number. More recently, the Patriot Act and anti-money-laundering regulations require full population and the highest level of data quality for specific data points in both retail and commercial data. The quality of the data fields intended for inclusion in data analysis may need to be cleaned up prior to analysis, or you might want to think about removing these fields from your analytical studies so as to not bias the research findings. Issues with factors such as availability of data, data quality, and database construction can add unanticipated delays to your analytic timeline, and you may need to add additional time or streamline your analytical activities to meet direct marketing timelines.

Your database should be designed to support a reporting tool such as SAS or SPSS, or Microsoft Excel, which will allow you to not only analyze the data quickly, but also produce graphical representations of the analysis ready for use in preliminary reports (Scarisbrick-Hauser, 2006). It has been noted that there still is a lag on the part of some companies to adopt technologies, for example, business intelligence architecture and tools for analyzing data to produce actionable intelligence (Pettit, 2004).

Data Analysis

Let us review some of the key activities associated with data analysis. Usually, you create high-level customer demographic profiles to create a preliminary detailed picture of each and every client, retail or commercial, summarizing the data. These profiles may or may not contain historical detail, which adds another layer of information to the results of your analysis. Profiles also provide an early warning alert of data quality issues before you move into more sophisticated analyses. Once profiles have been validated you usually proceed with additional analysis involving segmentation analysis, multivariate analysis, regression modeling, and hypothesis testing, using statistical analysis techniques to test the scenarios or business research questions posed by the business or direct marketing team. [Further detailed descriptions of how to conduct data analysis are available in the Parr-Rudd text *Data Mining Cookbook: Modeling Data for Marketing, Risk, and Customer Relationship Management* (2001)].

Ideally, marketing campaigns should include a number of test and control groups designed to provide useful data that can be used for response differentiation analysis. However, statistically valid "test and learn" activities are not easy to implement, particularly for small companies. Fortunately, small business Web sites are continuing to discuss ways and means of incorporating the best practice of test and learn with small sample sizes into small business direct marketing analysis, so this practice should increase over the next few years.

The next question is who will do this type of analysis for you? Marketing personnel are not usually trained to do these kinds of analyses, and many have not considered analytics as part of a marketing department until now. While a number of universities and corporate executive colleges are beginning to provide marketing courses in analytics, there is a noticeable lag in the availability of qualified personnel. The increase in demand for advanced marketing analytics, including e-commerce analytical skills, has highlighted a lag in skill sets among current marketing staffs. Major companies spend millions of dollars funding analytic consultant firms to cover their needs as they recruit internal resources to support their analytic needs. Consider asking your local business school for assistance via internships or consulting to get your data analytics process up and running. Students really appreciate real-life problems to work on, and you gain by having the benefit of their analytical skills; consultants provide doctoral-level contract workers and are very willing to engage in a modest amount of knowledge transfer to newly hired internal teams. Using an interim resource solution provides you time to decide the breadth and depth of analytical skills you require to support your direct marketing programs; you may decide to create a small group in-house to do the analysis or retain consulting organizations on an as-needed basis.

Report Publishing and Presentation

Results of data analysis are usually reviewed and discussed internally by the analytics team to ensure that the analysis has answered the questions posed by the marketing team and business managers. Once the results have been verified and are ready for review by the business, a summary report or presentation outlining the business questions, the steps of the analytic process, the results, and the interpretation are created. These reports usually include graphical summary representations of the data accompanied by appendices of raw data results for review. Be prepared for requests for additional analysis, and ensure that the analytical database and results are stored in a safe storage area for review and validation later.

Using Test and Learn Methodologies to Test Models

Once the direct marketing teams have reviewed the analytical results, they will decide how to incorporate the information into their programs and implement direct marketing campaigns. Data analysis can play a role in assessing the success of these programs through the use of "test cells" and control groups that receive differentiated treatments from the direct marketing campaign. There may also be those who decide to purchase the product for other reasons outside of the campaign, or "indirect" conversions.

In terms of marketing on the Internet, continual data mining is a critical factor for companies to participate in the competitive environment. Quickly understanding and adapting to shifts in the marketplace requires a commitment to test and learn methodologies. Data mining on the Web has already been engaged to administer a test treatment (offer) to a segment of customers generating analytical performance data in real time, assessing the success or failure of the test and establishing enhancements to generate improved performance, new revenue generating marketing offers all within a short period of time (Wasserman, 2000).

JP Morgan Chase has taken the organizational step establishing a culture encouraging the intelligent use of the test and learn model where failures do not have a negative personal impact on the staff. Testing and taking risk are encouraged as a means to identify innovative ways to solve problems (See, 2006). In terms of marketing on the Internet, continual data mining is a critical factor for companies to participate in the competitive environment. Quickly understanding and adapting to shifts in the marketplace requires a commitment to test and learn. Data mining on the Web has already been engaged to administer a test treatment (offer) to a segment of customers generating analytical performance data in real time assessing the success or failure of the test and establishing enhancements to generate improved performance all within a short period of time (Wasserman, 2000).

Direct Marketing Performance Testing

Following the implementation of the marketing campaign, how do you know what worked or did not work? Additional analytics to evaluate the success or failure of the campaign results are usually conducted during the campaign, at the end, and at regular intervals following the end of the campaign. The results are compared against expected results estimated by the precampaign analysis. Celebrate and analyze the winners and analyze the losers; there is always a better way to improve our direct marketing approaches.

For example, The Home Depot, Inc. is a lumber and hardware company with 1,911 do-it-yourself stores across the United States, Canada, and Mexico and approximately $73 billion in annual sales. The corporate offices receive daily sales data from the stores that are used to track sales performance on a daily basis and model the potential lift associated with changes or incremental investment in the marketing mix. Their analytics also take external risk factors, weather, world events or disasters, and competition pricing into account in the analytical modeling activities. Marketing analyses include continual assessment and evaluation of consumer trends, including lifestyle and demographic shifts in different geographies.

Sales activities are continually measured using metrics aligned with company strategic goals. Not only does Home Depot continually monitor sales and market performance, including market share, competitive activity, and brand strength, but also customer satisfaction with the shopping experience, measuring product depth, pricing, and service levels (Costello, 2006).

Analysis Complete: Follow the Information-Rich Road

In-depth customer analytics, which run the gamut from customer demographic profiling to creating customized marketing offers for current customers or potentially quality prospects, are critical tools for any direct marketing professional irrespective of company size. Armed with timely business intelligence, the direct marketing professional is better positioned to not only increase knowledge and understanding of the customer relationship, but also prepare to be responsive to changes in the market and customer preferences. Guided by a business strategy that prioritizes the degree of customer service offered, the level of customer value expected in terms of revenue and customer service, and the depth of product offerings the direct marketing professional will be better prepared to establish a data analytics process to support the corporate strategic direction.

Establishing a quality analytics process means much more than setting up a team of analysts or highly qualified doctoral-level researchers in an isolated area to produce reporting databases full of numbers and graphs. The production of the results of analysis is the second to last step in the analytic process and does not provide as much value to the business manager as the last step, which is the interpretation of the results within the context of the business question of interest or business initiative. Training your staff to interpret the results of analytics will be well worth the investment and will add value to the direct marketing role in the strategic business activities.

It should be noted that many marketing organizations are struggling to recruit the necessary skills to meet the changing needs to support an analytics group. A study of 120 senior marketing professionals in the United States and the United Kingdom was conducted in June 2006 to identify skills needed to perform the job, skills that have become critical over the past two years, and future skills that are needed to improve marketing activities. One of the most interesting findings to emerge was that 86 percent of the respondents indicated that their decision making has become more reliant on analysis over the previous two years. Half of those interviewed indicated that they felt underqualified to handle their evolving job requirements given the shift toward a more quantitative marketing environment. Furthermore, 86 percent of the respondents indicated that recruiting analytic skill sets was difficult, and 71 percent stated that opportunities for training and educational programs were not aligned with the urgent need to train their employees (American Management Association, 2006).

Analytics is a continual process of seeking new niches of intelligence that can be leveraged into business opportunities or experimenting with different test groupings in campaigns. Analytics will be only as good as the data available for use, so it is important to establish a culture of capturing quality data and maintaining the quality of that data going forward. Recognizing that marketing departments experience frequent staff turnover and the associated risk to retaining analytical knowledge, companies are beginning to establish learning groups within their marketing departments designed to retain that knowledge in a systematic way (See, 2006). It should be clear by now that one of the strongest indicators of business value is through the creation of fact-based direct marketing strategies, something that is not that difficult from planning and discipline.

Adoption of a test and learn strategy in analytics is a journey of continuous improvement and is adopted slowly due to some concerns about perceived failure and loss of reputation for the department. Team leaders have a responsibility to encourage and support this evolving process because it is important to measure factually the benefits of the chosen analytical framework for a marketing campaign and make adjustments based on market-based facts. Gathering metrics against a chosen strategy is a critical part of the direct marketing process, and such measurements are evaluated over time as opposed to traditional episodic analysis of marketing campaigns. Debriefing and understanding successes and failures from a factual basis provide useful information that can be leveraged in future campaigns. Lack of management support for initial failures or less than expected outcomes driven by analytic processes will impact credibility of both the analytics and the employees.

SUMMARY

In closing, let us review the main points of this chapter. First, conducting data analysis to support direct marketing is meaningless unless it is grounded within the context of a business strategy. Data analytic strategies are more than tactical approaches to discovering customer opportunities; they are part of a corporate cultural commitment to a fact-based sales and performance management strategy. As the economy has adopted an information-driven marketing framework, analytics have matured from a prior dependence on basic information gleaned from customer profiles to the timely processing of a customer's every transaction enabling faster deployment of customized marketing messages to current customers or offers to likely prospects. Being prepared to leverage the value of the available data means that a greater understanding of how these company data can be used to generate value from direct marketing is required by all direct marketing professionals today. Also, a better understanding of the potential value that can be generated leveraging customer information, including a tighter targeting of likely successful prospects, will contribute to enhanced results of direct marketing tactics. Analysis of customer data for direct marketing is much more than a repetitive report of their transactional or behavioral patterns. Customer analytics are enhanced by the combined analysis of behavioral, attitudinal, and demographic client data, and the more comprehensive a picture we can build of a customer's relationship with the company, his or her hopes, aspirations, and lifestyle, the higher the likelihood that we will successfully identify potential new opportunities as new customers. Establishing optimal data strategies to support direct marketing is an art and a science that require good teamwork and a commitment to capturing and maintaining quality customer data in internal databases. Data cleaning is not a substitute for sound data capture and data management practices.

The customer-centric approach has impacted the perception of a marketing department's business value in generating new business or return on investment. Marketing departments, in the product-driven marketplace, were long regarded as support areas, but now have come under close scrutiny as to their role and contribution to the company's bottom line. Proponents of the customer-centric approach are more likely to regard marketing as the medium for introducing prospects into the sales management process for the sales force to manage, placing a greater expectation on the marketing group to produce quality profitable prospects. Marketing teams have always stood at the forefront of merging business and technical needs into innovative marketing solutions. With work to reengineer the marketing skill encompassing a higher level of analytic skill, there is an opportunity for marketing teams to justify their business value.

REFERENCES

American Management Association, 2006. *Marketing Skills Lag behind Organizational Needs.* Marketing Matters Newsletter. Retrieved on September 13, 2006, from http://www.marketingpower.com/content-printer-friendly.php?&Item_ID=143133.

Associated Press. 2006. *Frequent Netflix Renters Sent to Back of Line: The More You Use, the Slower the Service, Some Customers Realize.* Retrieved on February 13, 2006, from http://www.msnbc.msn.com/id/11262292/.

Berry, Michael J.A., and Gordon Linoff. 1997. *Data Mining Techniques: For Marketing, Sales, and Customer Support.* 1st ed. New York. Wiley Press.

Berry, Michael J.A., and Gordon Linoff. 2004. *Data Mining Techniques: For Marketing, Sales, and Customer Support.* 2nd ed. New York. Wiley Press.

Coremetrics. 2004. *Coremetrics Extends Leading Web Analytics Platform to Address High-Value Marketing and Site Design Challenges.* Retrieved on September 17, 2006, from http://www.coremetrics.com/news/media/2004/pr04_02_24_extends.html.

Costello, John. 2006. Top Marketers Share Perspectives on Marketing Measurement. Retrieved on April 19, 2007, from http://www.marketingnpv.com/article.asp?id=1146&key=%233xVwdvSWLWn.

Dyche, Jill. 2005. *Making the Case for CDI.* DM Direct Special Report, June 16, 2005. Retrieved on August 28, from http://www.dmreview.com/editorial/dmreview/print_action.cfm?articleId=1030311.

Dyche, Jill, and Evan Levy. 2006. *Customer Data Integration: Reaching a Single Source of Truth.* Wiley Publishers. New Jersey.

Eckerson, Wayne W. 2006. *Performance Dashboards.* DMReview. June 2006.

English, Larry P. 1999. *Improving Data Warehouse and Business Information Quality.* New York. Wiley Press.

Fairfield, Craig. 2004. *Bringing Six Sigma to Customer-Facing Business Processes*. Retrieved on March 25, 2006, from http://www.destinationcrm.com/articles/?ArticleID=4054.

Koulogeorge, Paul. 2006. Top Marketers Share Perspectives on Marketing Measurement. Retrieved on April 19, 2007, from http://www.marketingnpv.com/article.asp?id=1146&key=%233xVwdvSWLWn.

Krol, Carol, 2006a. *Database Integration Key to Marketing Strategy*. Retrieved on March 10, 2006, from http://www.btobonline.com/printwindow.cms?articleId=10935.

Krol, Carol. 2006b. *Tying It All Together: Companies Help Clients Maximize List Impact with Integrated Tools*. Retrieved on March 10, 2006, from http://www.btobonline.com/printwindow.cms?articleId=27067.

Linoff, Gordon S., and Michael J. Berry. 2001. *Mining the Web: Transforming Customer Data into Customer Value*. New York. Wiley Press.

Martin, Justin. 2006. *Get it Right with Google: How Smart Entrepreneurs are Dealing with the Online Goliath That Can Make a Small Business—Or Break It*. Retrieved on September 22, 2006, from http://www/cnnmoney.com.printthis.clickability.com/pt/cpt?action=cpt&title=Get+right+with+-+September

Murphy, Maureen D. 2006. *Creatively Effective Direct-Mail Programs—Never Too Small to Test*. Retrieved on March 5, 2006, from http://www.smallbusinessresources.com/murphy.html.

Parr-Rud, Olivia. 2001. *Data Mining Cookbook: Modeling Data for Marketing, Risk and Customer Relationship Management*. Wiley Publishers. New Jersey.

Peppers, Don, and Martha Rogers. 2005. *Return on Customer: A Revolutionary Way to Measure and Strengthen Your Business*. New York. Currency Doubleday.

Pettit, Raymond. 2004. *The Importance of Marketing Analytics*. The Cutter Consortium. Retrieved on September 17, 2006, from http://www.Cutter.com/research/2004/edge040831.html.

Pettit, Raymond. 2005. *The Evolution of Marketing Analytics*. Retrieved on September 17, 2006, from http://www.b-eye-network.com/view/856.

Pyzdek, Thomas. 2003. *The Six Sigma Handbook*. New York. McGraw-Hill.

Scarisbrick-Hauser, AnneMarie, "Chapter 5: Data Mining and Profiling: The Right Information" in Andrew Thomas, et al. (editor), *Direct Marketing in Action: Cutting Edge Strategies for Finding and Keeping the Best Customers*. Connecticut: Praeger Publishing, 2006. Pp. 47–61.

See, Ed. 2006. *Reinventing the Marketing Organization: Five Critical Components*. Retrieved on September 17, 2005, from http://www.chiefmarketer.com/marketing_organization_01272006/index.html.

Syracuse, Amy. 2006a. *Co-op Databases Offer Savings, Services for Those Willing to Share*. Retrieved on March 10, 2006, from http://www.btobonline.com/printwindow.cms?articleId=27054&pageType=article&logopath.

Syracuse, Amy. 2006b. *Specific Needs Spur Demand for Private Databases*. B@B *Online Magazine for Marketing Strategists*. Retrieved on March 10, 2006, from http://www.btobonline.com/article.cms?articleId=27088.

Wasserman, Miriam. 2000. Regional Review: Mining Data. Retrieved on April 19, 2007, from http://www.bos.frb.org/economic/nerr/rr2000/q3/mining.htm.

Part III

IMPORTANT ISSUES IN THE FUTURE OF DIRECT MARKETING

CHAPTER 13

DOING THE RIGHT THING: ETHICS AND REGULATIONS IN DIRECT MARKETING

Steve Brubaker and Bruce D. Keillor

The terms "ethics" and "direct marketing" have come to be viewed by many people as being diametrically opposed. In the context of the U.S. business environment as a whole, it is not difficult to see how the public might look at any business or business activity with a skeptical, even cynical, perspective. Furthermore, the business community does not necessarily disagree with this viewpoint as shown by a survey of U.S. businesses, conducted by Touche & Ross, which concluded that a large proportion of the ethical problems in business that have been reported in the media have not been exaggerated. Unfortunately, due largely in part to its fundamental goal of establishing a direct interaction with consumers, direct marketing is a natural target.

A good case in point is Ryan A. Swanberg. For the past four years or so, Swanberg has made his living from suing telemarketers and debt collectors that in any way violate laws like the Telephone Consumer Protection Act of 1991, either inadvertently or on purpose. By late 2001, Swanberg, a high school dropout, owed over $25,000 on about ten separate credit cards, and he began getting calls from debt collectors. One was so abusive he thought he might have a legal case against the caller. He did, and won, but the settlement was nowhere near what he had been promised by his attorney. Recognizing that he might come upon other such opportunities, he decided to teach himself about the law. Eventually realizing the economic potential of turning his newfound talents on the telemarketing business, he made that a target. His sights were so keenly trained on telemarketing that he even installed additional phone lines to boost the volume of incoming calls, and he went out of his way to get on as many databases as possible.

Most of his cases are settled out of court, and he does not discuss specifics because of confidentiality agreements. Representing himself, he claims to have settled over 60 cases with debt collectors and more than 200 with telemarketers, with the average settlement between $1,500 and $2,000. Swanberg makes no distinctions between the big players and the little mom-and-pop operations in his efforts, reasoning that if they break the law, they break the law. But he does say he has accepted things like vacations, cell phone service, and carpet replacements as settlements in some cases. At the time of this writing, Swanberg reportedly was involved in 20 to 30 lawsuits and multiple settlements and had litigated over 300 cases representing himself.

The question then becomes, how did this happen? From a purely objective view, one could reasonably conclude that, given its objective of creating a one-to-one relationship with customers, direct marketing should have been at the vanguard of introducing and enforcing ethical business practices. Yet the record shows that, as is the case in many business activities, a short-term focus has creating a long-term problem. In the case of direct marketing, it has suffered from a bad reputation almost from the beginning.

Indirectly, at least some of this negativity toward direct marketing can be attributed to a disconnect between firms using direct marketing tools and their customers. Although direct marketers strive to establish and maintain close connections with customers, in practice it can be a very difficult thing to manage—resulting in a gap in expectations between the company and those it serves. At the same time, it would be naïve, perhaps even disingenuous, to suggest that the firms themselves were not in large part to blame.

A preoccupation with immediate revenue production, coupled with the tempting effectiveness of unethical practices, has resulted in direct marketing often being a convenient target in any discussion of ethics and business. Examples of maximizing short-term opportunities at the expense of producing long-term threats are not hard to identify. Practices such as providing free or heavily discounted products and then adding on significant hidden fees (for example, "shipping and handling"), fake or misleading testimonials, and the misrepresentation of products and services have contributed to the creation of a business environment where 60 percent of Americans are listed in the National Do Not Call Registry, over one-third employ pop-up blockers (with the number expected to rise significantly over time), and 80 percent report they generally do not trust most e-mail advertisements. If not addressed promptly, these threats to direct marketers will only increase. The key to solving the problem lies in understanding what the term "ethics in business" means, creating the mechanisms that foster ethical business practices, and then monitoring these mechanisms over time. It is a daunting task, but one which cannot be avoided.

ETHICS IN BUSINESS: WHAT DOES IT REALLY MEAN?

Defining "ethics" in business in general, and in direct marketing in particular, is a real challenge and has been for a number of years. From a theoretical stand-point, creating such a definition is relatively straightforward. The problem arises when it comes time to put the definition into practice. What fits nicely into an academic framework is often either so vague, making it unusable, or so idealistic it is unrealistic. Layer in the problem of reconciling "legal" behavior with "ethical" behavior and it is not difficult to see why many firms have trouble creating a functioning ethical culture.

It is generally accepted that a good working definition for "business ethics" would incorporate the means by which a firm integrates basic core values (for example, honesty, trust, respect, fairness, and so forth) into its policies, practices, and decision making. Further, the definition would recognize the importance of complying with legal standards as well as adherence to internal rules and regulations. Although the exact wording may differ, a practical definition of business ethics prominently features two key components.

First, it includes specific core values that will enhance the company's ability to establish *and* maintain long-term relationships with the important players in the marketplace—customers being at the top of the list. From a purely pragmatic point of view, the underlying motivation for acting in an ethical, socially responsible manner is largely irrelevant. Whether that motivation is an explicit recognition that being ethical is the "right" thing to do, or it is the result of more selfish motives, the benefits of attracting and retaining customers outstrips the costs associated with constantly having to attract new customers—which some have estimated costs as much as ten times more than keeping existing ones.

Second, the practical definition must recognize the clear distinction between ethical and legal. It is critical for both firms and individual employees to be aware that legal boundaries are, at best, the minimum baseline for establishing ethical guidelines. In short, while business behavior that is illegal is typically accepted as being unethical, not everything that is technically legal is always ethical. It is easy to demonstrate that blatantly false advertising statements are illegal, and therefore unethical, but claims that exaggerate or can be easily misinterpreted are much more difficult to judge—especially if legal standards are the only evaluative criteria.

ETHICS AND DIRECT MARKETING

The primary argument for direct marketing is based on the mutual benefits that are received by both the marketer and the consumer. On the one hand, the firm benefits by not wasting scarce resources on marketing to disinterested individuals or firms. Traditional marketing either disperses time, effort, and money toward people who are not interested in purchasing the product, or it expends resources on not accurately identifying the appropriate target market. This inefficiency leads to higher prices and/or lower shareholder value. At the same time, the customer benefits by receiving less clutter (that is, junk mail, pop-up ads, and unwanted phone solicitations) in favor of marketing approaches based on the potential customer's income, interests, past purchases, and other relevant information. Direct marketing therefore increases efficiency thereby serving the interests of both the producer and the consumer.

The argument against direct marketing is that it is essentially an intrusion on an individual's privacy. Even if overall economic gains result from appropriately targeted marketing efforts, the cost is a loss of privacy to the extent that either (1) an individual is observed without knowing that he or she is being watched (for example, cookies functioning without a computer user's knowledge or permission) or (2) an individual changes his or her behavior because of the knowledge that he or she is being observed. For example, a person might not visit a particular Web site if she realizes that tracking software will be automatically downloaded onto her personal computer. In either case, the violation of privacy that occurs can outweigh the utilitarian value of the economic exchange that may result from direct marketing.

It is important to note that people who respond favorably to direct marketing efforts are also more likely to be concerned about how firms use personal information. They tend to believe that companies should limit the amount of information collected from customers and should not provide customer lists to other firms or organizations without prior notice. The direct marketer is therefore constrained by the ethical imperative to respect the privacy of potential customers. By observing respect for privacy as a guiding principle, firms can enjoy the economic and efficiency benefits of direct marketing while maintaining their moral, ethical, and legal responsibilities.

CREATING AN ETHICAL BUSINESS ENVIRONMENT

The question now turns to how such a business climate can be created. In most cases the answer comes down to one of three solutions: a perfectly competitive market, more official regulation, or increased self-regulation by businesses themselves. In a perfect world a purely competitive market would be the answer. Unfortunately, this ideal option of a perfectly stable, self-regulating economy where corporations are forced to act ethically in order to obtain and hold market share is little more than fantasy.

The reality is that, particularly when it comes to direct marketing, legislation and government regulations have played a prominent role in creating the landscape for ethical business practices. These have been the result of the underlying assumption that businesses cannot be relied upon, existing internal ethical codes notwithstanding, to self-regulate. Official regulations, covering the various aspects of direct marketing, extend back to the 1970s and include customer requested removal from direct mail lists (circa 1970); the Federal Communications Commission (FCC) Telephone Consumer Protection Act (1991); Gramm-Leach-Bliley Act (1999) covering consumer financial privacy; the Telemarketing Sales Rule (2002); the National Do Not Call Registry (2003); and the CAN-SPAM Act (2003), with additional legislation and regulations being considered that would impact virtually all areas of direct marketing. Recognizing that a continued perception of unethical practices being tied directly to direct marketing activities will result only in ever-stricter rules of engagement in the marketplace, the industry as a whole has taken steps in recent years to address this potential threat.

At the forefront of many of the efforts to improve self-regulation has been the Direct Marketing Association (DMA), the oldest and largest organization in the direct marketing industry. In the past few years, the DMA has worked with the government in crafting anti-spam legislation (2002), developing plans to prevent telemarketers from targeting cell phones (2002), partnering with the American Association of Advertising Agencies and the Association of National Advertisers, Inc. to release guidelines for e-mail advertising (2003), and working with federal law enforcement officials to stop illegal or unwanted spam (2003). According to the DMA, the following principles should apply to any firm or individual involved in direct marketing in their interactions with both current and prospective customers, suppliers, and other businesses. These principles form the foundation for the DMA's *Guidelines for Ethical Business Practice*. Adhering to the framework means the following:

- A demonstrated commitment to customers' satisfaction,
- Clearly, honestly, and accurately representing all products, services, terms, and conditions,
- Delivering products and services as represented,
- Communicating in a respectful and courteous manner,
- Responding to inquiries and complaints in a constructive, timely way,
- Maintaining security policies and practices to safeguard information,
- Honoring requests not to have personally identifiable information transferred,
- Honoring requests not to receive future solicitations, and
- Following both the spirit and the letter of all laws.

This framework fits in nicely with the American Marketing Association's code of ethics, which is built on three principles: (1) marketers will do no harm, (2) marketers must foster trust in the marketing system, and (3) marketers must embrace, communicate, and practice ethical values including honesty, responsibility, fairness, respect, openness, and citizenship. While all of these principles are vitally important, they mean nothing without effective implementation.

DIRECT MARKETING ETHICS: PUTTING IT INTO PRACTICE

Before jumping into the implementation process, it is important to understand your firm's position in terms of its ethical maturity. Ethically analyzing any given situation, as we shall see, is a relatively straightforward process involving identification of the issue, selection of the standard to be applied, and then applying the standard. Introducing the organizational characteristics that will facilitate this process is paramount, but prior to embarking on a program designed to improve ethical decision making, it is advisable to first reflect on the organization's level of ethical development (see Figure 13.1).

The purpose of this progression is not to place negative labels on a given firm, but to enable the firm in question to reflect on the priority ethical behavior is given within the organization. Stage 1 is characterized, not necessarily by the presence, or existing pattern, of unethical behavior. Rather, companies at this stage are actively focused on maximizing profit. As firms progress upward from Stages 1 to 5, they begin to institutionalize ethics, and ethical behavior, into all aspects of corporate operations and activities. The most fundamentally important tools used to facilitate this progression are leadership, standards, good hiring practices, and promoting an ethical culture.

Figure 13.1
Organizational Ethical Development Model

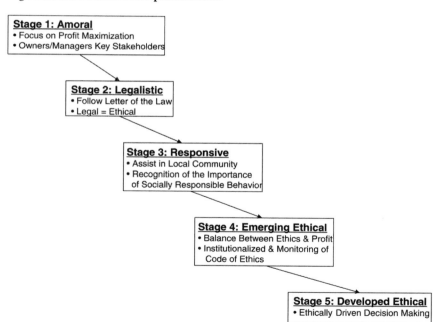

Demonstrate Leadership and Moral Courage

The first step in creating an ethical business environment for your direct marketing efforts is to make a conscious commitment that you and your organization will accept, and adhere to, high standards. The tone is set from the top, and it is the responsibility of the leaders of the company to create both the strategy and the boundaries through which a business achieves sustainable competitive advantage. Unless the management team makes a conscious and ongoing commitment to high ethical standards, the firm will drift to the lowest common denominator (that is, a short-term focus on profits) in the organization, regardless of pithy sayings on wall plaques or "ethics tips" in company newsletters.

Whether consciously or not, the CEO and the upper management team communicate a moral vision. The firm president who has little interest in ethical standards and pushes an agenda of sales at any cost will infect his employees with his amoral approach. Executives and managers lead by example. If ethics is important, managers must participate in ethics training or related events alongside firm employees. Managers must not only do the right things, but they must also speak the right language. For example, the manager of one large, midwestern direct mail company regularly sent employees to mandated sexual harassment training and made a show of attending these sessions himself. At the same time he tolerated and even participated in the crude jokes and discussions of several of the firm's senior vice presidents. As a result, his employees did not take the sexual harassment training seriously. Even after several lawsuits were threatened, this behavior persisted around the office. An important fact to remember is that 90 percent of leadership is communicated through the actions that you demonstrate to your employees day in and day out.

Leadership and moral courage displayed at the early stages of difficult or controversial issues will also help avoid trouble later in the process. For example, an initial problem that took place when automatic dialers were introduced in the telemarketing industry was that people would answer their phones only to be hung up on after a few seconds. Because of this technological glitch, many customers thought they were being stalked or harassed. According to DMA Senior Vice President Patricia Kachura, the probability of this happening was discussed at an early meeting of the big players in the industry. However, no action was taken to minimize this negative and clearly predictable outcome. In Kachura's words, "It doesn't make sense to make the quick buck today and ruin your reputation for the long term. If the president is not talking about the importance of doing the right things on a regular basis, there will be a real problem."[1]

Adopt Standards

In order to operate in a legal and an ethical manner, you must set and enforce standards throughout your company. Fortunately, as has already been discussed,

the DMA has produced a thorough set of ethical guidelines.[2] These are designed
to foster good consumer and community relationships and to protect direct marketers from potential legal problems. By formally adopting these guidelines and
actively monitoring their implementation, you are taking a big step toward pro-
tecting your firm from litigation. The complete DMA guidelines cover a wide
range of topics, including the terms of the offer, advance consent in marketing,
marketing to children, special offers and claims, sweepstakes, and order fulfillment. Many of these guidelines reflect common sense, "Direct marketers should
offer merchandise only when it is on hand or when there is a reasonable expectation of its timely receipt."[3] Other suggestions are less obvious: "The number,
retail value (of non-cash prizes) and complete description of all prizes offered,
and whether cash may be awarded instead of merchandise [and] the timing of
payments."[4]

   Implementing clearly defined standards is analogous to engaging in risk management to lower insurance costs. For ethical statements to be more than just
words on paper, management must be self-conscious in the implementation of
its ethical standards throughout the firm through specific actions.

Hire the Right People

   The best way to ensure ethical behavior among employees is to hire individuals
with a sense of personal morality and responsibility. In addition to appropriate
technical qualifications, the screening of applicants should include ethical criteria.
We suggest that potential employees be rated on items such as trustworthiness,
honesty, personal responsibility, and integrity. Assessing these characteristics is
the challenge. Fortunately technological solutions are available that are designed
to create personality profiles for applicants that can match personality dimensions
to the requirements of the job. In addition, electronic screening of applications
can detect red flags, such as misrepresentations or misleading information on
resumes.

Creating an Ethical Culture

   After hiring the right people, the best way to encourage an ethical environment
is through the creation and nurturing of an ethical corporate culture. A culture in
which ethical practice is the norm can result only from ongoing vigilance and
attention by both executives and line managers. In the book *Creating and Maintaining an Ethical Corporate Climate,* the Woodstock Theological Center states
that the role of a firm's leadership cannot be overstated.[5] Rather than imposing
standards by external edict, an ethical culture works best when it results from consensus and shared commitment. Such a culture is fashioned through explicit rules

and informal norms that alternately reward and punish, honor and dishonor individual actions.

DO NOT FORGET THE LAND MINES

By this point, it should be clear that legal behavior is not synonymous with ethical behavior. In addition to ethical concerns, managers face many compliance risks. These are ethical risks that have been codified into law. What follows are some of the most common (and dangerous) land mines confronting direct marketers and some steps that can be taken to avoid stepping in the wrong place.

Do Not Call List

It would appear obvious that everyone, businesses and customers alike, are aware of the National Do Not Call (DNC) list. Yet, according to the Federal Trade Commission (FTC), FMFC Inc., a Nevada bed company, made two years' worth (900,000+) of illegal phone calls to consumers who had registered with the DNC list. This firm had called potential customers falsely claiming that it was taking a poll about people's sleeping habits. While legitimate surveys are exempted from the DNC list, fake surveys are illegal under the DNC legislation.

The DNC covers all calls made to solicit consumers or sell goods through interstate phone calls. Calls from political organizations, legitimate telephone surveyors (where no sales pitch is included in the call), charities, or calls from companies with which a customer already has a business relationship are exempt. However, third-party telemarketing on behalf of charities is subject to the provisions of the DMC list. Direct marketers must access the DNC registry and update their calling list every 31 days. Compliance with DNC requirements is basic for firms that wish to avoid unpleasant entanglements with the FTC.

Racial Bias

Recently, the media has reported on an attorney general's office investigating a mortgage company because of racially biased lending practices. In most cases though, mortgage and lending institutions represent one of the best models for Equal Housing Lender and ethical business practices. The culprit probably lies in the chaotic and random use of customer database marketing practices. For example, a marketing manager may be preparing to send out a direct mail solicitation to target home buyers by mining their database for certain demographics. Though the criteria used for selecting the targets might have been approved by the legal department, there is often no control to ensure that the final query that was used actually conforms to the preapproved criteria. When the campaigns are audited, a racial bias may be interpreted even though it was never intended.

Misrepresentation

With the rapid product rollouts that take place in contemporary business practice it is not uncommon for little time to be available to marketers to fully review and verify that the information communicated to customers via product packaging, sales materials, and Web sites is consistent and accurate. Dangerous errors may occur. For example, a pharmaceutical marketer may unintentionally give improper dosage information, omit allergy-causing ingredients, or incorrectly label proper product-handling instructions. Clearly, these errors could lead to catastrophic results. Less egregious, but still illegal, is the practice of slamming, wherein a long distance firm changes provider service without the express permission of the customer. The FCC, which began regulating this activity in November 2000, provides for payments to authorized providers and customers of up to 150 percent of the slammer's phone charges. Even legal, but ambiguous, communication can lead to trouble for direct marketers. In one case a representative of a major long distance company induced a homeowner to switch to that company after making claims about the service that the homeowner later learned were false. The situation was not resolved until after the state Attorney General's Office became involved in the case.

Marketing Expenses

The Sarbanes-Oxley Act of 2002 requires communication about the effectiveness of internal controls related to financial reporting. Computing systems must protect the integrity of corporate, financial, and customer data. Marketing expenditures represent a significant percentage of overall company costs. Marketing managers are famous for ad hoc, unplanned operating expenses due to market changes and competition. Unfortunately, these unexpected expenses are very difficult to accrue accurately in the financial reports. Corporate profit and loss statements could have margins of error up to 10 percent directly attributed to marketing staff reporting discrepancies. Because of Sarbanes-Oxley, it is imperative for marketing departments to become financially accountable.

Privacy

It is important to remember that small businesses do not have to "reinvent the wheel" with regard to privacy and ethics. Perhaps the first source for standards should be a trade association within the firm's primary industry. As already noted, the Direct Marketing Association sets ethical standards for its members. Any business can use these as a good starting point for its own standards. A privacy policy creation template is available on the DMA Web site. It is also possible to obtain recommendations through the U.S. Small Business Administration and local business associations.

When developing a privacy policy you should include the following:

- A statement of how personal information is used and shared inside or outside the company.
- Steps to be taken to ensure consumer information is kept secure and private.
- Customers' choices regarding the use of their information.
- A way to contact your company.
- An unambiguous message that your firm is willing to discuss privacy issues.
- Full disclosure to consumers pertaining to when and why their personal information is collected.

It is also important to take a "jurisdictional" approach to compliance activities including consumer privacy issues. A small business should review the regulatory requirements of each jurisdiction in which it acts. Businesses operating solely in one state—New York, for example—should review federal, New York State, and local regulations. A regional business must review privacy standards in each state, especially if its activities are in states with active legislatures, such as California or Florida.

The *Florez* case provides an illustration. In this case a court held that a business could not ask for a customer's telephone number before she paid with a credit card. Nothing in the law bars a consumer voluntarily providing a telephone number, but California's law does ban requiring personal information as a condition of a credit transaction. The court ruled that because the telephone number was obtained before the credit card was given, it was implied that the number was required (even though it was not actually a required piece of information). The retailer has appealed.

To understand fully the implications for your business, three questions should be asked.

- What types of data do I gather from consumers?
- How do I use or intend to use the data I gather from consumers?
- How long do I retain data I have gathered?

Based on the answers to these questions, you can identify both what data you have gathered in the past, how it was treated, and what changes you might need to make in the future.

Another critical point to keep in mind is that your privacy policy should be designed to protect you from the most litigious individual. In court cases this is often referred to as the "least sophisticated consumer." When you review statements you make to the public regarding your privacy policy, you should ensure that it is written in a nondeceptive manner such that your least sophisticated consumer can understand its terms clearly.

SUMMARY

In summary, ethically sound direct marketing activities can be best fostered through

- leading with moral courage,
- adopting standards,
- hiring and promoting the right people, and
- creating an ethical culture.

Finally, be aware of both existing and emerging government regulations—they are coming at marketers fast and furious. These include laws governing racial bias, misrepresentation, financial reporting, and privacy, which are regulatory land mines that can literally "wipe out" firms that have not protected themselves with high standards of compliance and ethical decision making. By taking the high road, you not only will avoid needless legal entanglements, but your company will enjoy an enhanced reputation and you will be more likely to sleep with a clear conscience. In short—Good Marketing + Good Ethics = Long-Term Profitability.

NOTES

1. Federal Communications Commission, http://www.fcc.gov (accessed June 13, 2006).

2. Pat Kachura, Senior Vice President for Ethics and Consumer Affairs, Direct Marketing Association, personal communication.

3. www.The-dma.org/guidelines (accessed July 30, 2006).

4. Ibid.

5. Woodstock Theological Center, *Creating and Maintaining an Ethical Corporate Climate: Seminar in Business Ethics* (Washington, DC: Georgetown University Press, 1990).

CHAPTER 14

Nostradamus Knows Direct Interactive Marketing: Direct Marketers as 21st-Century Trend Messengers

William J. Hauser

During the 16th century, Michel de Nostredame (Nostradamus), a French physician, gazed into his crystal ball and made predictions that are debated and, in some cases, anxiously awaited almost four centuries later. Written in the form of rather obscure four-line poems or quatrains, Nostradamus and his work remains relevant today. Actually, one might look at the continued popularity of Nostradamus's work as an extremely successful direct multi-channel marketing campaign.

The predictions written as quatrains have and still make excellent copy. Because they are obscure, often written in a combination of languages, the reader is required to reread and study their contents many times over (stickiness). This obscurity also makes them adaptable to just about any recent historical time frame (relevance). Over the epochs the predictions (product) have remained the same; it is the delivery channels that have changed. Originally marketed by word of mouth and in limited print, Nostradamus's quatrains are universally marketed today via the Internet, books, television, movies, and other channels. Interestingly, unless some of Dr. Nostradamus's more dramatic doomsday predictions happen in the near future, there is no end in sight for this product. Think about it—a marketing campaign that has lasted for almost 400 years and is still going strong. I think we all might love being the account executive on this campaign!

As technology continues to breathe new life into marketing, especially direct interactive marketing, it might prove profitable to conjure up Nostradamus and his crystal ball to observe where direct interactive multi-channel marketing is headed in the first quarter of the 21st century. However, as with Nostradamus's earlier predictions, a caveat is offered here.

> Nostradamus's predictions come true
> As history allows them to.
> But a crystal ball's view clouded
> Makes predictions in uncertainty shrouded.

The following will view direct interactive marketers as the trend messengers of the 21st century. It will then borrow Nostradamus's crystal ball to look first at 21st century consumers. Next, it will envision the role of technology and its future impact on interactive multi-channel marketing. From this, we will delve deeper into the all-seeing orb in an attempt to predict the consumers' responses to it and any potential obstacles in the prediction.

THE MACROSCOPIC MILLENNIUM

Just a few years ago, you went to bed at night in one millennium and woke up the next morning in a new one. While this may not sound like it is a big deal, think about what was occurring. You were born in a century of rapid technological and social change. The 1900s were full of events that were unimaginable a century before. How many people in the 1800s even knew what an atom was, nonetheless understanding what it means to split it or make it a weapon of mass destruction? Similarly, how many 19th century thinkers would have ever fantasized that they could speak into a little mouthpiece and be able to communicate to anyone, anywhere in the world?

Where the 20th century has brought sweeping macroscopic innovations, the 21st century will foster in a trend toward understanding everything to the nth degree. Technology will continue to advance at even more accelerated speeds than it did in the past. With these advances our capacity to gather information and understand the environment around us will continue to grow and expand. Where we were once satisfied with a broad explanation, we will expect and demand the most minute of details. As we become inundated in our "intelligence society," even the simplest of relationships or transactions will become complex characterized by the need to have all the information available, even if it is just buying a gallon of milk.

In order to obtain this information, new tools will be developed that are beyond our dreams. Those bulky objects we call personal computers today will soon be museum pieces. In the very near future, computers the size of wristwatches will be able to hold more information than today's biggest Cray computers. Books, as we know them today, may become obsolete and exist only as antiques or collector's items. The communicative capacity of the Internet will be viewed by the late 21st century thinker in the same way that we currently view the technological advances of two cans and a waxed string.

These sweeping changes will be exciting for the direct marketer to identify and follow. The marketer will have new millennium tools available to track trends, understand messages, and ascertain the impact of these innovations on business and culture. More importantly, the marketer will thrive in an environment of rapid social and technological change which he or she can convert into actionable policies and actions. The direct marketers of the next century will also serve as the trend leaders for many of the new trends. Because of the plethora of information available to everyone, the marketer will want to take the time to thoroughly investigate and understand the short-term and long-term impacts of a myriad of trends. Because they are the ones with this information, they will become valued as the trend messengers.

DIRECT MARKETERS AS TREND MESSENGERS

Trend Messengers

Since trends are an integral part of a culture, the direct marketer can use the trends to define the likes/dislikes, current interests, "hot buttons," and general whims of the group. By definition trends are ideas, attitudes, or behaviors that reflect a current style or pattern of behavior within a group or culture. These trends reflect social conditions and demonstrate a direction in which these conditions are moving. Trends influence and are influenced by a number of groups in the culture or society. Finally, trends are time based and dynamically change within those time parameters.

The information given off by the trends is what is called trend messages. Like all messages, there is a sender and a receiver. The message must be communicated from the sender to the receiver in such a way that there is a shared understanding of the contents. If the receiver does not understand the message or translates it differently than the intended meaning, confusion arises.

Trends are complex messages and are subject to a wide variety of interpretations. This is why the direct marketer should not accept a trend message at its face value. A successful trend analyst will look at each trend from a number of different perspectives. This process, called triangulation, allows the analyst to understand the causes or conditions that helped the trend to emerge, the climate in which the trend exists, how individuals are responding to the trend and, most importantly, the trajectory or path the trend is expected to take over the next few years or months.

The intricacy of trend networks and the multiple messages generated from these networks further complicate the direct marketer's work. Since different groups and individuals will interpret trend messages differently, it is imperative that each meaning be placed in its own social context. Understanding the social context and the receiver's motivations/needs is as important as understanding the trend message itself.

In 21st century society and business, the individual who can identify trends and successfully convert the messages into programs and products is an extremely valuable asset. This person has the ability to define and shape the direction of the culture, group, and, especially, the business world. These individuals are called trend messengers. Trend messengers will take the multitude of messages given off by a trend, develop actionable interpretations of the messages, and then help others to develop successful responses to them.

Trend messengers play different roles at the different levels of society or business. At the national level, news commentators identify and define those macroscopic trends affecting the rest of us. Because their audience is so large, their interpretation of the trend is quickly shared by the group listening to them. Remember that the messenger's interpretation is not necessarily value-free or unbiased. The messenger's political, social, and religious backgrounds will help to shape his or her interpretation of the messages. Due to the near universal reach of the media, today's national trend messenger wields a great deal of power. Political office holders and their opponents spend great amounts of time and money trying to persuade the public that their interpretation of the trend is the only right way to view it. Similarly, commentators such as Paul Harvey, Oprah Winfrey, and others make millions of dollars each year by applying their "twist" or interpretation to the trends. Even the plethora of television talk shows are forums for trend messengers to discuss trends ranging from the economy to whether carrots will affect your sex life.

At the local level, similar trend messengers exist to help shape the opinions of the individuals who live or work in the area. While these individuals may not have the reach or power of the national players, they are still able to exert substantial influence in people's daily lives. One example may be the local chapters of Mothers Against Drunk Drivers (MADD). At numerous local levels this group was able to translate the messages being given off by a trend toward increased alcohol consumption and driving accidents and deaths. It was able to show local community members, through media messages and programs, that this trend existed in their community and was worse than most people would expect. As an outcome of how it interpreted and presented the messages, MADD was able to mobilize the community to action.

At the individual business level, trend messengers are essential. Most businesses work in an environment shaped by a large number of trends. These trends can be both beneficial or harmful to the business. Anyone can say that they have identified a trend and this is what it means. However, without understanding the numerous components of the trend, its networks, and its implications, the response may be wrong or, at the worst, damaging to the company. Business trend messengers develop a knack for identifying and interpreting trends. It becomes almost second nature to place trends in their social context and then apply their findings to program and product development. This second nature, however, comes from experience, that is, the expertise to identify, analyze, and interpret trend messages and translate this process into actionable responses. So, trend messengers rely on a blending of the art of trend identification and the science of trend analysis and interpretation.

Becoming a trend messenger and successfully interpreting trend messages is exciting, fun, and can be profitable for both the individual and the company. Trends and their messages are everywhere. The successful trend messengers will be the ones who can quickly and accurately turn trend messages into profit for their companies.

Trend Evolution

Today's trends are tomorrow's reality! Tomorrow's trends provide the material for today's science fiction writers. Our children giggle as they read turn-of-the-20th-century stories that talk about carriages that are not powered by horses and machines in which man can fly. In the early 1900s airplanes and automobiles were considered fads that would surely pass quickly into oblivion. As each of the decades of the first half of that century passed, older generations must have marveled at how dramatically things had changed in just the past ten years. Driving a horseless carriage was no longer a fad or even a trend. It had become a way of life in American society. Not only did the automobile evolve through a number of its own trends (for example, convertibles, large engines, rumble seats, tail fins, and whitewall tires), it also served as the incubator for a number of other related trends. Where would fast-food restaurants, gasoline stations, drive-in movies, 24-hour shopping, ATM banking, weekend trips, and even the suburbs be if the automobile had remained a fad?

Airplanes have followed a similar evolutionary trend trajectory. Orville and Wilbur Wright's first excursion must have seemed very strange to those who observed it or heard about it for the first time. Like the doubting Thomas's throughout history, there must have been a number of naysayers who went around espousing the fact that if "God wanted us to fly, He would have given us wings." But within a few short years, this futuristic phenomenon became interwoven into the fabric of our culture. All of a sudden airplanes were being used for entertainment, travel, and warfare. As the airplane's trend messages were heeded, the trend accelerated at lightning speeds. In less than 30 years after the Wright brothers, planes could now cross the country and, eventually, the oceans. People could travel distances in a day that used to take a week or more. But this was not enough. By the late 1940s, words such as "jet" airplanes and "rocket-powered" crafts began to enter our vocabulary. By the end of the 1990s, even the youngest pilot-in-waiting knew that you could now fly to Europe in about three hours and to the moon in a couple of days.

Studying the evolution of major trends is like studying the history of a culture. As the trends evolved to new forms, so has culture's reaction to them. Today's trends, as advanced as we may think they are, are only reflections of our culture at a given point in time. As time changes, so does this reflection. What will our trend reflections look like 50 or 100 years from now? Will trips to other parts of the world be in our own family "astromobile"? Will trips to the moon or other nearby stars become commonplace? If this sounds farfetched, look at the turn of the 21st century through the same glasses that your ancestors viewed the new 20th century. To the direct marketer in 2099 we may look as simple and unsophisticated as the horse and buggy.

Trend Messengers or New Age Prophets

The role of the trend messenger is still in its embryonic stage, but it will grow exponentially into the next century. Direct marketers must be prepared to take the lead in information gathering, trend tracking, and, most importantly, converting trend messages into actionable solutions to business needs. The role of trend messenger will become essential in those businesses where innovation and staying in touch with the consumer is important to their success. Understanding trends and how individuals and groups respond to them will be a skill that will be in great demand in the future.

Actually, the new age direct marketer could easily become a 21st century Nostradamus. Being able to explain current trends will give the marketer only entry into the trend business. Being able to predict the future with a high degree of accuracy will be the factor that will set the trend messenger above other social soothsayers. Once the trend messenger has gained credibility, he or she will be the person sought out to make the messages more profitable.

Since the beginnings of the human race, individuals have been trying to predict the future. Whether it was reading tea leaves, tarot cards, or crystal balls, our forefathers conjured up ways to try to figure out was going to happen next in their lives. Even if they were right a fraction of the time, they gained the reputation as being a seer of the future. Today, we still attempt to gaze into the future, but in a more scientific way. Computers have replaced tarot cards and telecommunications has replaced the crystal ball. But, today's direct marketing trend messengers are not all that different from their ancient ancestors. They are expected to give meaning to events and actions and to use the resources at hand to "show others the way."

The tools that future generations of direct marketers will have available can only boggle our minds today. Millions of pieces of information will be collated, analyzed, and interpreted within a matter of seconds. Decisions will be intelligence based and their outcomes will be evaluated at different times in different settings. The status of the future trend messenger will be elevated, and the role will become a prized asset for trend-centered companies.

THROUGH THE CRYSTAL BALL

The 21st Century Consumer

The year is 2010. The oldest Baby Boomer is 64 and the youngest boomer is 46 years old. Less than a century ago people in this age group (if they lived that long) would have been considered elderly. Now, ten years into the 21st century, the majority of these individuals live healthy, active lives, and few people would consider them "over the hill." These charter members of the new millennium club are still the largest and most powerful consumer group. However, their offspring have caught up. The children and grandchildren of the Baby Boomers have become adults and have emerged as very powerful consumer segments.

These two groups are integrally linked. The mature consumers have taught the younger consumers how to select the "best value" products and how to be brand loyal. Since both groups share information and opinions, they greatly influence each other's product awareness and purchase decisions. Thus, while these segments are major forces by themselves, together they form a strong network. Within this network the diversified consumer groups reside at different points on both the lifestyle and life-cycle continuum. More importantly, they provide different perspectives and strongly influence each other's decisions.

The key difference between the mature and young (45 and under) consumers is their different positions on the life-cycle continuum. Mature Baby Boomers are looking for products and services that help them maintain and enhance their lifestyles. Their key focus is convenience. Time is a precious resource, and anything that can be done to allow them to use this time to their advantage is appreciated and rewarded. The mature boomers are in the process of reengineering their nests. They are renovating their current living quarters or moving to smaller ones. At the same time, they are downsizing their possessions and reorganizing their lives to meet their current lifestyle needs. Most importantly, this mature consumer group spends a good deal of its time helping others, especially family members. The "peace, love, and happiness" philosophy of the 1960s, while somewhat subdued by the conservatism of age, has been firmly ingrained in their psyche. This feeling, coupled with the family focus of the late 1990s, has led the group to be very supportive of significant others in the form of financial assistance, gifts, and advice to family members. Like their parents and grandparents, the mature Baby Boomers relish the opportunity to give of themselves (emotionally and financially) to their children and grandchildren.

As the younger consumer groups born between 1964 and 1984 (that is, Generation X and the Echo Boomer Generation) have grown in size, the pendulum is gradually swinging back toward youth. Like their parents, these groups have their unique needs and lifestyles. While they appreciate the values taught them by their parents, they want to be different. This is reflected in the products and services they want and purchase. At the same time, these emerging groups are in the process of creating and feathering their own nests. In most cases these are their first homes, and coupled with the growth of their families is the need to make the nests meet their lifestyles. Because of their growing families and the resources they need to get started and maintain their lifestyles, this group relies on their parents and grandparents for help, support, and advice. It is here that brand support and loyalty are enhanced. The younger consumer's familiarity with products and services is reinforced by the wisdom they receive from their "trusted" elders.

The living environment in 2010 is similar for all the consumer segments. The pessimism toward government, politics, and business that was planted in the 1960s and germinated throughout the rest of the century remains strong in 2010. Highly active, highly stressed living environments are the norm. The average age of most houses is over 50 years, and many dwellings are in need of substantial renovation. More people are living alone due to the growth of Baby Boom widows and widowers, the growth of single-parent families in the late 20th century, and a trend toward singles living alone or in alternative arrangements. Not unlike the late 1990s, consumers in 2010 are fearful of victimization. Aging neighborhoods, aging consumers, and the uncertainty of random crimes keep the new millennium consumer on guard for his or her well-being and protection. Environmental awareness and activity are a normal part of the behavior, having been internalized into the culture by the youth who learned it in school and practiced it into adulthood.

The Consumer's View of the World

The "depression" psychology of the 20th century has been replaced in 2010 by a "preservation" psychology. As our consumers age, they become more aware of the changes going on around them and begin to yearn for "the way life used to be." These consumers feel the need to preserve the memories, feelings, attitudes, and behaviors with which they are comfortable. They strive to preserve security and well-being for themselves and their families. In an ever-changing world, they want to preserve the lifestyle to which they are accustomed. At the same time, they associate the family and family values with a more "peaceful" time during their youth and wish they could relive that time again.

In 2010, all consumers are intelligence-based consumers. The use of electronic information-gathering tools and techniques is commonplace and part of the consumer's normal daily activity. Gathering information on products and services and then completing the transaction have become the virtual reality of the computer, telephone, PDA (personal digital assistant), or even television. The experience and comfort the new millennium consumer has with electronic information has alleviated any fears about navigating through cyberspace. They are "smart" shoppers who know more and demand more. They seek information before purchasing a product or service and will change if they feel the product does not meet their "educated" expectations for it.

The new millennium consumers are global consumers, and they expect seamless integration of their products and services, no matter where they originated. They are very willing to purchase products from anywhere around the world if they feel these products best meet their needs. Awareness and information is available to them 24 hours a day, seven days a week, and they expect to transact business at the times most convenient for them, no matter when or where that is. Because these consumers think globally, companies are focusing on understanding culturally diverse consumer needs and then presenting solutions to meet them. Consumer relationship management is the reigning philosophy, and companies strive to achieve long-term loyalty with each of their customers. This means understanding customer needs, growing with the customer and his or her family, and seamlessly changing as the customer moves through life-cycle and lifestyle changes.

Consumers Define Value

Each consumer in the 21st century is driven by his or her own definition of "value." These definitions are learned from others and are based on individual experience and attitudes as the consumers attempt to deal with the world around them. Because their social environment constantly changes, their definitions of value are also subject to change. The notion of value is centered around the psychological feeling of making the "best deal." Delighted consumers are those who feel satisfied that they are the winners in the transaction they just completed. While price is important, it is but one of a constellation of factors that make up the value equation.

Because of their busy lifestyles, the new millennium consumers value superior solutions to their needs and problems. They have high expectations for product innovation, quality, and service. While switching costs (especially time and convenience) are high for most consumers, they will change to someone who they perceive is providing them a better solution. However, these consumers will support brands that continuously meet and surpass their expectations. The brands that have become a part of the consumer's family are the ones that will thrive and enhance consumer loyalty throughout the 21st century.

The new millennium consumers are actually an extension of the late 20th century consumer. They continue to demand more for less. They want more value and satisfaction for less time, effort, and money. They do their homework and demand to be treated as an intelligent partner looking for the best solutions. While they remain critical and somewhat pessimistic, each individual consumer expects companies to create solutions for "just my needs." Businesses that are able to do this on an ongoing basis will be richly rewarded.

The Power of Communications

The 21st century is the century of mass communications. From Marconi and Bell to geosynchronous satellites and the Internet, information is spread almost instantaneously from individual to individual, house to house, community to community, and nation to nation. Information that took weeks and, in many cases, months to get from one point to another now can be received as quickly as it is transmitted. An individual can pick up his or her telephone and speak to a friend or colleague in China and another one in Argentina. Not only can he or she talk with each one, the system is so configured to enable the three of them to carry on one conversation. Similarly, the Internet is currently at about one-tenth of its full potential. Its capacity to store and disseminate information will grow exponentially as the new technologies, markets, and needs continue to demand more of it.

If one thinks about it, the trajectory of the communication trend has accelerated almost exponentially during the past 50 years. Imagine living in the 1940s. Television was a novelty, telephones were rotary with party lines of many users hooked into one system, and radios and newspapers were the chief sources for information. Events were at least a week old before you saw them on the newsreels at your local theater. But, keep in mind that all of these forms of communication were light-years ahead of the technology even 50 years earlier.

Now look at the world almost 70 years later. Television is no longer a novelty and may even be considered a necessity in many parts of the world. Instead of one or two channels on a very small and fuzzy screen, you now have a choice of hundreds of channels on a large screen with a deciphonic (ten levels of stereo) sound system. Current events are transmitted "live" into your living room. Telephones have advanced to the stage where you can make calls, fax information, text message, take pictures, and link directly into your home computer. Telephones are no longer constrained to walls or booths; they are portable and cellular and can be taken anywhere you go.

Now look ahead to the year 2040. If the communication trend continues to follow its astronomical growth trajectory, one can only imagine what communication devices and media will be commonplace then. Futurists tell us that by this time everyone will have his or her own personal identification number. The number will be uniquely yours and, no matter where you go in the world, people will be able to communicate with you just by dialing the number. Along with this personal identifier will be personal communication devices that will go everywhere you do. These devices will be very small, powerful, and may even become a part of your wristwatch.

This communication trend is important to direct marketers for a number of reasons. First, it is the medium by which information is spread. Small, isolated events that in the past would not have moved any farther than 50 miles from the point of origin now achieve global impact within a matter of minutes. Second, because of the large audiences that receive the messages, the role of the direct marketer becomes extremely important. No longer is the messenger's sphere of influence small. Instead, the messenger may now be putting his or her spin on a message that is being received by millions of people. In today's environment, the messenger has the power to change the definition, interpretation, and direction of a trend in a matter of seconds. Third, the speed at which messages are communicated to the masses accelerates the life cycle of a message. With instantaneous communications the message has a very short incubation period. It also becomes subject to different interpretations quicker and, therefore, is more likely to be adapted to individual, group, or cultural needs.

All of this makes the marketer's job more difficult. There is little time to analyze the message and project its future. Decisions are made based on available information. However, most of this information will be outdated within a matter of days or weeks. Also, because of the size and diversity of the audience, the direct marketer must be prepared to examine the message from a number of individual and cultural perspectives. This can become a task of major proportions.

Thus, the 21st century telecommunication trend is integrally linked to most other trends. It affects how these trends are defined, grow, and are supported. Changes in the telecommunication field not only affect the acceleration of the trend trajectory, they also influence how the trend will be viewed and followed. As such, the telecommunication trend is and will continue to be one of the most powerful macroscopic trends in existence.

The Age of Aging

In 1945 millions of jubilant soldiers returned home to their loved ones and had babies. From 1946 to 1964, these babies came in record numbers. Little did anyone know at the time that this group would someday be the largest age cohort in American history. Not only is it the largest group numerically, it is also the most educated and the most powerful age cohort, both politically and economically. This group of "Baby Boomers" has influenced all aspects of American society and continues to do so well into the first quarter of the 21st century.

As the age structure of the population has continued to change, so has culture's view of it. Advertising, once focused on the young, upwardly mobile individual is now oriented toward the middle-aged consumer. While this shift has gradually evolved, businesses have been slow to understand and respond to the trend. This response is only now occurring, in earnest, with most companies. Perceptions are changing from viewing the "mature" consumer as a small niche group that has outgrown its need for most products to an ever-growing, powerful, and affluent group of consumers who may be looking for new products and services or may be purchasing products as gifts to help and assist others, such as their children or grandchildren.

The mature market has traditionally been viewed by the business world as a group of individuals who have accumulated all the material possessions they need and, therefore, are a less than viable market. Many businesses have erroneously labeled this group as "old" and view the mature segment as not being interested in or physically capable of using their products. Businesses have also assumed that this group of consumers does not have the financial wherewithal to purchase their products or services. This could not be further from the truth.

In 1996, the Baby Boomers began to cross the threshold into the 50 age bracket. As this group approached this benchmark age, the messages also changed. The new business mentality is to view the mature consumer of the early 21st century as a very important and influential segment. Today's mature consumers are looking for products and services that preserve and enhance their active lifestyles. This group no longer stops being active because "you're too old to do that," nor do group members mind "looking their age" because they are interested in looking and feeling their best no matter what the physical age may be. Thus, marketing messages concerning youthfulness are being redefined from the traditional life-cycle definitions to also include lifestyle definitions.

Mature 21st century consumers have more disposable income than the other consumer segments. More importantly, they have high levels of discretionary time. They gather information, study it, and then make informed decisions before they purchase a product. Probably the area most overlooked with this group is that of customer loyalty. While most businesses have long realized that established, satisfied consumers are the foundation of brand loyalty, they have neglected the loyalty of some of their most faithful and enduring supporters. Not only are older consumers among the most loyal, they are the key agents of socialization for other consumers. Social scientists have long demonstrated the importance of this intergenerational learning process, which can be parent to child, older adult to younger adult, or vice versa. Direct marketers need to use this interaction to better understand how consumers learn about products and become brand loyal. Older consumers are very influential in making younger consumers aware of products and services: either by using the product as the child grows up or by explaining the advantages of one product over another.

Thus, the macroscopic aging trend is affecting business attitudes toward older consumer groups. Marketers are beginning to realize the vast amount of power the aging consumer has. Mature consumers have a great deal of purchasing power;

that is, they have the financial ability to buy products that they feel meet their expectations, needs, and lifestyles. Aging consumers also have immense amounts of influencing power. They can influence businesses in the short run through their purchases and investments in the company. More importantly, they also have the ability to exert long-term influence over the company as they teach other generations of consumers about the value of the products.

But What About Generation X?

With the dawning of the 21st century comes the realization that Generation Xers have become middle-aged. This group of individuals, also known as the baby busters, was born between 1965 and 1986. Currently this cohort accounts for 17 percent of the total U.S. population and approximately 46 million individuals. While it is about one-half the size of the Baby Boomer (1946–1964) cohort, one must still remember that the 46 million individuals, if taken as a group, comprise a larger population than over three-quarters of the world's nations. In fact, this group actually would be the 24th largest country in the world.

For better or worse, Generation Xers are the by-products of their parents' generation. A number of factors influencing their parents in the 1960s and the 1970s helped to shape the way this group thinks and acts. As the first group to live through the Baby Boomer trends, the Xers are faced with the dilemma of dealing with their parents' youthful idealism turning to mature conservatism (that is, "do as I say, not as I did"). In a dialectical sense, the X Generation is the logical synthesis of the Baby Boomer philosophical and ideological struggles with the previous generation (Xers grandparents).

Numerous factors happened in the 1960s and 1970s that directly impacted the Generation X phenomenon. First of all, this era led toward an awareness among women that more options were available to them. This, in turn, led to both legislative and attitudinal changes in equality. Concurrently, men were beginning to have a general attitudinal shift that enabled them to support these changes. The overall effect of this was to change perceptions of traditional family roles, thereby changing the structure of the American family.

Related to the dynamic changes in social and political factors were changes in the educational institution. The 1960s and the 1970s witnessed the highest proportion of women attending college ever in history. This movement toward educational advancement had a number of direct effects on Baby Boomer women. First, the university setting and the advanced education opened up new avenues and options for additional opportunities. This is an extremely important factor. Attending colleges and universities meant obtaining new perspectives on attitudes and values. At the same time, the educational environment presented a forum where the time-honored ways of doing things could be debated. It is important to remember, however, that new learning goes both ways. Men attending college also had their eyes opened to the disparities in existing norms and traditions and gained the realization that changes in these traditional behaviors and attitudes were necessary and forthcoming.

A dramatic outcome of the growth in female educational advancement was the trend toward delayed child bearing. Not only was child bearing delayed due to the completion of undergraduate and graduate degrees, it was also delayed as women entered into the labor force and pursued career opportunities. This delay was one of the contributing factors for the lower number of births during this time frame. Three other factors are directly related. One factor was the introduction and mass usage of the birth control pill. Not only did it reduce unwanted pregnancies, it gave women new freedom in relationships and competition with men. More importantly, it allowed them to have better control over the planning of their lives (that is, school, career, and parenthood). A second factor was the legalization of abortion in 1972. Like the pill, it presented women with alternatives to child-bearing and did help to affect the smaller size of the succeeding generation. A third trend was the liberalized divorce laws of the 1960s and the 1970s. These laws allowed women additional freedoms and opportunities that did not exist under the traditional patriarchal system of the past. At one point during this time, 40 percent of all U.S. marriages ended in divorce. This trend was to directly affect the Generation Xers in that they became the products of broken homes and dis-solved marriages. As a matter of fact, approximately 50 percent of all Xers spent at least one year in a single-parent household before reaching the age of 18.

Finally, the above factors probably would not have occurred to the extent they did if economic trends had not been conducive to all of these changes. The expanded economies of the 1960s and the 1970s provided more jobs and oppor-tunities and enabled more women to pursue careers. In the 1980s the economy continued to affect women's growing entry into the labor force, but for different reasons. The prolonged recession during this period caused more women to enter the labor force to supplement family incomes. At the same time, the dissolution of many families created a large group of sole breadwinners. In this case, women's entry into the labor force became essential as they increasingly took on the single-parent, head of household role.

It is very important to remember that all of these factors are interrelated. Each was and is dependent on the others. Together they helped to shape not just the Baby Boomer generation, but also their offspring. However, the offspring (Gener-ation Xers), unlike their parents, had little to do with the development of these factors, but were required to face the consequences of them.

Among the consequences, Generation Xers were really the first latchkey gener-ation. Growing up in families with working mothers and, in many cases, absent fathers, members of this generation learned quickly how to take care of themselves and their siblings. This meant preparing their own meals and finding entertain-ment around the house. The Xers were weaned on the personal computer and arcade games. For the most part these skills were self-taught, and members of this group do not have the computer phobia prevalent among older generations. Television and VCR growth were a direct result of the need to find entertainment for latchkey kids while their parents were away from the house. When the parents were available, the kid's days were overly busy being chauffeured from one organized activity to another.

Generation Xers were also the first mall generation. Malls became the "in place" for meeting friends, eating, attending movies, browsing, and shopping. This was usually done without being chaperoned by the parents. Thus, Xers became very independent, experienced, and educated shoppers. Since work meant getting money to purchase things, most Xers worked during their school years. Parents, out of a combination of wanting to give their kids more than they had and guilt, created a generation of entrepreneurs, capitalists, and brand-conscious consumers. As the Baby Boomer parents moved away from the "five-and-dime" mentality of the 1950s, they became more brand conscious. While purchasing name brands for themselves, they also lavished their kids with "designer" products. This brand awareness was socialized into the Xers and then enhanced by them.

Finally, Xers, more than any other generation, have worked in ethically and racially integrated and diverse settings. As a group Xers are more tolerant of and comfortable with differences and are more likely to have friends outside their own racial group. Demographically, as a group, the Xers are more racially/ethnically diverse than the overall population.

America: Melting Pot or Stew Pot?

As many of us were growing up, it was common for us to hear that the United States was the great cultural "melting pot." That is, the best ideas, values, and attitudes from each culture are mixed into one assimilated blend that we call America. Recently, sociologists have changed this analogy from a melting pot to a stew pot. In the stew-pot analogy, each culture adds its unique flavor to the American blend. Like a good stew, however, each cultural ingredient maintains its own identity. To someone visiting this country in the first decade of the 21st century we are all considered Americans, but among each other we are very conscious of our ethnic backgrounds or heritage. Thus, it is probably more accurate to view ethnic diversity in the United States as accommodation (stew pot) rather than assimilation (melting pot).

America's history is one of ethnic diversity. Since our beginnings, the trajectory has swung back and forth between assimilation, distrust, and accommodation. In the early 2000s, the trend appears to be heading in the direction of accommodation. This is being brought on by changing attitudes and shifting demographics. Since the 1960s it appears that this culture has witnessed, to varying degrees, an attitudinal shift in favor of ethnic diversity. While this shift may not always be evidenced in relations between ethnic groups, it has surfaced in more subtle ways such as trends in ethnic foods and ethnic color and fashion motifs.

Demographically, over the last couple of decades, the major growth in the population in the United States has been among ethnic populations. Demographic projections indicate that the white population growth in the first few decades of the 21st century will continue to remain relatively flat. However, major ethnic populations such African-American, Hispanic, and Asian will grow at a relatively accelerated pace. Of these three, the Hispanic segment is expected to grow the fastest.

With the increased growth in population also comes an increased growth in social and economic power. Ethnic populations will continue to grow politically and, at the same time, wield more economic power. As this economic power is converted into purchase behavior it will be even more imperative for direct marketers to understand the nuances in attitudinal, behavioral, and cultural differences in each of these ethnic groups. For example, it would be quite erroneous to view an ethnic group, such as Hispanics, as one group. Mexican culture differs from Central and South American cultures, which differ from a Puerto Rican culture, which is different from a Cuban one. Similarly, there is no one Asian or African-American ethnic culture. As the ethnic groups differ from the dominant culture on the macroscopic level, so then do they differ from each other on the microscopic level.

In the 21st century ethnic diversity will continue to grow and manifest itself. The challenge that faces marketers is to decide when to emphasize the cultural stew or when to emphasize the individual ingredients. Do the various ethnic groups desire culturally specific products, or do they want mainstream products? Conversely, how much ethnic flavor will spill over to the overall culture? For example, Spanish-American colors are prevalent in the southwestern part of the United States. It is possible that this ethnic color palette has become the dominant color preference for most individuals living in the Southwest, regardless of ethnicity.

In order to successfully compete in the 21st century, marketers will need to understand each ethnic group's unique cultural heritage, values, and customs. To do so, they will have to understand the unique trend messages and interpretations associated with each culture and ethnicity. At the same time, they will need to be acutely aware of how the unique ethnic messages apply to the overall society.

We Have the Whole World in Our Hands

The 21st century will continue to manifest an ever-changing world. How many of us had heard of Bosnia and Herzegovina before 1990? What about Afghanistan, Darfur, and other trouble spots in the first decade of the new millennium? As you watch television or read your daily newspaper, you are observing changes on a daily basis that were unimaginable even a decade ago.

For the direct marketer the 1990s evidenced the opening of the global market arena. More appropriately, however, we should call it the global *markets* arena. With the formation of the European Union, the opening of the Eastern European and former Soviet markets, the strong advances of the Pacific Rim nations, the North American Free Trade Agreement (NAFTA), and the advancements in the standards of living in the developing nations of Central and South America, new and profitable markets are available to those companies that take the time and effort to understand them.

Even with the advent of major trading blocks (NAFTA, European Union, Association of Southeast Asian Nations, and the Southern Common Market), it is important for marketers to remember that they are really dealing with a multitude of cultures that are very different from their own culture and, also, from each other. Consumers in Mexico City may be dramatically different in their lifestyles and consumption behavior than people living in the United States and even from those consumers in other parts of Mexico or in neighboring Latin America countries.

Similarly, products and services that meet consumer needs in the United States may have to be adapted to meet the needs of other cultures. For example, many of the products used in U.S. households would be considered too large for most households around the world. Similarly, eating habits, food preparation techniques, and food storage requirements differ significantly from China to Ireland to Brazil.

Shakespeare once said that "the whole world is a stage." We are actors on that stage. Kind of overwhelming, is it not? How do you influence events in Japan, Germany, or Argentina? It may be more accurate, however, to view the world not as one all-encompassing stage, but as a series of "sets" at different "locations." For you, the direct marketer, this may even be more bewildering. You can no longer evaluate one role; you must learn to analyze a number of roles and, also, understand how the same role is played a number of ways on a number of different stages in order to achieve a great performance.

Our Children's World

What about the environment in the 21st century? While we have heard much recently about how nearly everyone considers himself or herself an environmentalist, the trend toward environmental concern and awareness in the early 21st century is still at an embryonic stage. Individuals are becoming more aware of environmental issues and concerns as they read and hear about them in the media. However, this awareness has still not been converted to real large-scale action. Numerous national studies have continued to show that over 70 percent of people in this country are aware of environmental concerns, but less than 15–20 percent actively do something (that is, recycle, drive less, and consume less) to remedy environmental problems.

The movement toward environmentalism is an excellent example of trend lag. Most individuals in the United States support the notion that environmental problems are serious and must be dealt with. However, when it comes to actually getting involved with the trend, the number of "doers" decreases immensely. There are a number of reasons why this discrepancy or lag occurs. First, messages are confusing. Individuals are confused as to the breadth and scope of environmental problems (that is, ozone depletion versus solid waste versus water pollution versus air pollution): confused as to what is being done about the problems and confused as to what they personally should be doing. These feelings of confusion are coupled with a notion that the environment is an abstract "public issue" that does not affect the individual as a "personal problem," and, therefore, they need do little or nothing about resolving it.

Other factors directly influence the environmental trend. First is the need for convenience. Individuals living in a fast-paced, stress-filled world are looking for ways to make their lives easier. From this need for convenience, a number of products and services have emerged. The use of prepared, fast foods and disposable paper products does make life a little easier for the active individual who has little time to shop, prepare meals, and wash dishes. However, this convenience comes at an environmental cost. All of these convenience items are made for a one-time usage and quickly end up in the trash, thereby adding to the solid waste problem.

Another way the drive toward convenience has affected the environmental trend is in the perception held that environmental behavior is time-consuming and inconvenient. For example, people in this society are accustomed to throwing trash into a container with very little thought about what they are doing or what will happen to it. When asked to begin separating this trash into recyclable and nonrecyclable items, the process becomes inconvenient and a waste of precious time. It is as if individuals assume that once trash is collected, someone else will do the environmental chores for them.

Ironically, another positive trend, consumers in search of value, has had a negative effect on the environmental movement. Consumers in search of the best deal or value are willing to travel from store to store to find it. In doing so, they are using up diminishing resources and adding pollution to the atmosphere.

Barring unforeseen ecological disasters, current attitudes toward the environmental trend will remain constant throughout the first quarter of this century. Small changes in consumer attitudes and behavior will gradually occur over time. However, these changes will be more concrete and enduring than the faddish behavior of the early 1990s, such as "green marketing." It is interesting that the long-term adherence to the trend will come from a nontraditional direction. Children, as part of their educational process, are being taught about the environment and how to become good environmental stewards. As they internalize the attitudes and practice the behaviors, the trend will become institutionalized in American society. These attitudes and behaviors will become part of normal daily living, and environmental sensitivity and activity will evolve to another level.

Thus, our children have become the environmental trend messengers. They bring home the information they learned in school and share it with members of their family. At the same time, they take on the role of monitor by influencing both the family's attitudes and environmental behavior. Children, as we know, can exert pressure and influence to do what they want or think is correct.

21ST CENTURY ADVANCES IN DIRECT MARKETING

Multi-Channel Marketing

Next, let us gaze into Nostradamus's crystal ball to see what the world of direct marketing will be like in the 21st century. Multi-channel marketing, a "new" idea at the end of the 20th century, will quickly become the standard-bearer for marketing in the 21st century. Customers no longer accept limited channels for both marketing and distribution. Instead they expect the direct marketer to "read their minds." That is, customers do not want to select among a number of alternative channels; they will expect the marketer to present them with the channel that best fits their needs and convenience.

This will be done by creating analytical profiles of the customers based on at least three integrated factors. The optimal profiling scheme will utilize a balanced combination of demographic, attitudinal, and behavioral factors. This will be necessary to obtain a well-rounded or triangulated view of the customer. It is essential to remember that these factors are interconnected. Demographic factors influence attitudinal factors and both, in turn, affect the customer's behavior. This is why it is limiting and, in many cases, misleading to use only one or two of the factors and not all three.

One of the best ways of looking at this combination of elements is to think of a three-dimensional chessboard. Make the top layer the customer's demographics, the middle layer the customer's attitudes, and the bottom layer the customer's purchase behavior. Not only do the unique elements move across each of the layers or boards, they also move up and down. Thus an element may indicate that certain customers with comparable demographic characteristics may share similar attitudes and acquire similar products. Conversely, even customers with similar demographic characteristics may have different attitudes and these, in turn, will drive their behaviors in different directions. For example, a 50-year-old may be interested in retirement planning. This individual may not have much knowledge of financial planning, not be actively involved in personal financial matters, be leery of advice, and not be open to taking much risk. The constellation of these factors would lead us to create a program or campaign specifically oriented to this cluster. On the other hand, if that same 50-year-old perceives himself or herself to be somewhat knowledgeable of finances, willing to seek and use advice, and willing to take some risks, another strategy would prove to be more effective.

Because the elements that go into a customer profile are subject to change, the overall profile must be viewed as a dynamic process. As the customer's lifestyle and life cycle change and as the demographic, attitudinal, and behavioral factors change, the overall scheme will need to be flexible enough to adapt to it. Static schemes will lose their robustness after a short period of time. Actually the best schemes are boxes within boxes, that is, larger schemes that can be reconfigured into a number of smaller schemes and/or vice versa. This enables us to maintain the structure of the larger foundation profile while being able to cluster and analyze the smaller pieces of intelligence to better understand and service the customer's needs. In this way, the profile becomes the easel on which we paint a number of unique customer pictures.

The multidimensional profiling, coupled with the ever-improving technological advances, will empower direct marketers to create true one-to-one marketing with their customers. Because they will know what the customer's needs and preferences are, marketers will be able to quickly customize the message and delivery channels in a way that the customer feels that he or she is understood and the company is looking out for him or her. Not only will this build a sense of trust, it will generate additional business from that customer and, most importantly, motivate the delighted customer to refer others to that business.

Of course the obvious concern here is to the amount and scope of customer information. What will be the tipping point at which the customer begins to feel that his or her privacy is being invaded and that the information is actually working against him or her? By the second decade of the 21st century information technology will have alleviated the vast majority of information theft occurring during the first few years of the century. At the same time, information gatherers and users will treat the handling of personal information as a sacred bond between the customer and the company. During the latter part of the first decade of the century, these attitudes and behaviors will change due to strong sanctions (fines) against the offending companies and even stronger sanctions (fines and imprisonment) against individuals who do not treat the information as part and parcel of another individual.

With these changes in place, 21st century customers will be more willing to share personal information because they know that it is secure and being collected in their best interest. The 20th century attitude of "who are you going to sell my information to" will be replaced by a new attitude of the best way to help the direct marketer to help me is to provide him or her with useful and accurate information about myself. As a customer, therefore, I will be receiving a profitable return on my information investment.

Life in the Information Cyber Maze

From a technological standpoint, we are only beginning to scratch the surface of the information technology in the early part of the 21st century. It is not too hard to imagine a time when you will have immediate, real-time access to every major global information base just by talking into your wristwatch. Think what you will be able to do with that power! Decisions will be made on the spot with accurate and timely information. Whether you are in the process of buying a new car or a loaf of bread, you will be able to scan current product and price information and negotiate your best deal in a matter of minutes. Businesses will be able to identify new markets and consumer segments and, given the breadth of data available, will be able to develop a profile of the market, evaluate how other companies have fared in the market, and develop a strategic market plan to successfully enter and grow that market. The wealth of information may actually make it possible for the market analyst to correlate all of the data and come up with projections that will indicate, with a high degree of accuracy, how successful the business will be.

While this sounds exciting, it is not without its pitfalls. Having all of this information available may actually create a trend away from information usage. Individuals, overloaded with data, may begin to feel trapped within their own networks. The information cybernet will then become the cyber maze. Once inside the maze, the individual may spend the majority of his or her time just trying to navigate or survive the maze. As tidal wave after tidal wave of new information continuously bombards the net, the individual may find that the overload is too much. When this happens, the trend trajectory may move away from information-based behavior to a more primitive instinctual behavior. New groups will surface with a "know nothing" philosophy of life. As this anti-information sentiment grows, a new trend will evolve. While the laws of *Fahrenheit 451* may be a little too dramatic, expect changes to range from "clear-mind" coffee klatches to "no net" protests to wide-scale information sabotage.[1]

Global Customer Relationship Management

By the end of the first decade of the 21st century, customer relationship management (CRM) is no longer a new concept; it is a way of life. Whether called customer lifetime value, one-to-one marketing, permission marketing, or mass customization, CRM has one underlying theme: The customer rules. Actually CRM is much more than a theme; it is a philosophy or way of thinking that must permeate through all levels of the corporate culture and processes. If not followed thoroughly and comprehensively across all aspects of an organization, it stands a very good chance for failure and, even worse, can be very unprofitable for a company.

Realizing that CRM is a strategic vision and not just a set of tools or processes has required a dramatic philosophical shift from how companies traditionally thought about and carried out their business. For many in the last part of the 20th century, CRM was thought to simply be the cross-selling of products and services. However, direct marketers today realize that this is only a small part, or actually the outcome, of a successful CRM philosophy. That is, in the course of knowing, understanding, and servicing customers you must be able to provide them additional products/services or unique combinations of the two that are "right" for them and profitable for your company. This profit is immediate in the sense of incremental products and services sold and, more importantly, is long term in the additional loyalty and business received from the customer over a sustained period of time.

In a nutshell, CRM can be defined as growing deep and enduring relationships with your profitable customers. In breaking down this definition into its component parts, one quickly sees that CRM needs to be a strategic vision and plan and not simply a set of processes or programs. At the heart of this definition is the customer. A customer-centric philosophy is exactly what it states. The customer is the center of attention, and everything done is centered around meeting and exceeding the customer's needs and expectations. During the 1990s retailer and manufacturer CRM programs focused on delighting the customer. By going past a product/service mentality and offering customers unique solutions that meet their needs and solve their problems, a company offers more than what is expected and, therefore, delights them. A delighted customer is a satisfied customer. A satisfied customer is more likely to acquire additional products/services and, therefore, become a more profitable customer. The satisfied customer is also more likely to maintain and grow the relationship over an extended period of time. Most importantly, the satisfied, delighted customer will become a loyal supporter and advocate, thereby bringing other customers to us.

The key term in the above definition is deep relationships. This means going past the list of products/services currently owned by the customers and understanding their aspirations, preferences, lifestyles, and life-cycle stages. It also means understanding their current needs, anticipating their future needs, and then communicating solutions to them in a nonthreatening, trusted advisor manner. That is, offer them the products/services that they will find the most personally useful via the channels they prefer to use.

By definition, deep customer relationships should be long-term growth relationships. As the customers experience continued delight with your solutions, they will continue to increase their level of comfort that you are providing them with the best solutions. The cumulative effect of these positive experiences will further solidify the relationship and, more importantly, allow it to grow. It is extremely important to remember here that good relationships are a reciprocal process. As you provide the customers with profitable solutions that meet and exceed their expectations, they become more comfortable with the idea that you are looking out for their best interests. As this comfort level builds, the customers will be more likely to allow you to provide them the expert advice that they have now come to expect. The unique blending and cross-selling of products, programs, and services becomes the logical outcome of this process. As with any type of relationship, the continuous meeting of expectations and the growth of trust will continue to deepen and strengthen it. In the end, these delighted customers are (and/or become) your most profitable customers.

Direct interactive marketing fits all of the above criteria for providing the customer with an optimal experience. By its nature, direct marketing is one-to-one marketing focusing on a unique customer's wants and needs. All 21st century direct marketers want to thoroughly understand their customers, anticipate their needs, exceed their expectations, and, most importantly, gain their trust. Due to exponential advances in telecommunications, the customer relationship management program of the 21st century will be global. By the second decade of this century, direct marketers will have mastered all of the problems and pitfalls of marketing and fulfillment. This will be in the form of global partnerships which by design "market globally, but fulfill locally." At the same time, the best direct marketers will have developed new strategies that will enable them to profitably compete against a global cacophony of competition. Direct interactive marketers will quickly become the trend messengers for the 21st century global CRM trend. Customers will come to expect a seamless process from beginning to end. Those companies slow to catch on to this established way of life will not be around by the end of the first quarter of the century.

NOSTRADAMUS: FULL CIRCLE

The year is 2107. Much has changed in the last 100 years. Advances in health care have caused the average individual to live to a young 104 years of age. Ironically, changing trends in the last 100 years have caused men to live longer than women. Lifestyle (for example, smoking) and employment (for example, stress) trends have actually lowered the life expectancy rates for women. It is now commonplace for four to five generations of family members to be alive and functioning within the family unit. Thus the nuclear family of the 20th century has become the extended family of the late 21st century.

The fuel-burning automobile can be found only in a museum. Environmental trends that started in the late 1900s and blossomed in the 2020s caused this form of transportation to be outlawed. The death of the car really passed unnoticed since most people found it more convenient and cost-efficient to use mass transportation. Specially designed units made it possible for each family to have its own private vehicle that links to a worldwide transportation grid making it possible to go to grandma's across town in seconds and to Europe in a matter of a couple hours. All of this is done without the family leaving the comfort of the vehicle.

All houses are now made out of stone. Researchers have observed a pattern where new homes moved from towering castles to ground-hugging, cave-like dwellings made from natural materials. Not only are these dwellings easier to maintain, they provide natural warmth and cooling, making them very fuel- and cost-efficient. Instead of adding floors on top of each other, the new avant-garde houses now add floors below each other.

After years of searching for the ideal convenience foods, scientists finally came up with water-soluble food strips that are added to your favorite beverage. The water supply, once a problem area in the past century, is now treated with vitamin supplements so that by drinking the water everyone is assured of receiving their optimum amount of required vitamins and nutriments.

What Would Nostradamus Think?

Upon digging through the basement of an obscure little bookstore in a tiny little alley in Paris, we come across some heretofore unknown manuscripts written by Nostradamus. As we begin to translate and interpret the quatrains we quickly see that Nostradamus has predicted what direct interactive marketing will be like at the end of the 21st century. First, he tells us that by the end of the 21st century all marketing will be direct and all marketing will be interactive. He also suggests that the tools direct marketers will have available then are unfathomable by today's standards. Technology- and intelligence-based decision making is as commonplace as putting on one's shoes. Global fulfillment issues have long been resolved due to global alliances, and he even hints at products being beamed around the world.

However, Nostradamus offers a few words of caution to the 21st century direct marketer. His crystal ball foresees a period of time in the 21st century where consumers revolt against technology totally intruding into all aspects of their lives. "Big Brother" notions of the 20th century have become the paranoia of the late 21st century. Only those companies that have truly built a strong bond of loyalty and trust with their customers will survive. Direct marketers will do well to heed this cautionary glimpse into the future for as Nostradamus says:

> As the new millennial century wanes
> And the machine's iron fist does life permeate,
> Only those in trust bonded
> Shall the dawn of the new day see.

NOTE

1. Bradbury, Ray (1953), *Fahrenheit 451*. New York: The Ballantine Publishing Group.

INDEX

flows of, 23. *See also* Ethics and regulations in direct marketing; Integrated
marketing
Customer retention, 161–163, 170–171.
See also Customer relationship
management; Loyalty
Customers. *See* Stakeholders
Customer satisfaction, 77, 146–147,
252–253. *See also* Consumer buyer
behavior; Customer relationship
management
Customer warehouses, 194. *See also* Data
collection and strategies
Customizing products, 153
Custom portals. *See also* Integrated
marketing
Czinkota, Michael R., 38

Dashboard reports, 203
Data collection and strategies, 192–215;
analytics, overview of, 200, 203–207;
anti-information sentiments, 251;
approaches to, 31–32, 207–214; challenges and limitations to, 195, 201, 202,
203; costs of, 197–199, 201; critical data
elements, defined, 196; database analysis,
13–14; database design, 209; data greed,
170; data latency, 197–200; data marts,
194; data mining, 200–203, 211–213;
decision analysis vs. data mining, 202;
direct marketing performance testing,
212–213; for eCRM, 171–172; identification of business strategies and, 199,
207–208; legal considerations, 195, 196,
200; mainframe databases, 203; management of, 208–210; multi-channel marketing and, 13–16; overview of, 192–
194, 207–208; personnel for, 211, 213;
post-data collection process, 213–214;
profiling, 138, 193, 200, 210, 249–250;
quality of, 194–195, 196–197, 201, 202,
205–206, 209–210; reporting, 210, 211;
secondary research, 29, 30–31, 34–35,
39–41; Six Sigma process, 195, 196–
197, 198t; social context and, 233; test
and learn methodologies, 210–212;
third-party data, 201–202; tools for,

199–200; triangulation, 233, 249–250.
See also Direct marketing research; *entries
at Market;* Integrated marketing
Davis, F.D., 76
Dean, Howard, 71–72
Decentralized marketing research, 31
Decision analysis, 202. *See also* Data
collection and strategies
Dell Inc., 119, 153
Demand curve. *See* Long-tail distribution
Demassification, 143, 153
Demographic segmentation, 15, 246,
249–250. *See also* Market segmentation;
Profiling
Differentiated marketing, 17, 19, 101–104,
108
The Digital Age, 63, 232–233
Digital communities, 69
Digital inventor systems, 150–151
Digital marketing. *See* Internet
Digital products, distribution of, 151
Direct mailings, 42–44, 127, 149–150,
185–186, 223, 253. *See also* Print
channels
Direct Marketing Association (DMA), 223,
225, 226, 228
Direct marketing research. *See* Marketing
research
Discover Card, 50–51
Dissatisfaction, 124. *See also* Consumer
buyer behavior
Distribution, 11, 23, 150–151. *See also*
Long-tail distribution
Diversified growth, defined, 18–19
Divorce laws, 244
DMA (Direct Marketing Association), 223,
225, 226, 228
DNC (National Do Not Call Registry),
220, 223, 227
Douglas, Susan P., 34
Drucker, Peter, 62

eBay, 66
E-catalogs, 67. *See also* Internet
Echo Boomer Generation (Generation X),
238, 243–245
E-commerce wave, 63. *See also* Internet

About the Editors and Contributors

GENERAL EDITOR

BRUCE D. KEILLOR is coordinator of the American Marketing Association's Office for Applied Research-Direct Marketing and Professor of Marketing and International Business at The University of Akron. He is also a research fellow at Michigan State University. Dr. Keillor specializes in international marketing strategy and direct multi-channel marketing and has authored more than 60 articles published in journals worldwide. He has also contributed to numerous books. In addition to his academic credentials, Dr. Keillor has also been an active entrepreneur as co-owner of a direct-marketing software company he helped found in 1994. Dr. Keillor also has extensive executive education and consulting experience as a copartner in BBA Associates, a global marketing consulting firm.

EDITORS

WILLIAM J. HAUSER is associate director for the Taylor Institute and Assistant Professor of Marketing at The University of Akron, where he teaches courses in creative marketing, marketing analytics, and marketing research. He has also taught at West Virginia University and Washington University in St. Louis and is an adjunct Associate Professor of Sociology at The University of Akron. Over the past 20 years, he has served as the manager of market research and business development for Rubbermaid, Inc., and its Little Tikes subsidiary, and, most recently, as senior vice president and director of research and planning for

KeyCorp in Cleveland, Ohio (the 13th largest bank in the United States). Bill has also completed numerous consulting projects for small businesses and social agencies.

DALE M. LEWISON is founding director of the Taylor Institute for Direct Marketing and Professor of Marketing at The University of Akron. He is the author of *Retailing* (6th ed.), *Essentials for Retailing*, and *Marketing Management* (2nd ed.).

CONTRIBUTORS

STEVEN BRUBAKER is Senior Vice President of Corporate Affairs for InfoCision Management Corp., where he serves as the company's spokesperson for media-related news and public relations events, oversees InfoCision's continued expansion and the deployment of all new call centers, and directs the company's department of regulatory compliance. A member of several professional organizations, including the American Teleservices Association and Direct Marketing Association, he is a frequent guest speaker for industry events. He has also contributed to numerous industry trade journals and publications, including *Call Center Magazine, Customer Interaction Solutions, DM News, DMA Insider, DMA Teleservices Council Newsletter, Fundraising Management*, and *Journal of the American Teleservices Association*.

MARK COLLINS is the Creative Director at Suarez Corp. Industries (SCI). At SCI, he oversees a creative staff responsible for more than $100 million in annual sales. Since 1997, Mark has instructed courses in direct marketing and copywriting at The University of Akron.

JEFFREY C. DILTS is an Associate Professor of Marketing and a Fellow of the Fitzgerald Institute for Entrepreneurial Studies at The University of Akron in Akron, Ohio. His areas of specialization and research include marketing strategy and Internet marketing.

JOSE MANUEL ORTEGA EGEA is a lecturer in Marketing at the University of Almeria (Spain).

ANDRIA EVAN is a professional marketing researcher in Canada. Following a diverse retail and wholesale management career, she eventually progressed to market research. At first she was the Account Executive for the New York–based NPD's *Canadian Apparel Market Monitor*. During her tenure, notable clients included Gap, Sears Canada, Levi's, Nike, and Reebok. Thereafter, she became Manager of Customer Research and acting Customer Insights Director at the

Liquor Control Board of Ontario (the world's largest merchant of beverage alcohol). Her broad research experience encompasses customer segmentation; store location, design, and assortment; product format, packaging and positioning; advertising testing in TV, cinema, outdoor, print, and radio; magazine design; opinion polling and customer satisfaction studies; as well as highly controversial topics, such as teen alcoholism, and the effects of theft on frontline employees. She has also served as a consultant for Appleton (Jamaica), E&J Gallo, Smirnoff, Johnny Walker, Alizé, and the Ontario Wine Council. Presently, she is completing an MBA degree at The University of Akron, Ohio.

MARIA VICTORIA ROMAN GONZALEZ is a Professor of Marketing at the University of Almeria (Spain).

MARIO MARTINEZ GUERRERO is a lecturer in Marketing at the University of Almeria (Spain). He is also the New Development Coordinator in the Department of Direct Channels at Cajamar Cooperative Bank.

PARAMJIT S. KAHAI is an Assistant Professor of Management Information Systems in the Department of Management at The University of Akron in Akron, Ohio. He teaches Telecommunications, Database, and Information Strategy courses. His research interests include e-Business in small firms, Internet access and use in small businesses, wireless local area networks, and information systems decentralization.

TOBY MALONEY is a lifelong media junkie and entrepreneur whose passion for newspapers and magazines first surfaced when he launched a neighborhood paper at age six. The former head of Internal Communication for SmithKline Beecham (now GlaxoSmithKline) and KeyCorp, he is a graduate of John Carroll University and has graduate degrees from Miami University (Ohio) and Case Western Reserve University. He is the Vice President, Business Development, for Mental Floss LLC and spends 24/7 thinking of ways to introduce more people to the company's products.

MELANIE MALONEY grew up on building sites helping her father in his construction company and has been building things ever since. She shares Toby's entrepreneurial spirit, but does not read four papers each day. As Vice President, Operations, for Mental Floss LLC, she has been instrumental in setting up the processes that have enabled Mental Floss to grow from a dorm room idea to a multi-million-dollar business. A graduate of SUNY-Oswego, she also has a graduate degree from Fairleigh Dickinson. Toby and Melanie are the primary investors in Mental Floss LLC.

ANNEMARIE SCARISBRICK-HAUSER is Senior Vice President and Manager of Enterprise Business Intelligence at KeyCorp in Cleveland, Ohio, where she is responsible for enterprise information management for the nation's 13th-largest banking institution. Before joining KeyCorp, she was the associate director of the Survey Research Center at The University of Akron. She is currently an adjunct professor at The University of Akron, where she teaches courses in research methods, collective behavior, public administration, and emergency management. Over the past 20 years, she has completed more than 125 research projects for a diverse group of internal and external clients, presented papers at numerous domestic and international academic and professional conferences, published articles in a variety of journals, and co-authored a book on applied sociology.

MICHAEL SCHILLER is a principal with Schiller, Benson and Polo, a digital brand-management and strategy firm. His career spans over 25 years of marketing and technology. He is currently a Lecturer at The University of Akron. He is a graduate of Arizona State University and holds an MBA from Western International University.

TIM SEARCY is the CEO for the American Teleservices Association. His past endeavors include executive positions with West Teleservices, APAC Teleservices, Transcom Worldwide, and Rapp Collins. Tim has been inducted into the Teleservices Hall of Fame and is a highly sought after international speaker and published author on CEO leadership, sales and marketing, and the future of the direct-marketing industry.

JOEL SOBELSON is currently practicing what he preaches, creating true integrated marketing solutions for Schick razors, Trojan Brand Condoms, Arm & Hammer, Crest SpinBrush, Mentadent Toothpaste, and Halls Cough Drops. After a successful career in general advertising, where he managed the creative output on brands such as AT&T, Citibank, Jamaica Tourism, Marriott International, Bolla Wines of Italy, and Alamo Rent A Car to name a few, Joel was most recently the Executive Creative Director for a global direct marketing agency in New York City. There he built and managed its staff of 100 creatives, including its interactive efforts. Under his leadership, the agency has been recognized with winning the most industry awards in its history for such brands as Citibank, Microsoft, IBM, AT&T, Pfizer, Kraft, Club Med, Hewlett-Packard, the New York Philharmonic, and Toys "R" Us. All the while he continues to write blogs about marketing, lecture about advertising at trade events and universities, and work on a book on creative marketing.

NADJI TEHRANI is the Founder, Chairman, and CEO of Technology Marketing Corporation. He is also the Executive Group Publisher and Editor-in-Chief of *Customer Interaction Solutions Magazine*. Educated at the Sorbonne (University of Paris), in the Middle East, and in the United States, Nadji has an undergraduate degree in Chemistry and has completed graduate studies in Business Administration. As founder of Technology Marketing Corporation in 1972, he has been publisher of more than a dozen periodicals, books, and buyers' guides in the high-tech field, including radiation curing. In doing so, he has established himself as the preeminent spokesman in these important and highly scientific fields. In 2003, Nadji was inducted into the American Teleservices Association Hall of Fame and in 2006 was the recipient of an award recognizing 25 years of excellence to the industry. Nadji is owner of the registered trademark for the term "Telemarketing" and is acknowledged as one of the visionary leaders that has helped the call-center industry grow into a $2 trillion business employing more than 15 million people worldwide.

YING WANG is Assistant Professor at Wichita State University. Her research focuses on international marketing, marketing communication, and research methods. She has recently investigated consumers' attitudes toward online advertising in multiple countries. Her research has been published in *Journalism and Communication* and *Marketing Survey and Research*. Before becoming a professor, she worked in industry for seven years as an international marketing consultant. She has conducted consulting for many international companies such as 3Com Corporation, IBM, Motorola, Fujifilm, Compaq Computer Corporation, Hewlett-Packard, and Marriott International.

TIMOTHY J. WILKINSON is Associate Professor of Marketing and International Business at Montana State University–Billings. He studies export promotion, international market research, and the international aspects of direct marketing. His papers include publications in *Long Range Planning, Journal of Business Research, Journal of International Business Studies*, and *Journal of Small Business Research*.